Friendship, Altruism and Morality

International Library of
Philosophy

Editor: Ted Honderich

A Catalogue of books already published in the
International Library of Philosophy
will be found at the end of this volume

Friendship, Altruism and Morality

Lawrence A. Blum

University of Massachusetts, Boston

ROUTLEDGE & KEGAN PAUL

London, Boston and Henley

First published in 1980
by Routledge & Kegan Paul Ltd
39 Store Street, London WC1E 7DD,
9 Park Street, Boston, Mass. 02108, USA and
Broadway House, Newtown Road,
Henley-on-Thames, Oxon RG9 1EN
Set in IBM Press Roman by
Columns
and printed in the United States of America
by Vail-Ballou, Inc.

British Library Cataloguing in Publication Data

Blum, Lawrence A

Friendship, altruism and morality. —
(International library of philosophy).
1. Friendship
2. Altruism
I. Title   II. Series
177'6   BT1533.F8   80-49942

ISBN 0 7100 0582 2

To my mother
and the memory of my father

CONTENTS

ACKNOWLEDGMENTS

I owe a great debt to many people who helped directly or indirectly in the writing of this book. Over the years scores of conversations with my good friends Marcia Homiak and Vic Seidler have pointed the way towards new approaches to moral theory, emphasizing character, emotion, and human relationships; the present work is one outgrowth of that collaboration. My teachers and mentors, Stanley Cavell, Rogers Albritton, and Hubert Dreyfus shaped the way that I approach philosophy. Bernard Williams's work in moral philosophy and moral psychology, and the unpublished work of Jerry M. Cohen (now Swami Anand Purodha) on reason and emotion were fundamental intellectual influences on my perspective in moral philosophy.

Richard Norman, Alan Montefiore, Tony Skillen, Bernard Williams, Barbara Herman, Michael Friedman, W. David Solomon, Howard Cohen, Martin Andic, and Jennifer Radden read all or most of one or another draft of this book, made invaluable suggestions and criticisms, and gave personal support. Jennifer Radden was particularly generous in going over a later draft page by page with me. Robert Shope and Jane Martin made some astute criticisms of some chapters in an early draft. Ted Honderich proffered important structural suggestions on the penultimate draft. My ethics students at the University of Massachusetts in Boston helped keep the issues of the book especially alive for me during 1977-9.

Research for this book was partially supported by a Faculty Development Grant from the University of Massachusetts. Elisabeth Bouche did a superb typing job on the manuscript. Bernard and Betty Miller allowed me to use their lovely house in New Hampshire where I wrote much of the book.

To all of these people I am very grateful.

Finally I want to thank my wife Judy Smith for sharing her life with me, and for help with this book as well.

I

ALTRUISTIC EMOTIONS AND THE KANTIAN VIEW

This book focuses on sympathy, compassion, and human concern, considered primarily as emotions but also as character traits, and on friendship as a context in which these emotions play a fundamental role. Contemporary moral philosophy in the Anglo-American tradition has paid little attention to these morally significant phenomena. In fact the 'altruistic emotions' (as I will call them) have not played a significant role in moral philosophy within this tradition since the empiricist moral philosophers of the eighteenth century, such as Adam Smith and David Hume. Partially accounting for this neglect within moral philosophy and moral psychology are powerful traditions of thought and philosophic orientation which militate against according sympathy, compassion, concern, and friendship a substantial role in the moral life. A major task of this work will be to articulate and to come to terms with some of these major lines of thought. Doing so will point the way toward an adequate account of friendship and altruistic emotions, and of their moral significance.

I

It may be useful in this introductory chapter to present in schematic form some of the lines of thought which will be discussed separately and in detail in subsequent chapters. Taken together they yield a familiar conception of morality and of the emotions, in particular the altruistic emotions. I will refer to the view as 'Kantian,' for it has its roots in Kant's writings, undoubtedly expresses some lines of thought

1

within Kant's philosophy, and is often associated with Kant. On the other hand I do not claim that it represents a full and balanced articulation of Kant's views, taking into account all his writings bearing his moral philosophy; it could justly be regarded as an unsympathetic version of Kant's views.[1] Though 'Kantian' is more than merely a convenient label, my main interest is less in Kant's own views than in some lines of thought, associated with him, which have been influential in moral philosophy. Hence I do not intend to take sides in the dispute over the correct reading of Kant's views.

The general conception of emotions and feelings involved in the Kantian view is this:

Emotions and feelings are transitory, changeable, and capricious. They are weak, subject to variations in our mood and inclinations. They are controlled by and responsive to considerations other than moral or rational ones. Emotionally motivated conduct thus is or is likely to be unreliable, inconsistent, unprincipled, or even irrational.

Feelings and emotions are entirely distinct from reason and rationality. They do not yield knowledge, and can in fact divert us from morally directed thinking and judgment. In order to obtain a clear view of the rights and wrongs in a situation we must abstract or distance ourselves from our feelings and emotions.

We are passive in respect to our feelings and emotions. They are not in our control, and thus we are not responsible for them. They lie outside the scope of our will. We do not choose to have the feelings and emotions we do have. And so, as moral agents, our feelings and emotions cannot reflect on us. We cannot be blamed or morally praised for having or failing to have particular emotions and feelings.

Emotions, in particular the altruistic emotions, are directed towards and occasioned by particular persons in particular circumstances. They do not have the generality or universality required by morality. Thus they involve 'partiality.' They are not based on principle. I might feel compassion for A, but not feel it for B, though A's and B's situations are entirely analogous.

To act from altruistic feeling or emotion is to act out of an inclination or desire. Though the inclination is towards the good of another, action thus prompted is fundamentally egoistic in its motivation. For the agent acts beneficently only because he happens to have a particular inclination to promote the other's good.

The Kantian view of feelings and emotions is correlative to certain general conceptions of morality and 'the moral point of view.' Morality

2

is first and foremost an enterprise of reason and rationality. Morality must apply to all (rational) beings, and does so because and insofar as they are rational. The moral point of view involves impartiality regarding the interests of all, including oneself. It involves abstracting from one's own interests and one's particular attachments to others. To be moral is to respect others as having equal value to oneself, and as having an equal right to pursue their own interests. One acts contrary to morality in preferring one's own interests, or the interests of those whom one likes and is connected to, simply because they are one's own, or one's friends', interests. Moral principles must be universal, or universalizable. They must be valid for all and compelling to any rational moral agent.

Morality has primarily to do with obligation, with action we are morally bound to perform. That which cannot be made an object of obligation, such as emotions or feelings, can have only peripheral moral significance, entirely derivative from its connection to obligation.

The moral motive — that is, a motive which is to have moral value — must have a certain strength and must be reliable. It must be capable of standing up to contrary inclinations, and must not be dependent on our changing moods. Morality must involve self-control. The moral motive must be capable of leading us consistently to morally right acts. It must be available whenever it is called upon.

The moral motive must be a non-egoistic one. It cannot depend on our own particular interests, desires, emotions or attachments. The morally motivated action must be prompted by the actual moral considerations of the situation, not by particular and fortuitous aspects of the agent.

Taken together, the Kantian view of feelings and emotions and its view of morality constitute a powerful and influential tradition of thought, which would deny a substantial role to sympathy, compassion, and concern in morality and moral motivation. It is important to see that these lines of thought do not spring solely from explicit philosophical thought. Rather, they have roots also in our own moral culture. The Kantian view has obvious affinities with a definite Protestant tradition of morality — the emphasis on subjection to duty, on control of feelings and inclinations, on strength of will in resisting impulses and inclinations from one's selfish lower nature, on conscientious action on principle, rather than emotional spontaneity. That tradition has deeply affected the moral thinking and experience of Anglo-Americans. Thus part of the usefulness of focusing on the Kantian view is that one is thereby dealing with many of our own moral views, intuitions, and ways in which we experience and assess ourselves and others morally.

II

A brief outline of the argument of the book is as follows: In chapter II I consider the Kantian claim that feelings and emotions are capricious, changeable, transitory, and weak, and are therefore unreliable as moral motives. Clearly distinguishing altruistic emotions from some other psychological phenomena shows these views to be unfounded. Altruistic emotions are not like changeable moods, such as good-spirits and exuberance, which might on occasion lead to acts of beneficence. Acting from altruistic emotion is not characteristically acting 'on impulse' or 'impulsively'; nor is it acting 'on inclination' or doing what one is 'in the mood' to do. Altruistic emotions must be distinguished from some other-regarding sentiments (such as well-wishing), which involve weaker dispositions to act beneficently and which aim at less significant aspects of a person's good than do altruistic emotions. Negative states or moods such as depression or sadness can weaken altruistic emotions, but do not necessarily do so, nor do they typically extinguish them.

Altruistic emotions are distinct from personal feelings, such as liking and affection. The former are grounded in the weal and woe of others, whereas the latter are grounded in personal (but not necessarily moral) characteristics and features of the other person. Altruistic emotions towards someone can occur in the absence of personal feelings towards him; and vice versa. That altruistic emotions can sometimes be weak, transitory and capricious does not mean that we should shun emotional motivation in favor of duty and rational principle. For altruistic emotions are themselves capable of the strength and reliability which the Kantian demands of moral motivation. Moreover, in their actual operation reason-based motivations are subject to many of the same defects and distorting influences as are altruistic emotions. It is misleading to compare the ideal potential operation of Kantian motivations with mediocre specimens of the altruistic emotions.

Chapters III and IV deal with friendship and morality. In chapter III I focus on a central claim of the Kantian view of morality – that impartiality is a principle and a perspective which defines 'the moral point of view.' I use the case of friendship to argue that impartiality constitutes only one among other moral principles, perspectives, and virtues.

The Kantian view objects to our being beneficent towards friends on the grounds that in doing so we distribute our beneficence according to personal interest and attachment rather than need or desert. Against this objection I argue that impartiality as a moral stance and principle is appropriate only in certain circumstances, which do not generally include those of friendship.

Thus it is morally appropriate for us to favor our friends with our beneficence, simply because they are our friends (and outside of any moral obligation to do so); and this is not to be explained through appeal to some higher-order principle of impartiality. The good we do for our friends cannot be expressed within Kantian categories.

In chapter IV I develop the view that it is not only morally appropriate but morally good to care for one's friend and to have the disposition to act beneficently towards him. Friendships of a high degree of moral excellence involve a deep caring and strong identification with the good of the friend. But friendships can exist at different levels of moral value, of caring and commitment. Caring for a close friend is not a form of extended self-interest but (in healthy relationships) involves an appreciation of the other in his separateness from oneself. Friendship and other special relationships are morally good insofar as they involve concern for the other for his own sake, even if such concern would not exist towards the other in the absence of the relationship.

In chapters III and IV generally I argue that friendship has significant moral dimensions; yet its human importance is far from exhausted by its moral significance.

In chapters V, VI, and VII I elaborate a positive view of the moral worth of altruistic emotions, counterposing it to the Kantian view and defending it against Kantian objections.

In Chapter V I argue that action motivated by altruistic emotions is morally good because it involves 'direct altruism' — a direct concern for and responsiveness to the weal and woe of others. This view contrasts with the Kantian view, according to which moral action must be grounded in universal principles morally binding on the agent; the latter view, I argue, cannot encompass more than a small range of morally good beneficent action. A weaker version of the Kantian view would require only that we test our proposed actions for moral permissibility, as determined by a universalization test. Though this view would encompass beneficent action excluded by the stronger view, it cannot provide a full explanation of why such action is morally good, and so would have to allow for non-Kantian forms of moral value (such as that put forth in the account of direct altruism).

Altruistic emotions not grounded in universal moral principles do not typically lead us to action which conflicts with moral demands, nor does such action typically involve inconsistency. (But inconsistency is, in any case, only one sort of moral defect among others, and is not undermining of moral value in a person's behavior.) Nor does altruism not grounded in universal principle typically lead to undeserved beneficence.

Action grounded in altruistic emotion is no less directly altruistic than action grounded in purely rational altruistic motivation, nor does the emotional element render such action in any way egoistic. Action from altruistic emotion may in a sense be said to be done 'for a reason,' but the notion of 'reason' here must be understood much less rationalistically than is customary.

In chapter VI I discuss the role of perception of others' weal and woe as a factor in beneficent action. The compassionate or sympathetic moral agent differs from the Kantian moral agent not only in the nature of his motives to beneficence but in the greater likelihood of his perception of the conditions which make beneficence appropriate.

In chapter VII I argue that what makes some actions morally appropriate is inseparable from the emotions which prompt them, so that in a sense the emotions must be seen as part of the action (morally viewed); or rather the two together (emotions and action) must be seen as part of a unity, which I call a 'response.' Responses convey a good to the persons responded to, and the altruistic emotions are essential to conveying that good. Altruistic emotions can convey a good even when they do not lead to acts of beneficence.

The good conveyed by altruistic emotions takes us beyond a consideration of altruistic emotions merely as motives, and their full moral value cannot be appreciated without taking this into account, as even non-Kantian defenders of altruistic emotions have usually failed to do.

In Chapter VIII I contend with a fundamental Kantian criticism of my enterprise in the book, namely the claim that our emotions and feelings cannot be relevant to a moral assessment of us. For we are entirely passive with respect to our feelings and emotions; they are not in our control, and lie outside the direct scope of our will.

Against this I argue that our emotions are integral to our general attitudes, values, and orientations towards others (with regard to their weal and woe) — what I call our 'being-towards-others.' Our being-towards-others must be seen as part of our moral self; and yet it is not an outcome of the will, of deliberate decision and choice. Our altruistic emotions contain an element of both 'activity' and 'passivity.' Yet the familiar philosophic understanding of these terms must be revised if they are to express the way that our emotions reflect on us morally.

The Kantian view's emphasis on choice, decision, will, and rational deliberation yield an inadequate view of moral change. Moral change generally involves engagement with and reorientation of our emotions, and, more generally, of our being-towards-others.

III

The argument builds on what I take to be a widely shared sense that it is good to be sympathetic, compassionate, concerned, and caring for other human beings, and that to say of someone that he has these qualities is to say something about him from a moral point of view. The moral position to be argued for is simply this one, and it can thus be seen as in conformity with the deliverances of the 'ordinary moral consciousness.' It is not that I begin with this judgment, but rather that my argument is guided by it. My concern is that moral philosophy, especially contemporary Anglo-American moral philosophy, has found it difficult to give philosophical form and expression to this aspect of the ordinary moral consciousness, much less to give it a firm philosophical grounding.

In speaking of the 'ordinary moral consciousness' I mean to call Kant to mind. (He called it 'moral knowledge of common human reason.') For, in his *Foundations of the Metaphysics of Morals* he regards himself as beginning with precisely this sort of knowledge, in order to articulate its presuppositions, thereby giving it a philosophical foundation of which the ordinary person is unaware. This aim I share with Kant. But there are three crucial elements of Kant's endeavor which differ significantly from my own. First is Kant's desire to articulate the fundamental principle of morality; he assumes that morality is a human enterprise with a unitary nature, for which a single 'foundation' can be found. Second, related to this, is the assumption that 'the moral knowledge of common human reason' is essentially unified, that it has no internal tensions or contradictions. Third is Kant's starting point, namely the experience of obligation, of being unconditionally bound to do something simply because it is the morally right thing to do.

In contrast to Kant I do not claim that morality is of a unitary nature. When I argue that it is morally good to have sympathy, compassion, and concern, I will not need to be committed to regarding these altruistic emotions as the most fundamental moral phenomena, in terms of which others must either be reducible or discarded. I will not deny that it is also morally good to be rational, just, principled, impartial, conscientious; nor will I claim that the grounds of the moral worth of these Kantian virtues is of the same nature as the grounds of moral worth of the altruistic virtues. What I will want to say is that there are irreducibly different and varied types of moral goodness. Thus in defending the moral significance of the altruistic emotions I will not also be attacking the moral significance of some of the moral qualities important to the Kantian view. Another way to express the relationship between my view and the Kantian view is that much of the Kantian view of morality (though not of the emotions) is true — if confined to its proper scope or arena within the moral life. I will not be so concerned to work out this truth, though I hope not to deny it.

In rejecting the view that morality is of a unified nature, I am also departing from Kant in not attempting to give anything like a foundation to morality. For I do not think there could be such a foundation. In this I depart also from Schopenhauer (in *On the Basis of Morality*), whose views are otherwise closely akin to my own. Schopenhauer is right, I believe, to see compassion as a morally good motive and to lament its neglect in other systems of morality (primarily Kant's). But he makes the further unsupportable claim that compassion is the *only* morally good motive and, in addition, that it is the basis of morality as a whole. I am not attempting a totalistic view of morality of the sort that either Kant or Schopenhauer puts forth.

I disagree also with Kant's second assumption, one which seems to be widely shared; and that is the notion that the common moral consciousness, on its most fundamental level, is essentially without internal contradiction. On the contrary, it seems to me unlikely that all the deliverances of the ordinary moral consciousness, even our most deeply held ones, are entirely compatible with one another and can be brought together within a common system. This is connected with the fact that the concept 'moral' itself cannot rightly be given a unitary meaning, but rather bears the heritage of different moral traditions from which it gathers different sorts of meanings.[2] More generally, the assumption of

8

unity seems to me an article of faith, not borne out by experience. Iris Murdoch warns against the 'spurious unity' which she sees as an occupational hazard of moral philosophy.[3] I mean to preserve the sense that when I argue for a morality of sympathy, compassion, and concern, I am seeing this as only a part of an overall 'pluralistic' view of morality.

To give up the notion that there is one unified perspective which can be called the moral point of view is to abandon one of the sources of the view that the distinction between the moral and the non-moral is radical, categorical, and firm. And I will not want to make any *general* claims about the distinction between moral considerations, judgments, and standpoints and non-moral ones. Nevertheless, I will want to maintain one distinction, namely the difference between concern for others and concern for self, and will want to see this distinction as having moral significance.

The non-unified nature of the ordinary moral consciousness allows an argument for the moral significance of altruistic emotions without inflating that significance to cover the whole of morality; nevertheless the same lack of unity means that to argue for the moral value of the altruistic emotions is inevitably to do more than merely to support a deliverance of the ordinary moral consciousness and to give a rationale for it, while leaving everything else intact. It must also involve countering some other deliverances of the ordinary moral consciousness (mostly, ones enshrined within the Kantian view) which are genuinely in tension or contradiction with the viewpoint which I am defending. In this way my endeavor is in no way morally neutral.

This leads to the third element of Kant's endeavor — the starting point of the experience of obligation. While such a starting point is not in itself strictly incompatible with the morality of altruistic emotions which I am articulating, in fact it orients moral inquiry in an entirely different direction. I will be concerned to show how the notion of obligation makes it difficult, if not impossible, to see one's way clear to understanding the moral significance of sympathy, compassion, concern, and friendship.

IV

The notions of 'altruism' and 'altruistic' will play a central role in this work, and bear some delineation at the outset. By 'altruism' I will mean a regard for the good of another person for his own sake, or conduct motivated by such a regard. This meaning corresponds, I think, to customary philosophical use of the term as well as to what Butler meant by 'benevolence.' But it departs from ordinary use in not carrying the connotation of self-sacrifice or, at least, self-neglect. Because of this usual connotation, 'altruism' is in many ways an unfortunate term, yet it seems the most suitable among the options available. But it should be remembered that, in my usage, to say that an act is altruistic is only to say that it involves and is motivated by a genuine regard for another's welfare; it is not to say that in performing it the agent neglects his own interests and desires. (The implications of this point are specifically addressed in chapter IV.)

By calling sympathy, compassion, and concern 'altruistic' emotions I mean to imply that they involve a genuine regard for the good of the person who is their object. But I do not mean, simply by my choice of label, to rule out the view that all emotions, hence altruistic emotions, are in some way fundamentally self-regarding, that acting from them is, ultimately, acting egoistically.

In contending with the Kantian view, one is dealing with more than an explicit set of arguments and positions. In addition, and not readily distinct from these, are certain concerns, general orientations of thought, intellectual tendencies, metaphors, and the like which do not necessarily congeal into definite views or positions. Iris Murdoch seems to be making a similar point when she speaks of the unavoidability of metaphor in moral philosophy.

> The development of consciousness in human beings is inseparably connected with the use of metaphor. Metaphors are not merely peripheral decorations or even useful models, they are the fundamental forms of our awareness of our condition . . . .
> Philosophy in general, and moral philosophy in particular, has in the past often concerned itself with what it took to be our most important images, clarifying existing ones and developing new ones. . . . it seems to me impossible to discuss certain kinds of concepts without resort to metaphor, since the concepts are themselves deeply metaphorical and cannot be analyzed into non-metaphorical components without a loss of substance.[4]

Kantian notions and metaphors do not always exclude the moral significance of sympathy, compassion, concern, and friendship, but they do at least distract us from it. Because of this, the considerations I bring to bear against the elements of the Kantian view will not always be detailed arguments or counter-arguments, but rather alternative perspectives, constructions, and examples. These will all, I hope, be considerations capable of moving the intellect and of loosening the profound grip which the Kantian view has on our moral thought.

This approach will make substantial use of certain examples, which will be described in more detail than is often done in moral philosophy. On some occasions these will be merely illustrative, that is, will be merely heuristic devices to help bring out the force of a point which could nevertheless be readily understood without the example. But more often they will have a broader function. They will be meant to describe moral situations which Kantianism does not characteristically speak of and which its categories are poorly suited to describe. They will thus serve as points of reference for the development of alternative views.

II

ALTRUISTIC EMOTIONS AS MORAL MOTIVATION

I

This chapter will aim at an account of the altruistic emotions which brings out their immunity to some of the Kantian criticisms. I will begin with some preliminary remarks, noting aspects of the altruistic emotions which are important to keep in mind from the outset. Some of these remarks will be elaborated in later sections, and additional aspects will be noted as the full account of altruistic emotions emerges in our discussion.

One purpose of this preliminary account is to indicate some of the complex structure of the altruistic emotions as psychological phenomena. Part of the source of neglect of these emotions in philosophy lies in oversimplified views of them.

Altruistic emotions are intentional and take as their objects other persons in light of their 'weal' and, especially, their 'woe.'[1] Sympathy, compassion, or concern are directed towards others in virtue of their suffering, misery, pain, travail. And so the altruistic emotions have a cognitive dimension: the subject of the emotion must regard the object as being in a certain state (e.g., of suffering). A person's woe involves elements of differing degrees of importance or seriousness; for example, suffering is more serious than inconvenience; one cares more about avoiding the former than the latter. Compassion, concern, and sympathy are distinguished from one another and from other other-regarding sentiments or attitudes partly by the different levels of woe which they can take as their objects. I have sympathy for or feel sorry about someone who is mildly inconvenienced by a detour or who misses a good film; but I cannot (barring unusual circumstances) feel compassion or concern for him on those grounds alone. Compassion and concern take more serious levels of woe as their object.[2]

The cognitive dimension is not sufficient for an altruistic emotion to be present, for someone could believe that another is suffering yet not be roused to compassion or sympathy for him. The subject must be 'affected by' the plight of the other, and so there must also be an 'affective' dimension to altruistic emotions. Occurrence of these emotions on particular occasions involves some feeling-states or sensations. But each altruistic emotion does not have one single or distinct feeling-state which constitutes its affective dimension or component. For example, the affective state of mind which is involved in concern is not a single feeling, but comprises elements such as being upset at this or that aspect of the other's plight, worrying about the effect of the other's condition on him, hoping that no greater harm will befall him, etc.

Emotion-terms can be used either episodically or non-episodically. Someone can have compassion, concern, or sympathy on specific occasions, fairly well delimited in time. But 'to be concerned about' and 'to have sympathy for' do not refer to distinct emotion-episodes.[3] Usually when we speak of 'feeling (a certain emotion) for someone' we are referring to a specific episode involving some affective state, whereas we use 'having' and 'being' constructions non-episodically. We say, 'I am concerned about X, but I am not feeling that concern at the present moment.' But this is not always the case; sometimes 'feeling compassion for X' and 'having compassion for X' are not really different; and both can be used either episodically or non-episodically.

Both episodic and non-episodic uses of altruistic emotion terms involve cognitive and affective elements, as well as the other features described below.

Altruistic emotions are more than passive feeling-states which have a person in a state of woe as their object. They involve an active, motivational (or 'conative') aspect as well, relating to the promotion of beneficent acts aimed at helping the other person. In general, if person A fails to be motivated to help B (who is suffering), whom he is in a position to help at no cost and with minimal inconvenience to himself, then A does not have concern, compassion, or sympathy for B.

It is important to recognize this connection between the altruistic emotions and beneficent action, since prominent traditions in moral

13

psychology have pictured emotions purely as states of passively 'being affected by' something. Altruistic emotions are both affective *and* conative.

Yet in making this point some philosophers have overstated and misconstrued the conative element. For example, Philip Mercer claims that concern and sympathy for a suffering person involve 'being disposed to do something about' the person's condition.[4]

Let us distinguish two types of situations in which compassion, concern, or sympathy can occur. In the first, the object of our emotion is someone whom we are not in a position to help, such as those remote in distance from us (e.g., victims of natural disaster, disease, or crime, whom we learn about through the media). By 'not in a position to help' I mean 'not in a position to help without extraordinary rearrangement of priorities, disruption of our lives, or sacrifice.' The second category of situation includes those in which we *are* in a position to help, at minimal inconvenience and with no sacrifice. There are many situations falling between these two types, in which helping the other would require various degrees of cost, inconvenience, or disruption.

While, in the second type of situation, compassion, concern, and sympathy do involve being disposed to help, they do not in the first, i.e., where one is not in a position to help; at least, to say that they do is quite misleading, for there is no help for one to render. Perhaps in having sympathy, concern, or compassion one is disposed to do something until one becomes convinced that there is nothing for one to do. One might then wish that there were something one could do, regret that there is not, etc., but it seems odd to say that one is 'disposed to help' when one is convinced that one cannot.

Mercer's view extends an important truth about some situations of sympathy, compassion, and concern, to all situations. In doing so it overstates the 'practical' or action-oriented nature of these phenomena and obscures the moral importance of the altruistic emotions. This importance, discussed in detail in chapter VII, depends on recognizing that the value of altruistic emotions is not exhausted by their capacity to motivate acts of beneficence.

Common to the altruistic emotions in situations in which one is in a position to help and those in which one is not is a desire for, or regard for, the good of the other (for his own sake). This desire prompts (intended) beneficent action when the agent is in a position to engage in it. Failure to so act is a sign that the desire is absent.

The motivational aspect of altruistic emotions stems from this desire

14

or regard for the other's good; yet the desire or regard can exist when one has no scope for beneficence. In that case, symptoms of that desire would be to bemoan or feel sorry or sad about the other's plight, and to wish and hope that those (if there are any) who are in a position to help do so.

II

The remainder of this chapter will focus specifically on the motivational aspect of altruistic emotions. We will leave aside until chapter VII those situations in which the altruistic agent is not in a position to help.

On the Kantian view altruistic emotions are unreliable as moral motives, for they are too transitory and changeable. One acts according to how one feels — one's moods, impulses, and inclinations — and not according to the moral requirements of the situation. Our feelings for different people differ, independently of how we ought morally to act towards them. And so sympathy, compassion, and concern cannot be counted on to lead to morally right acts.

On the Kantian view, a moral motive cannot be unreliable in these ways. It must always be available to us and guide us consistently and reliably to morally right action. Only a purely rational motive, independent of the vagaries of our feelings, can do this. So a moral agent ought to look to reason or duty, and not to emotions of any sort, to guide him unfailingly to moral action. Therefore, according to the Kantian, a moral theory which places sympathy, compassion, and concern in a central role must be inadequate; only the sense of duty — of acting for the sake of what is right or obligatory — can meet the requirements for moral motivation.

In the next five sections I will argue both that the altruistic emotions, in their role as motives to beneficence, are incorrectly characterized by the Kantian view, and that they are not unreliable as moral motives. In particular I will discuss the relationship between the altruistic emotions and other psychological phenomena, such as moods, impulses, inclinations, personal feelings, and other altruistic sentiments. These latter phenomena do suffer from the moral defect of being unreliable as motives of significant beneficent action, and my argument will be that it is a failure to distinguish these phenomena from altruistic emotions proper which supports the Kantian view of the latter as morally unreliable.

15

III

Let us first consider certain moods which may lead to beneficent action. As part of a happy, joyful, and exuberant mood, I may be feeling very expansive and generous, and may therefore be more inclined than I normally would to give, e.g., money or possessions, to people around me. But such a mood might well pass, causing my generous feelings and inclinations to disappear.

Moods of exuberance, or joyfulness, or general warm feelings towards other people are certainly capricious, transitory, and changeable. If beneficence had to depend on them it would rest on a very precarious basis.

Such moods are significantly different from altruistic emotions. They may be sources of such impulses as would prompt us to lend someone money, buy drinks for others, etc. But they might just as readily fail to prompt any beneficent act whatever. I may be excited and exuberant yet (except perhaps for a general cheerfulness) fail to do anything of benefit to anyone.

Altruistic feelings and emotions involve an internal connection with the good of the particular other person who is their object. They involve an appreciation of another person's situation regarding his weal and woe. The acts of beneficence prompted by altruistic emotion grow out of this appreciation. By contrast, the moods in question do not involve such an appreciation of the other's situation. Such moods do not take as their objects other persons in light of their weal and woe, as altruistic emotions do. In fact it seems misleading to say that they take 'objects' at all; rather they involve a kind of tone or coloring of the way in which we experience the world when we are in such moods.

Therefore, that acts of beneficence can flow from such moods as excitement, high spirits, exuberance, and expansiveness is no indication of genuine concern, compassion, or sympathy for the person who is the object of the beneficence. Hence the capriciousness of the moods is not by itself an argument for the capriciousness of altruistic emotions.

Next consider the view that sympathy, compassion, and concern are like impulses, and are hence unreliable as moral motives, since impulses cannot be counted on to be there when we need them, and are liable to prompt inappropriate acts. I will discuss this view by considering whether acting on altruistic emotion is acting impulsively, on impulse, or on an impulse.

What is it to act impulsively? At the least it involves acting spontaneously and without deliberation. Even in this sense much action motivated by sympathy or concern is not impulsive, for these emotions can impel me to deliberate how best to help someone in need, and the action eventuating from this process, though deliberate and not spontaneous, will nevertheless be motivated by altruistic emotion.

Still, much action from altruistic emotion surely is spontaneous and undeliberate. Suppose that I am waiting in a check-out line of a supermarket with a cart full of groceries. I notice that the man behind me has only about eight items and, without giving the matter any further thought, offer to let him in front of me in the line.

Is this act impulsive, or done on impulse? I think not, for these locutions seem to imply that the agent has an insufficient grasp of his situation and of his act. This condition goes beyond merely acting spontaneously and without deliberation, for we can have an adequate grasp of a situation and, on the basis of that understanding, act well without having to deliberate about it. The mistake here, encouraged by an over-intellectualized picture of moral action, is to think that acting impulsively and acting with deliberation constitute an exhaustive disjunction. Much sympathetic or concerned action falls into neither category.

This is not to deny that sympathetic or compassionate action can also be genuinely impulsive. I can plunge into a quarrel between two acquaintances, intending to help out, yet because I really do not understand what is going on I cause more harm than good. But that to act from altruistic emotion can be impulsive does not mean that it typically or characteristically is.

Moreover, acting on a sympathetic impulse does not entail acting impulsively, in the sense delineated here. The former expression seems to carry, along with the notion of spontaneous and undeliberate action, some implication of a suddenness or an unanticipated quality, but not the implication of inadequate grasp of one's situation. Hence the former avoids the particular moral deficiency of the latter, though, again, not all sympathetic action is done on a sympathetic impulse.[5]

So action motivated by altruistic emotion does not typically suffer the deficiencies, as moral motivation, that impulsive action does.

Another way in which altruistic emotions are assimilated to moods is conceiving the acting out of altruistic feelings as the doing of something which one is 'in the mood' to do (or, what seems almost equivalent, of what one 'feels like doing'). This phenomenon seems also to correspond to what we mean by 'acting according to one's inclinations', in at least one sense of that protean term 'inclination'. This usage of 'mood' seems distinct from what has been discussed above. Still, moods in this sense are evidently capricious, and if acting from altruistic emotions entails being in the mood to do something, it would follow that altruistic emotions are capricious and hence unreliable as motives to beneficence.

But this view of altruistic emotions is incorrect. I am by no means in the mood to do everything which I do out of sympathy, compassion, or concern. Out of concern for a friend I might spend an evening helping him to sort out a difficult situation, when this is not at all what I am in the mood to do. I might really be in the mood to stay home and watch television. Quite often the acts naturally prompted by an altruistic feeling will involve us doing what we are not in the mood to do, and not doing what we are in the mood to do. (This is not to deny that sometimes we are in the mood to do that which we do out of altruistic emotion.) That in having an altruistic feeling I desire the other's good does not by any means entail that I am necessarily in the mood to do, or that I feel like doing, what will bring about that good. In this particular sense of mood, in acting out of altruistic feeling I can act contrary to my mood. So not all altruism comes from altruistic moods. Hence we do not have here an argument for the capriciousness of altruistic feelings.

This point comprises part of a response to the Kantian view that in acting from emotion one acts egoistically, hence without moral value in one's action. For what I have argued here is that in acting from altruistic emotion one is not acting egoistically in the particular sense of doing what one feels like doing or is in the mood to do. In fact in acting from altruistic emotion one can act contrary to one's moods. One can even act self-sacrificingly in acting from altruistic emotion. (The issue of egoism will be discussed further in chapter IV, pp. 75-7 and 83.)

IV

Let us now discuss some other altruistic sentiments which, while not impulses, inclinations, or moods, nevertheless suffer a deficiency as motives to significant beneficent action.

Altruistic emotions, sentiments, and attitudes all involve a desire for the good of another person; this is what makes them altruistic. But they differ in the strength of this desire. Some altruistic sentiments involve a stronger desire for the other's good than do others and therefore involve a stronger disposition to help the other person (when the agent is in a position to do so).

'Well-wishing' is an altruistic sentiment. One wishes the other well, is pleased at his pleasure and happiness, does not want things to go badly for the other person. Well-wishing involves a genuine regard for the other's good, yet this sentiment does not imply a strong desire for the other's good. If the other were suffering, well-wishing would not imply a substantial willingness to help out if doing so would take some trouble or inconvenience.[6]

In contrast, compassion and concern do prompt acts of beneficence which take time, trouble, and effort, and involve inconvenience and perhaps sacrifice on my part. If I perceive that someone is in trouble or danger, compassion or concern for this person can lead me to go out of my way, to sacrifice some of my own desires to help him out.

Of course the altruistic emotions themselves vary on the dimension of the strength of desire for the other's good. I can have weaker or stronger concern for different people, implying a lesser or greater desire for their good, and willingness to act so as to foster it. Yet there is a threshold of the strength of this desire below which an emotion cannot go and still be compassion, concern, sympathy. For example, having compassion for someone implies a greater strength of regard for their weal than feeling sorry for or being mildly upset about someone's plight; yet the latter sentiments do involve a genuine regard for another's weal and are thus altruistic.

The strength of desire present in an altruistic attitude or emotion is related to the issue of reliability as motivation to beneficence in this way: the weaker the desire, the less the disposition to engage in beneficent action — that is, the less likelihood there is of beneficent action (e.g., because the less the cost, sacrifice, and inconvenience to oneself one is willing to countenance in order to help the other). Hence, the weaker the desire, the less reliable as a moral motive.

So the altruistic emotions are more reliable than altruistic sentiments which involve a weaker degree of desire for the good of the other. And the stronger the sympathy, compassion, or concern, the stronger the desire, hence the greater the reliability.

This difference among altruistic sentiments is connected with a distinction noted earlier between different levels of importance or centrality within a person's weal or woe (p. 12). Though the same altruistic emotion can take different levels of woe as its focus, in

19

general compassion, concern, and sympathy take more central aspects of woe as their focus than do some other altruistic sentiments, such as well-wishing, feeling mildly sorry for, etc. Often it is because one is helping to relieve a strong negative condition of the other that one is more willing to put oneself out to help than one would if the other were in only a mildly negative condition.

The foregoing account and arguments have largely emphasized those features shared by the altruistic emotions, for the argument of the book concerns what is common to the altruistic emotions and to the altruistic virtues associated with them. It is worth pointing out, therefore, that interesting and morally significant differences exist among these altruistic phenomena, which can not be explored within the confines of my argument. For example, while compassion involves the apprehension of someone as in pain or suffering, generosity does not. One helps an injured person out of compassion or concern, but not out of generosity. It is perhaps generous, but not compassionate, to give a gift to someone to whom one stands under no obligation. Generosity necessarily involves giving up something which is a good to oneself, while acting from concern, kindness, or sympathy does not. An act of concern, but not of generosity, can conform to (though not be motivated by) one's duties or obligations. Some altruism involves a subordination of one's own interests to those of another; some does not.

These remarks indicate some of the important distinctions among compassion, benevolence, generosity, kindness, sympathy, thoughtfulness, charity, love — all of which share the feature of 'altruism'. An important task for moral philosophy is to explore these differences.[7] Yet the dominant tendencies in moral philosophy and especially Kantianism have directed us away from this general moral territory.

V

Up to this point I have been concerned to distinguish between altruistic feelings and some other feelings, moods, and impulses, in order to get clearer on aspects of the nature of altruistic emotions relevant to their reliability as moral motives. In considering this issue of reliability it is worth focusing also on the causal effect of our moods on our altruistic emotions.

I will examine the relationship between certain negative moods or states of mind — such as sadness, depression, sorrow, 'bad mood' — on our altruistic emotions and feelings.

My general claim is that though negative moods and states of mind can have an effect on our altruistic feelings, they do not typically extinguish existing ones nor necessarily prevent potential ones. Let us consider an example: I have a friend, Jean, whom I know well and to whom I am devoted. Lately she has been behaving in a strange and (so it seems to me) somewhat self-destructive manner. I am concerned about her. I try to keep in touch with her, to see how she is doing, and to help her when I can.

Then suppose that a sour mood overtakes me, or that I become depressed about something. This negative state would not necessarily undermine my concern for Jean. It might not at all keep me from being worried about Jean's state, or being affected by the things which Jean does which are the grounds of my concern for her. My own mood might affect my direct inclination to help her out, though it would not necessarily do so. In fact it might even strengthen it, giving me (as I see it) an opportunity to 'get out of myself' and thus to snap out of my own bad mood. But even if it did affect my direct inclination to help, it would not necessarily affect the concern itself, with its attendant willingness to help. That is, I might be absolutely willing — because of my concern for Jean — to help her, though my own psychological state prevents me from being in the mood to do so.

The same argument could be made for sympathy or compassion. A sympathy or compassion well grounded in an understanding of someone's situation — whether a friend or not — is not necessarily undermined or even substantially affected by negative moods such as sadness, depression, sourness.

One source of the view that there is a direct general connection between 'negative states or moods' and altruistic feelings might be the conception that negative states always involve a self-absorption which does not leave any room for attention to others. But this is not typically the case, except perhaps for very extreme depression, grief, or sorrow. Mild depressions, bad moods, or sadness do not prevent us from being attentive and responsive to others in sympathetic and concerned ways.

This argument relates to a well-known passage in Kant's *Foundations of the Metaphysics of Morals* in which he portrays a person whose sympathy for others is extinguished by a personal sorrow, and who, out of a sense of duty, helps those for whom he is unable to sympathize.[8] A personal sorrow, unless it were very extreme, would not typically extinguish my sympathy for persons whom I regard as being in bad straits and for whom I have felt sympathy. Thus if I performed a beneficent act in such a situation I might do so out of sympathy. This is not to say that the act could not also be performed out of duty, as Kant envisages; nor is it to deny the possibility that one's sorrow could extinguish one's sympathy. It is only to deny that this happens necessarily. Some of the plausibility of Kant's view of duty as the sole worthy moral motive comes from failing to see that our altruistic feelings and emotions can survive our negative moods and states, and can motivate us to act counter to our mood of the moment.

Thus the capriciousness of negative moods, the fact that they come and go regardless of moral considerations, does not carry over to altruistic feelings; for altruistic feelings, though to some extent affected by moods, are not controlled by them.

But the effect of negative moods on altruistic emotions might be thought to fall less on already existing ones than on the likelihood of our coming to feel sympathy or compassion when we are in such moods. I might naturally be more likely to sympathize with someone else's troubles if I am feeling good about myself than if I am troubled and depressed.

There is something right in this line of thought; but it must be treated with caution as a general statement of the effect of our moods on our altruistic feelings. First of all, persons of low self-esteem or who are often or chronically depressed can still be quite kind or concerned about others, willing to give of themselves to help others, genuinely emotionally responsive to and caring about others. In fact, to place little value on one's own interests and goals and yet to care genuinely about the good of others is a moral character structure often found in women insofar as they are generally considered inferior to and less important than men.[9] Though such a character structure is quite unhealthy in many ways, this unhealthiness does not necessarily prevent genuine sympathy, compassion, care, and concern for others.[10]

A person's receptiveness to being moved to sympathy, compassion, or concern by the plight of others can certainly be affected to some extent by negative moods.[11] But this effect does not show that altruistic emotions are capricious or generally unreliable as moral motives, for they can also withstand changes in those moods.

What causal effect does exist between negative moods and altruistic feelings does not in any case provide unequivocal support for the Kantian view, for rationalistic or Kantian motives, such as a sense of duty, are susceptible to the same effects. That is, as a psychological fact, the likelihood of our acting according to our duty is also affected by our negative moods. Sorrow or grouchiness might cause someone to fail to act in accordance with what he knew to be his duty. One step further back, such moods might affect the likelihood of the agent even thinking, or thinking seriously, about what his sense of duty tells him to do in the situation. His sorrow may blind him to the moral dimension of the situation in the first place.

VI

Let us next consider altruistic emotions and personal feelings. By 'personal feelings' I refer primarily to affection, friendly feelings, liking, and being drawn or attracted to (personally rather than sexually). These are feelings directed towards others which can exist either inside or outside the context of friendship or a similar personal relationship. In chapters III and IV, personal feelings will be discussed within the context of friendship. In the present chapter I will discuss them outside of that context.

From a Kantian perspective personal feelings, like moods and impulses, are capricious. For our likings and affections for others can be subject to all sorts of vagaries and personal idiosyncrasies. W.D. Ross, for example, refers to 'instinctive affection' as a 'wayward capricious motive.'[12] Beneficent acts motivated by personal feelings are not typically grounded in moral considerations, or considerations of rational principle.

Personal feelings are subject to an additional moral defect, 'partiality.' We often help people we like, rather than people who need or deserve our help. 'Suppose that I want to relieve a certain man who is in distress, simply because I like him personally,' C.D. Broad says, describing what he regards as a case of non-morally motivated action.[13] Action motivated by personal feelings thus violates one important requisite of the Kantian view of morality and of moral motivation, its impartial character.

Both altruistic feeling and personal feeling are types of positive feelings for others which can lead to beneficent acts. The Kantian view does not draw the distinction between them. I will argue that altruistic feelings are in important ways a different type of feeling than personal feelings.

Altruistic feelings are directed towards other people in light of or in regard to their weal and woe; whereas personal feelings are directed towards others in light of their personal features. These features may be personal qualities, such as sense of humor, vitality, integrity. Or they may be aspects of the person which stand in some special relationship to myself, e.g., interests which we share (politics, movies, popular music), or experiences we have shared (growing up in the same neighborhood, attending the same college). It is in virtue of such features that I have affection for someone, or like him, or am drawn to him; but not that I have sympathy, compassion, or concern for him.

I am not always able to say or even know what about a person is the source of my liking of him. I might say 'It is a certain quality he has — I can't put my finger on it.' Or I may even like him without having the notion that there is some feature which is the source of my liking, even a feature which I am not able to name or to explain. But even in these cases it would still be in virtue of certain personal features or qualities of the person that I liked him.

A person's personal qualities can play a part in activating my sympathy or concern. For example, Frank's infectious good humor can make me more liable to feel sympathy or concern for him, when his situation warrants it. But the sympathy is still directed to Frank not in virtue of his personal quality of good humor but in virtue of his weal or woe.

In one sense we can say, to emphasize this categorical difference, that altruistic emotions and personal feelings have different objects. That is, an altruistic emotion is directed towards a-person-in-light-of-his-weal-or-woe (or, in-light-of-his-situation-as-it-bears-on-his-weal-or-woe); whereas a personal feeling is directed towards a-person-in-light-of-personal-features. But we must keep in mind that in both cases it is the whole person who is the object of these feelings, as I am defining them. Personal feelings are directed not to the person's qualities themselves, but to the whole person in light of his qualities. It is John whom I like, and not merely John's wit or vitality. One can readily imagine liking a certain quality in someone but nevertheless disliking the person overall, because of his many other qualities which I find objectionable; but I am not concerned with this sort of liking.

An aspect of the categorical distinction between altruistic and personal feelings is that they can occur independently of one another. I need not like, nor have affection for, someone with whom I sympathize or for whom I feel concern or compassion. I may actually dislike him and yet feel sympathy for him, insofar as he is having a rough time, or is suffering. Conversely I can be attracted to or feel affection for someone without being sympathetic towards him in every situation, e.g., one in which he feels that my sympathy is called for. I may feel that in this situation he is not worthy of sympathy, that for example he has behaved badly and is only getting what he deserves. This does not mean that I do not like him or feel affection for him. Thus there can be affection (or liking) without sympathy or compassion, and also sympathy or compassion without affection.[14]

A second point, regarding the independence of altruistic emotions from personal feelings, is that many of the natural contexts for much of our concern, compassion, and sympathy are ones in which the issues of liking or disliking the other person do not arise. Envision a person doing volunteer work for a local tenants' organization in his community. Let us say that he investigates complaints of people about their housing situations. It would be natural that feelings of sympathy, compassion, and concern towards the different tenants whose cases he works on would often be aroused. But the issue of whether he likes or dislikes the particular people might seldom come up. It may be that for many or even most of the people he sees he does not feel particular affection. He is not personally drawn to them. He has no particular desire to get to know them better, or to spend time with them. He does not find them particularly pleasant or appealing as persons.

Nor, we can also imagine, does he dislike the people or find them unattractive. Though not drawn to them he is not repelled or put off by them either. In this way we can say that personal feelings towards the people in the community are minimal or non-existent in him. What is salient for him is not the people's personal features, but their weal or woe, particularly in regard to their housing situation (e.g., whether their stairways are in good repair, whether they are getting sufficient heat, etc.), which is the focus of his work. It is this feature of the people's situation which arouses his altruistic feelings for them. In this way one can emotionally respond to the people without personal feelings being involved. Thus in many contexts people who arouse altruistic emotions in us will not necessarily arouse personal feelings. (In real life the feelings would probably not be kept as separate as I have portrayed here. It would be more natural for the volunteer housing worker to be personally drawn to some of the people, while disliking others.)

An objection can be brought to the argument so far. For surely, one might feel, at least some personal feeling is naturally aroused towards a person for whom one is feeling sympathy — some kind of liking, or very mild affection. It would hardly be humanly typical to feel entirely personally indifferent to or uninterested in the people. Altruistic feeling and personal feeling would not be as separate as I have claimed, for contexts in which altruistic feelings are aroused will also arouse some form of personal feelings.

There is a kind of ambiguity in the terms 'personally indifferent' and 'disinterested' as they are used here. In one sense, to have sympathy, compassion, concern, or care for someone is already not to be personally indifferent and disinterested. One cares about their welfare, about how they are doing. Even if it is primarily housing which our man is dealing with, I have not imagined him as being concerned only about the 'housing dimension' of the people's lives. Rather, he is concerned about the people themselves as whole people. He is interested in their general weal and woe, even if it is only a specific area of it to which his work and his main attention is directed. In this sense he is certainly not disinterested in or personally indifferent to the people.

But this sense of 'personal interest' — essentially connected with the people's well-being — is merely correlative to altruistic emotion; it does not, I would argue in the manner above, imply any substantive personal feelings towards the people: enjoying their presence, wanting to get to know them better, thinking fondly of them, being drawn to them, etc. Kant and Sidgwick claim that helping people naturally gives rise to feelings of liking towards them,[15] but this could be only a very weak or mild sense of liking or affection. The way in which our man likes almost everyone for whom he feels sympathy (and whom he does not dislike) must be a different sense of liking from one in which he really or especially likes only a few among the people whom he works to help and feels sympathy for.

More directly relevant to our argument, it is only the stronger sense of like which is appropriate to the issue of the capriciousness of personal feelings. It is clearly this sense which Broad and Ross have in mind in this regard (see p. 23 above). For liking in the weaker sense is essentially subsidiary to or supervenient on the altruistic emotion. It arises because of them, rather than being an independent source of beneficent acts. Hence it cannot be personal feelings in this sense which are claimed to be a source of the capriciousness of the altruistic emotion and the beneficence to which it leads. I will thus restrict 'personal feelings' to this stronger sense of liking and affection.

If we distinguish personal feelings from altruistic emotions we can see that arguments for the capriciousness or partiality of personal feelings, whether valid or not, will not apply *ipso facto* to altruistic feelings. Part of the tendency to see altruistic feelings as capricious, or otherwise morally suspect, stems from a tendency to assimilate altruistic feelings to personal feelings, or to fail to distinguish clearly between them.

An aspect of the difference between altruistic feelings and personal feelings is that altruistic feelings are grounded in moral considerations in a way in which personal feelings are not. Altruistic feelings have as their object another person in light of (and for the sake of) his own good. The good of others is a moral consideration; and so altruistic feelings are grounded in moral considerations. The moral significance of altruistic feelings, then, lies not only in their promotion of morally good acts, in particular the acts of beneficence, but also, and at a deeper level, in the fact that their objects are the good of other persons.

Thus altruistic emotions and feelings have a kind of moral significance which personal feelings lack. In two ways personal feelings are not grounded in moral considerations: (1) The qualities of the other person which are the source of one's liking of him are not necessarily or typically moral ones. They can be his wit, warmth, vitality, certain interests of his, etc. (2) The object of personal feelings is not the good of the person to whom the feeling is directed.

But the fact that personal feelings do not have this moral grounding is not a moral defect in personal feelings, nor is it grounds for moral suspicion. It only seems to be so if one has the view that all feelings, or actions, ought to have moral grounding. But such a 'moralized' view of the morality of personal feelings and attachments is an inappropriate one. There is nothing morally unacceptable about liking people for qualities which have nothing to do with morality, or with having feelings towards them which are not directed at their good. This point is separate from the defense against the view that as a moral motive personal feelings are capricious and unreliable.

VII

Failure to distinguish clearly between personal and altruistic feelings can be seen in Kant's discussion of love. Kant's views on love are undeveloped. I will discuss only one strain in his views, though it is a major one. Kant distinguishes two kinds of meanings of love: 'practical' and 'pathological,' or love from duty (or will), and love from inclination.

Practical love is the doing of beneficent acts (from the motive of duty or on principle.)[16] Love as inclination is a feeling for others which leads to beneficent acts.[17] Kant seems to envisage these two kinds of love as exhaustive of altruistic motivation generally.[18] Given this dichotomy, the altruistic feelings will tend to be regarded as love from inclination. Yet Kant tends to regard such love as a direct affection for another person.[19]

On the one hand 'love' refers to a kind of motivation to beneficent action, a motivation which is a feeling. On the other hand, love as a feeling is also thought of as an affection for another person. Thus we are encouraged to see Kant's view of altruistic feelings in one of two ways. Either he is picturing all feelings which prompt beneficent acts, and *a fortiori* altruistic feelings, on the model of affection and liking (personal feelings); or he is simply leaving altruistic feelings out of consideration altogether, excluding them from his definitions of either pathological or practical love. On either interpretation, that personal feelings are serving as a model for love gets in the way of a clear focus on altruistic feelings as distinct from personal feelings.

Even though the two kinds of feelings are distinct, it is true that personal feelings do give rise to altruistic emotions. We are in general more likely to feel sympathy or concern for (and hence are more likely to benefit) persons whom we like than those towards whom we have neutral or negative personal feelings. I will argue in chapter III that there is no moral deficiency in this fact by itself, but only if other moral strictures (duties of impartiality, specific obligations to others, etc.) are violated. There I will take up the issue of 'partiality'.

That argument will acknowledge the evident fact that personal preference may lead us to favor with our beneficence a less deserving to a more deserving person when justice might seem to demand that we favor the latter. But in regard to the support which this admission lends to the Kantian view, it should be noted that whether we act from a sense of duty or rightness can itself be affected by personal feelings. Our personal affection for X can lead us to convince ourselves that X is more deserving than Y (when the reverse is the case). Or it can lead us simply to overlook the desert-features of the situation altogether, so that the question of moral rightness never gets raised. We can convince ourselves that we are morally permitted to make an exception (in favor of our friend) to a general rule of justice in this particular case. Or, because of our feeling for a particular person, we can simply and knowingly act counter to what our sense of duty prescribes.

As an actual human motive, the sense of duty is no more immune to the distorting, rationalizing, self-deceiving, and weakening effects of personal feelings than it is to negative moods (see above pp. 20-3). It shares these susceptibilities with sympathy, compassion, and concern, though on the other side they share the ability to operate independent of our moods and our personal feelings.

VIII

The previous sections have purported to show that sympathy, compassion, and concern are not subject to the same moral unreliability as other phenomena, from which they are generally insufficiently distinguished. They are not impulses nor inclinations to perform helpful acts for their object. They are different from moods. Altruistic emotions can remain focused on their objects, motivating us to act beneficently towards them, despite changes in mood and impulse, and in the absence of inclinations to perform beneficent acts.

Altruistic emotions involve a stronger motivational component (a stronger desire for the other's good) than do weaker altruistic sentiments; hence they are capable of leading us to act contrary to our inclinations and interests, for the sake of the other's welfare.

Altruistic emotions involve a focus on the other's good in a way that personal feelings do not. And so they can be present towards someone regarding whom one has negative personal feelings, or no personal feelings at all.

Do the arguments of the previous two sections show that the altruistic emotions are reliable as motives to beneficence? To answer this we must focus more closely on the notion of reliability here, and on the concern which the Kantian has to exclude incentives which are unreliable. Our concern is that the motive in question, when acted on, actually lead to morally right action. There is a strain of thought within Kant's writings which implies that any incentive other than the moral law leads only accidentally to morally right acts. Though Kant generally has self-regarding motives in mind when he says this, he explicitly includes altruistic emotions and feelings as well.[20]

Such a view appears to deny any essential connection between an altruistic emotion and the relief of the woe of the person who is its object. But if we acknowledge that these emotions do have objects, and that their objects are other people in regard to their weal and woe, then it cannot be said that the actions motivated by such emotions lead only accidentally to morally good action, i.e., action aimed at promoting the other's good. It is true that in particular cases acting from sympathy or compassion will not lead to the promotion of beneficence. But this does not mean that the connection between the sympathy (as a motive) and the beneficence is merely an accidental or contingent one.

If it is acknowledged that beneficent action is, *ceteris paribus*, morally good, then a motive which naturally leads to it (i.e., a person acting from it aims at beneficence) is not, on the criterion in question, unreliable as a moral motive.

A second aspect of unreliability has been addressed in these sections; not whether if someone acts on altruistic emotion he aims at something morally good, but whether if the motive is present to an agent he can be counted on to act from it. Here the Kantian view implies that because of the transience, capriciousness, and weakness of emotions in general (and of altruistic emotions in particular), the presence of the motive is not reliably followed by the agent acting in accord with it.

Against this I have argued that altruistic emotions are in fact reliable, or, in any case, are not significantly less reliable than the sense of duty. For they are not essentially transient, weak and capricious, but rather are able to withstand changes in mood and impulse, and can motivate us to act contrary to our inclinations and interests.

IX

But there are further conditions which the Kantian view places on an acceptable moral motive, and the relationship between these and reliability bears examination. These stem from the Kantian view that the moral motive must be something available to any moral agent at any time, this in turn deriving from the notion that acting morally or being a moral person must be equally within the reach of anyone.[21] This availability can be broken down into two components. The first ('summonability') is that we must always be capable of summoning up the motive before our mind. The second ('efficaciousness') is that if the motive is present to our mind, and we aim to act in accord with it, then we are always capable of so acting; that is, the motive is always capable of withstanding any contrary inclination.

Let us consider efficaciousness first. The Kantian thought here is that our sense of duty is capable of withstanding any contrary inclination;

for we *can* do what we know unconditionally that we *ought*. No matter how tempted we are to act wrongly we are always in fact capable of acting morally,[22] whereas this is not so for any emotionally based motivation. Sympathy or concern which we feel for someone cannot (as a motivating force) necessarily withstand a strong desire for something incompatible with what sympathy or concern would lead us to do.

This Kantian view seems overstated in both directions. First, it is at least doubtful that we are actually capable of withstanding every inclination, temptation, or desire by means of our sense of duty (our firm conviction as to what is the right thing to do).[23] Some desire may simply be too overwhelming for our sense of duty to contain. Secondly, the altruistic emotions are themselves capable of withstanding quite strong counter-inclinations. Concern for someone can lead me to forgo activities which I strongly desire to engage in, or to make great sacrifices of my possessions, money, even my life, for the sake of the object of my concern.

More important, the significance of efficaciousness as a condition for adequate moral motives is doubtful. If what we want from a motive is that it in fact leads us to morally good acts, we should be more interested in the extent to which the given motive actually does this, in the face of the counter-inclinations which we as human beings actually face, than in whether the motive is capable of withstanding any possible counter-motive.

Let us grant for the sake of argument that there are some strong anti-moral inclinations which agent A's sense of duty would be able to counteract, but his altruistic emotions would not. This would, it seems, show that in situations in which such inclinations would arise, duty would be more reliable than altruistic emotion. But it would hardly show that the latter were *un*reliable, if my argument up to now is right. Perhaps it is not thought to be reliability which is the issue here but rather the view that any incentive which can be called moral must simply be able to stand up to any counter-motive. But separated from the other elements of the Kantian view with which it is associated, this notion seems arbitrary as setting a necessary condition for any moral motive.

Let us now consider 'summonability,' as the second aspect of availability. On this ground the Kantian excludes emotional motivation as moral. For, it is claimed, we cannot summon up our feelings, we simply have them; whereas we are always capable of bringing before our mind the thought that something is right or is our duty. (Part of the view here is simply that we can summon up a thought but not a feeling).

The factual claim here too is overstated. For, as we will discuss in a later chapter, sometimes we can summon up feelings of sympathy or other altruistic emotions, and can do so more than the Kantian conception of emotions will allow for. But this admission still leaves part of the Kantian claim, namely that while we are always capable of summoning up our sense of duty we are not always capable of summoning up our sympathy.

This seems to me possibly true. A consequence is that I do not assert that what I am claiming to be moral motives, namely the altruistic emotions, are always available to a moral agent. Someone may simply be unable to get himself to feel compassion when it is appropriate for him to do so (and even when he acknowledges this appropriateness); but to feel compassion is no less morally good for that.

But the significance of summonability as a necessary condition for moral motivation is questionable, for two reasons. First, the fact that we can summon up the consideration of duty or obligation does not mean that it will actually be efficacious in motivating us to act. A person may be aware that something is the right thing to do, yet choose not to do it. This may be, as mentioned before, because though he attempts to or intends to do it, he has desires against doing it which are too strong and which prevent him from successfully carrying out his attempt. But this familiar phenomenon of weakness of will is not the only way in which one can fail to do what one knows to be right. One can simply choose to ignore or act against what one knows.

So the fact (if it is a fact) that we are actually able to summon up the thought that something is our duty does not mean that this thought will motivate us to act. Thus the availability of the sense of duty is actually two steps removed from the production of morally good acts — the first being the genuine attempt to so act, and the second being the overcoming of any resistances to that attempt. Hence the kind of availability granted here is some distance from genuine reliability as a moral motive.

A second reason why summonability seems both less related to reliability and less significant as a condition of moral motivation is that moral agents may and often do simply fail to summon up considerations of right and wrong, duty and obligation, in the first place. That is, that any moral agent is capable of bringing before his mind the thought of what he ought morally to do does not mean that agents inevitably do this. People often simply fail to bethink themselves of what, in the situation they are facing, is morally forbidden, permissible, or obligatory. They fail to perceive a moral dimension of this sort in the situation at all. After all, one must already regard a situation as possibly presenting a question of morality before one even raises the question of what is morally right (or wrong) for one to do, that is, before one even consults one's conscience or sense of duty.

That we are able always to summon up our sense of duty is significant for the issue of an agent's actually acting from his sense of duty, only given that the agent does attempt to summon it up; that is, only if he raises the question for himself of what he ought morally to do. But this question may fail to occur to him, just as an agent may fail to be aroused to sympathy or compassion in situations in which others' weal and woe is at stake. And it is as characteristic of (certain types of) selfish people that they seldom think about what they ought morally to do as it is that their altruistic emotions are so rarely touched by the woe of others.

One important strand of thought within the Kantian philosophy pictures the agent as always concerned with, or at least fully aware of, the moral status of his actions — whether they are morally right, wrong, or permissible. I am arguing that this is decidedly not true of every moral agent.

So if we are looking for motives which will lead us reliably to good or right acts, that a certain motive is always capable of being summoned up is less significant than the extent to which it actually is summoned up.

Exploring the notion of reliability, then, we find that according to two significant aspects thereof — that, *ceteris paribus*, the motive aim at morally good acts, and that the motive be capable of withstanding contrary inclinations — altruistic emotions are reliable moral motives. Two further conditions — summonability and efficaciousness — are seen to be very weakly related to reliability, questionable as showing a significant advantage of the sense of duty over altruistic emotions, and arbitrary as necessary conditions for moral motives.

There is a systematic ambiguity in the way the Kantian view thinks about the moral adequacy and inadequacy of motives beyond the more straightforward issues of reliability discussed in this chapter. Against emotion-based motivation the Kantian argues that such motives are, so to speak, not always there when we need them. We might simply fail to be roused to sympathy or concern, even when another is in need of beneficent action on our part. Yet in favor of rationalistic, obligation-based motivation it is argued only that we are always capable of summoning it up as a motivating force. Masking the ambiguity, one can say that our emotions are not always available to us as motivation, whereas reason and duty *are* always available.

The ambiguity is that the emotions are criticized for how they actually operate (though we have seen that the Kantian view does not get this right), whereas the rationalistic motives are not scrutinized for how they do operate, but are put forward only for how they are capable of operating. Obviously these are two quite different things. Once one asks how a sense of duty actually operates as a human motive, the great gulf which the Kantian view portrays between it and the altruistic emotions virtually disappears (in regard to the issues discussed in this chapter).

My argument here depends on driving a wedge between the motivational capability of a certain motive or consideration, and its actual functioning within our lives. In one sense Kant and many of those who have followed him are concerned to draw this distinction themselves. Kant says that we cannot be certain in any individual case that someone has in fact acted from duty; but we can be certain that we ought to so act, hence that we are capable of doing so.[24] And more generally, the point of a Kantian theory of morality is not to speak of what considerations do move us to action, but of ones which ought to.

But, on the other hand, there is an important strand within Kantian thought which sits uneasily with the sharp distinction drawn here; and that is the notion that considerations of moral rightness are in an important sense unavoidable or inescapable. Certainly one motivating force behind Kantianism as a moral philosophy is the desire to ground morality in considerations to which no agent can fail to be susceptible.[25] No one can claim to fail to be moved by these considerations simply because, for example, he lacks certain desires or sentiments (or other variable and contingent features of human nature).

On this line of thought, a sharp line cannot be drawn between what we as moral agents are in fact moved by and what we are capable of being moved by; for the considerations in question, in order to meet the demands of the theory, must be ones to which we are unavoidably susceptible.

I have argued that considerations of moral rightness (and, by implication, any other considerations) do not and cannot meet this condition. We are always capable of failing to be moved by a sense of rightness or duty, just as we always might fail to be moved by sympathy or compassion. And by this I mean more than that a sincere attempt to act in accordance with such considerations might fail (i.e., weakness of will). I mean first that a person can simply choose to act against what he acknowledges to be his duty, and second, and more significant, he can act within the situation without any thought at all to considerations of moral rightness, permissibility, or impermissibility.

What I think a Kantian would want to say here is that an agent can ignore moral considerations only on pain of irrationality, and that it is this notion of rationality which underlies the inescapability of moral considerations. The thought is that, at the very least, if such a perspective were brought to the agent's attention, he would be unable without irrationality to reject its applicability, i.e., he could not simply choose to ignore right and wrong. A stronger view here is that independent of the issue of right and wrong actually being brought to his attention, the agent offends against rationality merely by failing to consider it in his action in the first place.

This takes us to a line of inquiry which will be pursued in chapter V. But even if the Kantian were correct here about rationality (which I deny), such a notion of rationality could not do the trick of making considerations of rightness inescapable or unavoidable, and thus cannot assure the presence of Kantian motivations in a way in which (as I grant) the presence of emotional motivations are not assured. For doing so would require it actually to be unintelligible, and not merely irrational, for someone to act (consciously and intentionally, i.e., not mere random body movements) while failing to consider the Kantian-moral dimension of his situation, or to act contrary to such considerations while acknowledging their applicability. Only this would show Kantian-moral considerations to be actually unavoidable. But, as I have argued, this is not at all unintelligible. There is simply no way to find within the notion of an 'agent' or of 'action' the resources to exclude such possibilities. And in fact most of us at some time or other act knowingly and willingly contrary to, or failing even to consider, the thought of what is right in the situation facing us. Whether such an action is morally objectionable is a wholly different question, which will be taken up at a later time. I argue here only that it is possible, i.e., not unintelligible.

In this chapter I have tried to articulate some lines of thought within Kantianism which, taken together, view the sense of duty, as an incentive, as always available or summonable (and in fact

inescapable), and as efficacious, i.e., as being at least capable of standing up to any contrary inclinations. It was Schopenhauer's insight to
identify the presence of this thought in Kant, and there is important if
overstated insight in his ridicule of Kant for thinking that in the moral
law (and its formulation in the categorical imperative) he had found a
moral incentive which was always 'at our service.'[26]

I follow Schopenhauer here in abandoning any search for the omni-
available moral incentive, while broadening the search for those incentives which do in fact lead to morally desirable action through showing,
by an examination of the structure of such motives, that they possess
features required or at least desirable in moral incentives. I depart from
Schopenhauer only in his wholesale rejection of duty as even a possible
moral motive, and in his concomitant view of compassion as the only
moral incentive.

X

The argument of this chapter does not deny the evident fact that
altruistic emotions are sometimes capricious, and the next few sections
will explore the moral significance of this. For the Kantian, that significance is that we should not look to our emotions at all as moral motivation, but only to purely rational motives, i.e., sense of duty. For only a
sense of duty can avoid the deficiencies of changeable emotions.

I will begin by describing two examples in some detail. These examples
will serve only partly as illustrations of concrete claims; more significantly they will serve as points of reference and reorientation, in this
and subsequent chapters, for a discussion of altruistic feelings and their
role in morality.

Example 1: Jones, a college instructor, is visited in his office by
Clifford, a student who has not been getting his work in on time.
Clifford explains that he has been having some troubles with his family,
which have been making it difficult for him to find the time and con-
centration to get his work done. Jones generally regards Clifford as a
competent and serious student and believes what Clifford is telling
him. As Clifford begins to talk more about his situation with his family
it becomes evident that it has been causing him pain and distress.
Moreover, as the conversation progresses Clifford goes beyond explaining why his work has been late and Jones can see that Clifford is
beginning to talk and would like to continue talking about the problems

themselves. Jones lets Clifford go on, feeling some sympathy for Clifford in regard to the evident difficulties he is facing.

However, after a short time, Jones looks at his watch and remembers that there is a lecture beginning in a few minutes which he would like to and had been planning to attend (though it is not really important to Jones that he do so). Unable to easily cut the conversation off he begins to feel irritated, and his sympathy disappears. He stops Clifford, dismisses him from his office and rushes to the lecture.

Example 2: While at work Bob hears that a friend Sue has had an accident and is in the hospital. He feels concern about her and intends to visit her when he finishes work. However, when he actually does finish work the drive to the hospital seems very long (as he thinks about it), and some fellow workers ask Bob to come out and have a beer with them. His feelings of concern weaken and he does not visit his friend Sue in the hospital, but rather joins his fellow-workers for a beer.

Both of these examples illustrate how altruistic emotions can be weak, changeable, capricious, unable to withstand conflict with convenience, self-interest, inclination. In both situations the response of the agent leaves something to be desired, from a moral point of view. Clifford's situation warrants a more fully sympathetic response than Jones gives him; forgoing the lecture in order to remain talking with Clifford would seem the morally appropriate, or at least preferable, thing to do. In the second situation, Bob shows less than admirable sensitivity to his hospitalized friend's situation. Sue would be very pleased if he did visit. Perhaps she would be disappointed if he did not (though he has no actual obligation to visit). Certainly he would be doing the morally better thing by visiting Sue.

XI

According to the Kantian view such examples are typical of how emotions operate. But, as the argument of the previous sections has indicated, sympathy does not necessarily operate in this manner. Jones's sympathy for Clifford could persist despite his desire to attend the lecture. Bob's feelings of concern could withstand his tiredness, his desire to join his friends, in sufficient strength to motivate him to visit Sue. Contrary to the Kantian view, it is not only the sense of duty but the altruistic emotions themselves which are capable of the steadfastness, strength, and persistence necessary to withstand changes in mood and circumstance over time, and to overcome contrary inclination, in order to motivate an agent to act in a morally appropriate way.

This suggests that, at least in many situations, it is not altruistic emotions in themselves which are capricious, but rather instances of sympathy or concern which are inadequate as sympathetic or concerned responses to the situation. For if Jones's sympathy for Clifford had been as substantial as Clifford's situation warranted it would not have been so readily extinguished by Jones's remembering about the lecture; and similarly for Bob's concern for Sue. In fact, it could even be questioned whether it could genuinely have been sympathy in the first place if it were so readily extinguished;[27] in any case a genuine and substantial sympathy would have remained, though this would not preclude Jones from regretting missing the lecture or even having to struggle against the desire to leave. It is a Kantian prejudice which assumes that the only motivating thought capable of withstanding or struggling against a desire to do something incompatible with a morally good (e.g., beneficent) act is the thought of it as our duty. In fact, direct concern or sympathy for another can equally well do this.

So changeableness and capriciousness are not so much a characteristic of all altruistic emotions as they are of weak, superficial or otherwise inadequate instances of them. It reflects morally on Jones and on Bob that their sympathy or concern is not as substantial as the situation warrants (or, if this is too strong, not as substantial as would be desirable). But the Kantian cannot allow for this inadequacy to be a failure of emotional response itself, but only a failure to act from duty in the situation.

Since the Kantian sees emotions as essentially changeable and capricious, he will not see that 'weak,' 'inadequate,' 'superficial,' 'capricious' function as specific terms of moral criticism of a person's emotions and emotional responses themselves (on particular occasions or in general). A's response to B's plight may be too weak for the compassion or sympathy which B warrants. C's concern for D may be inadequate as a response to the danger which D faces. E may be someone whose sympathy for others generally remains at a superficial level. The form of moral assessment and criticism in all of these cases presupposes that there are appropriate emotion-based responses, which the agents in question fail to give.

The Kantian view will therefore not allow for the range of possibilities necessary for an adequate moral assessment, or at least an understanding, of the agent in light of his emotional response. Let us look at some possible plausible accounts of Jones's response to Clifford.

Jones might simply have failed to listen attentively to Clifford and thus not have grasped his situation fully. This in turn might be because, in general, he does not take students' personal lives seriously, or does not pay attention to aspects of their lives not directly related (in his mind) with academic concerns. This would not necessarily be a fault, but it would be an explanation of absence of sympathy.

Alternatively it may be that Jones has the view that it is improper for teachers to relate to aspects of students' situations other than purely academic ones. He might not necessarily blame or think it wrong of the student to have brought up personal matters, but the fact that he does not regard it as appropriate for himself to respond to them will affect his capacity and willingness to be sympathetic, to be fully open and receptive to what the student is saying.

A different picture would not have Jones with a clear view of what is and what is not appropriate, either for a student to bring up or for him as a teacher to respond to. He might be perfectly open to hearing about and responding to students' personal problems — i.e., until doing so conflicted with something which was interesting to him intellectually (such as attending this talk). Jones would then be a person who regards his own intellectual pursuits as more important than his students' personal lives. We can imagine Jones as a man to whom it would hardly occur to choose to remain listening to a student's personal problems when there was an event of intellectual interest to him going on at the same time.

Another possibility is that Jones is just generally not a sympathetic person, not only to students but to people in general. Thus his sympathetic responses would generally be fairly weak and superficial and would seldom withstand the press of a desire for something which he wanted.

In another direction it may be that Jones's behavior in this situation is not a symptom of these wider attitudes towards others, or towards a particular group of people (students). He may simply be tired, and this may be what keeps him from fully taking in what Clifford is saying. This would account for the weakness of his sympathy. Perhaps if he were listening fully he would be strongly sympathetic to Clifford. If Jones was not up to his usual standard of sympathy, our moral assessment of him in regard to this situation would take that into account.

Whatever explanation is given of Jones's sympathy will connect with his general attitude towards others (or particular groups of others). But the Kantian view, in virtue of regarding feelings as by nature capricious, will not be led to try to understand the situation in terms of what it says about Jones. It will not encourage us to look for the connections between Jones's sympathy and his beliefs about the situation, his general ways of regarding people, his values.

Further, connecting an agent's particular emotional response with his attitudes and values will point the way to possibilities of change, should that be desirable. If the lack of sympathy is connected with a constricted view of one's professional role, then a change in that conception might open one up to a fuller and more extensive sympathy towards those whom one serves in that role. (The issue of emotions and moral change will be considered in detail in chapter VIII).

According to the Kantian view only a purely rational motivation, in terms of a sense of duty, can correct for the deficiencies of emotion-based motivation. I have argued that this is not so; but it may be worth spelling out by means of an example how sympathy can have the required features of strength, tenacity, and ability to withstand contrary inclination, without actually itself being a duty-grounded motive.

The example concerns Brown and Casey, whose situation is identical to that of Jones and Clifford up to the point where Jones (Brown) realizes that the talk he would like to attend is beginning momentarily.

Example 3: Brown realizes that the lecture which he would like to attend begins momentarily. But through the conversation he has come to feel sympathy and even some degree of concern towards Casey regarding his situation with his family. This sympathy means that he does not even feel inclined (or tempted) to have the conversation end in order to be able to attend the lecture. He feels that Casey's problems are genuine and that they are causing him distress. He would like to be able to help Casey out. The importance to Casey of the plight he is describing is appreciated by Brown, and he is moved by it. It is this appreciation in which his sympathy, and concern, is grounded. The lecture, when the thought of it comes to him, does not present itself as being of nearly sufficient importance in comparison with Casey's situation. And so it is not even the case that Brown chooses – needs to choose – not to attend the lecture. Rather the thought of it passes from his mind and he focuses fully on Casey.

Later, Brown may be sorry to have missed the lecture. But he will not resent having done so unless he somehow feels that he had to do so. Nor need he even be sorry that Casey talked with him at a time which caused him to miss the lecture. He more feels pleased that Casey did talk with him at all, and he accepts the unfortunate coincidence of events with only mild regret.

In example 3 Brown's sympathy is not capricious in the way that Jones's is. It is not weak or transitory. It possesses strength and steadfastness. It is not controlled by events external to its proper object (Casey). It withstands the desire to go to the lecture. (Rather, because of the strength of the sympathy, the thought of the talk does not even become a desire which needs to be withstood.) The sympathy is an appropriate emotional response to the situation, and it leads to the morally good act of listening sympathetically to Clifford (and trying to help him).

It is not necessary that Brown be acting from any sense of duty or obligation here. He need not regard himself as under any obligation to Clifford to listen sympathetically to him. He may, but need not, see it as part of his professional, or even merely human, responsibilities or obligations to forgo the lecture for Clifford's sake. He may but need not regard his action as 'the right thing to do' for anyone in his situation. Rather, his direct sympathy for Clifford may simply be strong enough to move him to forgo the lecture in order to listen to Clifford and try to help. (I do not argue here either for or against the view that it would be better to act from duty than from sympathy in this situation.)

XII

In summary: although our sympathetic and concerned responses can be transitory and capricious, this is not so much a defect in the altruistic emotions *per se* as it is a sign of an inadequacy in the particular responses of the particular person in question. The possibility of correcting these inadequacies lies so to speak within the altruistic emotions themselves. One need not turn to a rationalist, duty-based motivation for such a corrective, nor, as we saw in previous sections, are such Kantian motives immune from the effects of changes in mood, inclination, and circumstances.

An upshot of the argument is that altruistic feelings and emotions possess many of the features demanded by the Kantian view of a motive adequate to morality; thus one important element in the Kantian view's case against the moral value of altruistic feeling is undermined, and the Kantian view of altruistic emotions is shown to be false.

This does mean that sympathy, compassion, concern, and care are much more like rational moral principles or the sense of obligation than one might have thought; and so the contrast between my view and the Kantian view may seem not so great as it did originally. This should not be seen as detracting from the force of the alternative view which I am developing; but rather should undermine some of the sources of adherence to the Kantian view itself. Admittedly, so far the Kantian view of morality itself has been only minimally criticized, and in fact it is partly in its name that the altruistic emotions have been defended. Let us proceed, then, to consider the Kantian view of morality, and thereby to bring out its differences from and inferiority to a morality of altruistic emotions.

III

FRIENDSHIP, BENEFICENCE, AND IMPARTIALITY

I

So far we have examined the Kantian view of emotions against the background of the Kantian view of what moral motivation must be. It might be thought that the argument, while yielding a greater understanding of the altruistic emotions themselves, has dealt with only the periphery of the Kantian arguments against the moral significance of emotions. The central arguments draw on a conception of moral action itself which excludes emotionally motivated action. In this and subsequent chapters, we will look at the Kantian view of morality itself – of what the moral point of view is and of what it requires of us in the way of action.

In light of the Kantian conception of morality we will look at the phenomenon of friendship. Friendship is a phenomenon of great complexity. While desiring to avoid simplistic accounts of it, there are two aspects of friendship which will be important for the discussion. One is the personal importance which our friends have to us – the fact that friends are people we like, enjoy being with, trust and rely on, that they are part of what in our lives is valued by us.

The other aspect is that friendship (or, anyway, most genuine friendship) involves a substantial concern for the good of the friend for his own sake, and a disposition to act to foster that good, simply because the other is one's friend. In this sense friendship is an altruistic phenomenon, and a locus of the altruistic emotions. This altruistic aspect is essential to friendship; a relationship based solely on mutual advantage (even if it involved mutual liking) would not in this sense be a friendship.

Moreover the kind of personal importance which friendship has to us requires the genuine concern for the friend's good. Without it there could not be the trust and reliance, and the substantial mutual personal involvement between the friends. In friendship one desires and acts for the good of the friend, not simply because he is another human being but precisely because he is one's friend.

I will call these two aspects the 'personal' and the 'altruistic' aspects of friendship, though the personal implies the existence of the altruistic. What I called earlier the 'personal feelings' — liking, affection — are part of the personal dimension of friendship, though they take on a greater significance and are embodied in a richer web of emotions, attitudes and sentiments than they usually do outside of friendship.

In the Kantian conception of morality, impartiality and impersonality are central notions, definitive of the moral point of view. Moral rules and principles embody a perspective which excludes no one, and which takes everyone's good into account. Every human being, simply in virtue of being human, is worthy of equal consideration, and his good is equally worthy of being promoted. Moral rules and principles must reflect this fact. So taking the moral point of view in one's actions and judgments means regarding them from an impartial standpoint, not giving weight to one's own preferences and interests simply because they are one's own, but rather giving equal weight to the interests of all. The viewpoint is impersonal because it gives due consideration to all, favoring none simply because of personal preference, but only according to principles which can be vindicated from that impartial perspective. This line of thought draws also on a notion of fairness as central and definitive of morality: it is unfair to accord a benefit or burden simply because it accords with one's own preferences or interests. Action which fails to stem from, or to be justifiable by appeal to, this impartial standpoint is, on the Kantian view, contrary to morality.[1]

The Kantian view implies that we may not pursue our own interests simply because they are our own. But it implies no less a condemnation of acting for the sake of one's friend, simply because he is one's friend; for it equally violates impartiality to favor or benefit someone based on one's personal feelings, attachments, and relationships. For example, when one is in a position to benefit either one's friend or another person who is much needier or more deserving, it would be wrong to prefer the friend. We must take equally into account the interests of all whom we are in a position to benefit. Only if benefiting our friend can be justified according to such a perspective of impartiality is it morally acceptable.

The point is not that the Kantian view necessarily condemns benefiting one's friend. What it condemns is benefiting one's friend simply because he is one's friend. Similarly, morality does not condemn all acting for the sake of one's own interest; what it condemns is doing so simply because it is one's own interest. For such benefiting gives no guarantee of being justifiable from an impartial perspective; yet it is such a perspective which, on the Kantian view, morality requires.[2] But friendship itself does at least appear morally condemned on this view, for it appears to be an integral part of what friendship is that we do often act for the sake of our friend's good simply because he is our friend, and without thinking that such action is or needs to be vindicated from an impartial point of view.

Let us examine, then, whether morality does make the demand that we be able to vindicate all our actions by reference to impartiality, i.e., whether 'the moral point of view' is coextensive with an impartial and impersonal standpoint.

First, does friendship offend against any moral requirements not stemming from impartiality? We want to clear this issue out of the way to make certain that we have isolated impartiality from other possible sources of moral objection to friendship.

One might have a duty to another person stemming from a (non-personal) relationship with him — e.g., a professional relationship — or from some commitment made to him, such as a promise. Friendship for another party might lead one to violate such an obligation, e.g., to fail to show up for an appointment with a client because one wants to remain with one's friend who is feeling down in the dumps.

Second I could have a 'natural duty' to another person, not in virtue of any special relationship, but simply in virtue of being a fellow human. Sidgwick states such a duty of beneficence in the following way, as 'a positive duty to render, when occasion offers, such services as require either no sacrifice on our part or at least one very much less in importance than the service rendered.'[3] Our friendship for someone could lead us to neglect this natural duty of beneficence in favor of helping out our friend.

There is no global or fundamental moral criticism of friendship itself involved in either duties of commitment in non-personal relationship, or in natural duties of beneficence. For situations in which such duties arise are restricted to special circumstances, which do not ordinarily include those in which we help out our friends.

In any case the possibility of conflict of our attachment to our friends with our more impersonal duties (and let us suppose that we are not speaking here of cases in which a duty to the friend is involved, for then we would have a conflict between duties) does not mean that we will necessarily violate those duties. A person might well do the morally right thing by adhering to his more impersonal duties in the face of the 'temptations' of friendship. Nor will this typically mean that he is any less of a good friend to his friends. It is possible to have strong friendships to which one is loyal, friends to whom one is devoted; and yet to be conscientious in fulfilling one's more impersonal duties towards others. The possible difficulty of achieving such a state has less to do with any inherent tension between conscientiousness and devotion to friends than with the difficulty of achieving these separate virtues.

II

Turning now to the issue of friendship and impartiality, I will argue for essentially the same view as I just did regarding natural duty and duties of special relationship — namely, that impartiality is a moral requirement only in certain restricted sorts of situations. It is not a morally incumbent perspective to take up in every situation. In particular, friendship does not typically involve us in situations in which impartiality between the interests of our friends and those of others is a moral requirement; hence in acting beneficently towards our friends we do not typically violate a duty of impartiality.

Certainly attachments to particular persons can lead us to violate impartiality, and thus to be unfair to others. Someone in an official position to dispense jobs can use his position to get jobs for his friends and relatives, independent of their qualification for the jobs. And we may imagine a doctor who because he likes a particular patient devotes too much of his consulting time to this patient, neglecting the others who are waiting to see him.

But such situations do not point to a general conflict between helping one's friends and helping others. It is no violation of impartiality if I phone my friend to see if he is feeling better, knowing that he has been ill. Such a situation of acting from concern for a friend does not impose on me the obligation to take into account the interests of all the people whom I *might* help at that point in time, and to choose according to some impartial criterion whom to benefit. The examples so far given point to one of the primary sorts of situations in which such impartiality is demanded — namely, an official capacity within some public institution or practice.

A judge, a captain of a ship, a doctor, a nurse, a teacher, all occupy roles or positions in which a certain kind of impartiality is demanded of them regarding the interests of certain parties whom they serve or for whom they have some responsibility. This impartiality extends to persons to whom they have special attachments. The benefits or burdens dispensed by these persons are to accrue to persons not on the basis of some personal attachment of the holder of the role to them, but on the basis of some impersonal criterion, connected with need, qualification for a position, established and rational procedure, or the like.

Thus, to take the most obvious case, a judge is meant to dispense justice impartially. He is meant to make his decision on the merits of the case and not according to his attachment to one of the parties involved. A teacher is not supposed to grade a student higher because he likes him or has a special attachment to him. A nurse is supposed to help his patients according to their individual needs, not according to his own personal likings and attachments.

It is an important part of our understanding of the duties of impartiality attaching to these roles that persons who assume the roles are aware of what those duties entail; in particular, aware of how they might impinge on the interests of those to whom they are attached. Thus a doctor or nurse knows that by virtue of his position he is forbidden from attempting to secure for a friend of relative some drugs or other medical care which are properly meant for others, or which fair procedures would allot to others.

A person might refuse to (or not be allowed to) put himself in a position in which he would be required to dispense a benefit or a burden according to an impartial rule, where a friend would be one of the candidates for the benefit or burden. This could be either because he did not feel he would be capable of such impartiality, or because, if he were, he would find it too difficult or painful to be required to dispense the benefit to someone other than his friend.

For this sort of reason it is a general policy that judges not sit in cases in which they have some special connection to one of the parties (or in which they have a self-interest in the outcome). The temptations of conflict between their impersonal duties and their personal attachments would be too great and would place an extraordinary personal burden on the role-occupiers and on the friendships; so for the good of everyone such a situation is best avoided.

Institutional roles and positions are an obvious arena of life in which a certain kind of impartiality between the interests of all, including those to whom we are personally connected and attached, is demanded of us. Equally obvious is the fact that situations covered by such roles are very untypical of those in which we interact with and benefit our friends. And so the existence of such roles does not betoken a common, much less a fundamental, moral problem regarding the beneficence dispensed to our friends.

This conclusion is strengthened by the fact that even within these institutionalized roles there is a limit to the demand of impartiality, and in most cases a scope outside of that limit for benefiting those whom we choose for whatever reason (e.g., personal attachment or liking) to benefit. Thus if a doctor, having fulfilled his obligations to his patients, spends extra time on the case of a friend, this would not be a violation of impartiality, but on the contrary would be admirable behavior on his part. A teacher is permitted to give more attention to some students than to others (not merely on pedagogical grounds), as long as he gives full and adequate attention to all. The criterion here, vague though it may be, of when it is morally permissible to depart from strict impartiality, has to do with what is regarded as the duties of one's role, in contrast to what is regarded as going beyond those duties (and is in that sense supererogatory). In the latter situations, what one does for those one chooses to help is regarded as giving something of oneself, rather than as depriving others of what one owes to them by virtue of one's institutional relationship with them.[4] The line between these is extremely difficult to draw, is not in general fixed but is subject to change (e.g., redefinition of what constitutes the responsibilities of a role), and is not applicable in all situations. But that it exists is significant for our argument. For what it shows is that even in contexts in which impartiality between the interests of one's friends and those of others is demanded, this demand is limited in its scope, and there remains an area in which we are able to express our natural care and concern for our friends, our desire to do what is good for them, outside of the constraint of impersonal considerations.

It should be noted that this argument applies not only to actual friends and personal relationships but also to people whom we like but have no substantial or developed relationship with; i.e., it applies to beneficence from personal feelings. Here too we are morally permitted to benefit them, and this benefiting is not in general required to be justified through an impartial perspective or procedure. Morality does not in most situations demand of us that we justify such beneficence with regard to the interests of others whom we could have served but did not.

III

I have claimed that institutional-role contexts are ones in which impartiality is demanded of us. What I have not yet done is to show that the demand of impartiality is limited to such institutional-role contexts. Nor, related to this, have I given a general characterization of the conditions in which such a demand is an appropriate one, from a moral point of view.

To help gain some clarity regarding the non-institutional contexts in which impartiality is incumbent upon us, it is necessary to make an important distinction. The fact that impartiality does not demand that we constantly appraise our potential beneficence to our friends by an impartial standard does not mean that we are justified in totally disregarding the interests of others when the good of our friends is at stake, even outside contexts in which strict impartiality is demanded. To take an extreme example, suppose that I am in a train crash in which many people are injured, including my best friend (but not myself). I am certainly generally justified in giving my first attention to my friend. But it seems also required for me to give some attention to others. Some weighting is evidently called for here. The point is that strict impartiality is not required or appropriate, but neither is ignoring the interests of others simply because the weal and woe of one's friend is at stake.

Suppose I pass two persons on the street digging their cars out of the snow, and one of them is my friend. Surely I am justified in choosing to help my friend in preference to helping the stranger, though it would also perhaps be the decent thing to do to attempt to help both of them. But if, say, the friend could very easily dig the car out by himself, and in fact had almost finished doing so (though there was still room for assistance from someone else), and the other person obviously could not do so without some assistance, then another factor will have been introduced which must be weighed against the desire to help the friend. Here it might be more appropriate that one help the other person. (One would imagine that the friend would agree that this was appropriate.)

49

We then have three different sorts of situations. In the first we are required to treat the interests of the relevant parties from a strictly impartial perspective, even if one of the parties is our friend. Personal attachments must be entirely overlooked (though only up to a certain point). In the second, we are required to give some attention to the interests of others, but are not required to regard those interests strictly impartially or as having equal weight to the interests of friends who are involved. In the third type of situation consideration to the interests of others is not at all appropriate or relevant. In such situations it is morally permissible to act solely for the benefit of one's friend.

The existence of the second category helps to define the limits of impartiality, while giving credence to our sense that in some situations the presence of friends does not or should not preclude attention to the interests of others. For we see that in some situations there is some moral constraint on us to attend to the weal and woe of others, even though the weal and woe of friends is also at stake; and yet the grounding of such moral constraint need not be located in a demand for impartiality. In the train crash example just described, I have claimed that one ought to give some help to injured persons who are not one's friends, though one's first concern is properly with one's own friend. Some might see this help as a strict duty (of beneficence) on the ground that great harm to others can be avoided with little sacrifice to myself (or to a person to whom I am attached). But even if one does not see this as an actual duty, it is possible to recognize some element of moral constraint in the consideration that my ability to help the injured persons ought to weigh with me in my actions.

Thus, that I ought to help the injured persons seems in many contexts to stem not from a general demand of impartiality between the interests of all concerned (including myself or my friends) but from something like a duty of beneficence. That this is so can be seen if we imagine the situation without the friend's being injured. There would still be moral constraint for us to help the other persons; yet this moral constraint cannot stem from a demand that we treat the interests of everyone, including those to whom we have a special attachment, impartially. What the presence of the friend does to the moral configuration of this situation is not so much to undercut this moral quasi-demand of attention to the weal and woe of others, but to bring into play another consideration against which it is to be balanced. It is still true that we ought to attend to the interests of the injured strangers, but it is entirely proper for us to attend first to our friend. It would be inappropriate for us to give our entire attention to our friend, when further attention to him would produce minimal good to him compared to the much greater good which could be produced by attention to others. But, on the other side, it is also inappropriate for us at the outset to apportion our help impartially – solely according to need – ignoring the fact that one of the persons is our friend.

It could be responded here that this argument applies only to situations where the interests of others are substantially threatened – such as in a train crash – so that attention to their interests is urgent enough to be morally incumbent upon us. The same argument would not seem to hold for the case of digging the car out of the snow (above, p. 49), where there would seem no demand that we attend to the interests of the person who is not our friend merely because he could use some help.

Yet it seems that whatever consideration is appropriate regarding the weal and woe of the stranger is unaffected by the presence of the friend, and so is not connected to impartiality. Though there is no *duty* to help the stranger, perhaps there is some moral deficiency or inadequacy in failing to do so, if one has nothing very important to do and could help fairly readily. Yet whatever force of 'oughtness' one attributes to the consideration of the man's weal and woe (regarding digging his car out) exists independently of whether the friend is present in the situation or not.

The presence of the friend merely interjects another factor which changes the overall moral configuration of the situation. We might properly not help the other, choosing instead to help the friend (assuming we cannot do both). But we do not thereby repudiate the moral consideration of helping the other.

Thus even in cases (involving friends) in which there is nothing like a duty of beneficence, a consideration to the interests of others does not stem from a requirement of impartiality; for, first, that consideration exists even when the friendship issue does not, and, second, impartiality between the interests of the friend and of the other(s) is not actually required.

IV

If the argument of the previous section is right, then in non-institutional contexts at least some of the morally appropriate regard to the interests of others can be accounted for without appeal to the principle of impartiality. This is a step towards defining the scope of the principle of impartiality in non-institutional contexts.

I suggest that we can learn something of that scope by asking in what the nature of impartiality, justice, and fairness consist, as virtues or traits of character exhibited in one's non-institutional (as well as institutional) life. Here the definition given by Sidgwick seems to me close to the mark:

> What then do we mean by a just man in matters where law-observance does not enter? It is natural to reply that we mean an impartial man, one who seeks with equal care to satisfy all claims which he recognizes as valid and does not let himself be unduly influenced by personal preferences.[5]

This definition brings out that impartiality or justice has to do with overlooking personal preferences in circumstances which have to do with according burdens and benefits to persons.

For example, suppose I am helping to settle a dispute between two persons, one of whom is a friend. Both persons are looking to me for mediation in the quarrel. This is a circumstance where justice or impartiality is required, or appropriate. We are not to favor the friend simply because he is our friend. Rather we are to overlook our personal attachment and consider only the factors relevant to the dispute. Hearing the claims made on both sides, it might turn out that I feel that the non-friend's claim has more merit, and that he is more deserving of the benefit regarding which there is a dispute.

Sidgwick's definition suggests why impartiality is not always required of us, nor required in every situation in which our actions are of a potential benefit to someone. For the application of impartiality depends on the pre-existence of claims on the part of persons involved (though the claim need not actually be made, or even recognized as existing, by the person who has it). It is only when someone has a certain claim on a benefit that it is a matter of impartiality to give due regard to his interest in that benefit. If he has no claim to it then such regard is no longer a matter relevant to impartiality. (These claims can be grounded in a person's meeting the criteria relevant for relegating a certain benefit within a certain procedure − e.g., the criteria for producing the soundest argument in a dispute, or the criteria for meeting a certain job specification.) A just person is one who can be counted on to overlook personal interest and preference, where others might tailor their views of the claims involved to their own preferences.

It is thus not impartiality regarding interests *per se* which defines impartiality, as it is impartiality regarding interests in which the parties involved have some claim, the honoring of which might require the overlooking of personal ties and preferences. This claim is not itself grounded in impartiality but is rather the grounds of it.

This is why it is not a violation of impartiality if I help my friend in preference to the other person also digging his car out of the snow. For this other person has no claim on my help. It may be good or decent of me to help him; to do so may be something which one could expect of a decent person. But it is not a claim. It is thus not a violation of impartiality if I fail to help, preferring to help my friend.

In the train-crash case the other injured persons also have no claim on my beneficence; or, rather, if one wants to argue that a duty of beneficence exists, which is thus correlative to a right or claim on the part of the injured persons, this is not the kind of claim which demands that we overlook or abstract ourselves from our personal attachments, apportioning our attention and help purely on the basis of need. (If this is so, then not every claim can be a basis for impartiality.)

Impartiality is appropriate therefore only in certain situations. It is not a perspective which defines what it is for us to act morally, to take up a moral point of view on our actions (regarding our friends). To refer to an example from Telfer,[6] if I choose to visit a pensioner (to help decorate his flat) rather than my friend, determining that the pensioner is in greater need of my visiting, this behavior is not in accordance with the virtues of justice or fairness; for the pensioner has no claim on my visit, which requires me to overlook my relationship with my friend and make my decision purely on the basis of which one will benefit more from my visit. Depending on other factors in the situation, my visit to the pensioner can evidence a commendable concern for a particular person to whom I have no relation; and, again depending on the situation, my friend may be able to acknowledge that it was a good thing for me to visit the pensioner rather than him. But if there is some virtue here it is not the virtue of justice or impartiality. (In other circumstances the visit to the pensioner can show an insufficient regard to the friend and to the friendship.)

The same can be said of impartiality in non-institutional contexts as was said above about institutional ones, namely that in most cases in which we can act to benefit our friends, but in which it is also within our power to benefit someone else, there are no claims on our beneficence the honoring of which requires us to overlook our personal ties. Thus there is no general demand of impartiality.

In fact Sidgwick's definition could be taken to apply to institutional as well as non-institutional contexts. Institutional contexts can be seen as an application of the general definition to a certain category of situation. For we can look at institutional contexts as helping to define the claims which some persons have, with regard to their interests, on other persons. For example, the claim which a patient has to be treated in a certain way by a doctor; or the student to be graded according to certain procedures by his teacher; or an applicant to be given a certain kind of consideration by the personnel officer. Part of what characterizes such institutional contexts is that they define more precisely than is often done in ordinary life what the relevant considerations are for allocating benefits to persons. This is why institutional contexts seem so appropriate for impartiality.

Finally, it should be remembered that even in contexts in which impartiality is demanded, there is almost always some room for the person of whom impartiality is demanded to benefit the friend in a way appropriate to friendship. (See above, p. 48.) For example, in the case of the quarrel mentioned above (p. 52), suppose I feel that the non-friend's claim to benefit is greater than that of my friend. Impartiality requires me to overlook my attachment to the friend in deciding that the benefit properly goes to the non-friend. But impartiality does not prevent me from showing special attention to my friend if he is disappointed, trying to do something to cheer him up, comforting him, etc., while not doing the same for the other person.

Thus impartiality is limited not only to certain sorts of situations. In addition, even within the situations in which it applies, it applies, so to speak only up to a point, and generally there will be room left over for extra beneficence to be shown to the friend.

To summarize the argument so far: according to one important strain of thought within the Kantian view, a principle definitive of morality is impartiality. To take up a perspective of impartiality regarding any of one's actions which impinge on the interests of others is to take up, and act from, the moral point of view. To fail to do this is to fail to act morally. A corollary is that it is contrary to morality — because contrary to impartiality — to favor the interests of oneself or one's friends simply as such, i.e., simply because they are one's own or one's friends.

Against this I have argued that it is not in general contrary to the demands of morality to prefer our friends' interests as such, i.e., to act for the sake of R's good simply because R is my friend, even if there are other persons whom it is in my power to help and who are in greater need than R. In fact it is entirely morally appropriate to do so. Such action does not typically violate the demands of impartiality; for that perspective is appropriate only in certain contexts, which do not include most friendship situations. There is no general demand of impartiality. Rather the demand of impartiality rests on prior claims to some benefit, the acknowledging of which requires the overlooking of personal preferences and attachments.

Thus acting morally is not always or fundamentally a matter of equality or impartiality towards all. For this is not what it is to act morally within friendship.[7]

Thus in one sense it is actually misleading to say that we are necessarily or typically partial to our friends, if this is meant to imply a deviation from a morally requisite norm of impartiality. For such a norm is not typically in force in regard to our benefiting our friends. In another sense, however, we are partial to our friends, in that we benefit our friends without testing that benefiting against a norm of impartiality with respect to others; and we are not morally remiss for doing so.

If this argument is right then impartiality does not define 'the moral point of view.' Rather, it defines a moral viewpoint appropriate in certain circumstances but not in others. When acting from friendship it is neither required nor appropriate (normally) to look to impartial or impersonal considerations to guide our actions. Impartiality, fairness, and justice are personal virtues, but they are merely some virtues among others. They are not definitive of moral virtue altogether.

V

One source of the view that a general stance of impartiality between the interests of friends and those of others is morally required comes from a picture of non-friends as in competition with friends for our beneficence, so that we are typically choosing between them. It is important to see that this picture is very misleading.

This is partly so because, as Telfer points out, some of what we do for our friends, such as 'the proffering of advice or criticism,' is not thereby rendered unavailable to others.[8] More fundamentally, it is because it is not the case that the kind of benefiting which we do for our friends is generally such as it makes sense to speak of doing for strangers. What we do for our friends is very particular to our relationship to them, both in the sense of being particular to friendship as a type of relationship, and in being particular to a particular relationship with a particular person. What is involved in comforting one's friend, for example, is particular to the friendship and grows with the friendship. It is only in the context of friendship that the friend is sufficiently open to allow someone to comfort him, and the particular ways in which the friend comforts are particular to those two people and to the relationship. I cannot just pop over to someone's house who is in need of comfort and comfort him, in the way I can to my friend. This is not to say that one can never comfort someone who is not a friend; but the contexts for it are much more restricted than in friendship.

Thus in comforting my friend I am not doing something which I could typically be doing for another. This is even true for Telfer's example of decorating a house (above, p. 53). I cannot simply go over to an old age pensioner's flat and help him to decorate it. I must have a certain kind of relationship with him, perhaps only an institutional one mediated through a certain kind of program. And so decorating my friend's house and decorating the pensioner's house are not equivalent activities from my perspective, and it is misleading to see a choice between them as one between the same kind of thing done for a friend and for a non-friend.

It is not only a matter of the trust, intimacy, and personal understanding involved in friendship which makes various kinds of 'doing for others' possible and appropriate within the friendship, while being impossible or much less natural outside of it. It is also that it is integral to the significance to the friend of what I do for him that my act is an expression of our particular friendship, of the particular concern and care which I have for my friend; rather than, say, an expression of a general human responsiveness.

The lack of comparability between what I do for a friend and for a non-friend holds for many activities in which we please our friend or make him happy. If we go out together to drink or to a film, what pleases my friend is essentially bound up with the fact that the activity is something shared with his friend. What gives the activity the particular kind of meaning and particular kind of pleasure that it has is in important ways bound up with how we relate to and participate in it together as friends. This is true even if we merely sit in the bar together and hardly speak a word to each other. The experience is still different from sitting alone, or with someone one hardly knows.[9]

Thus not only activities which relieve a negative condition of the other person, but also ones which bring about a positive one, are particular to the friendship; and therefore when we do something for our friends it is wrong to picture us as choosing not to do the same or something comparable for someone else.

This point is obscured by looking at friendship as involved 'beneficence' (or 'rendering services') as philosophers we have discussed (e.g., Sidgwick, Telfer, Kant) have tended to do, using the terms to cover all the different kinds of good which we bring about for others. The concept of beneficence is more appropriate in reference to kindness and generosity towards non-friends, to interaction in more impersonal situations than friendship. I want to gesture at some ways in which the notions of beneficence and of rendering services are ill-suited to express the good which friends do for each other.

First, beneficence is too individualistic a concept. It does not suggest something shared between two people. But, as we have seen, the good to our friend of what we do for him is bound up with its involving something shared, or its being an expression of a relationship between people.

Second, beneficence is too impersonal for friendship. It carries the implication that the giver and the recipient have a certain distance from, and stand external to, one another. But friends are bound up with each other. A related implication of beneficence is that of a good which could be a good for anybody and which could, as it were, be given by anybody. (That is why charity, and money generally, are often used as examples of beneficence). But we have seen that what makes what someone does for his friend a good for the friend is often (though certainly not always) very particular to the relationship, to the two particular people. It is a very personal good.

Thus the concept of beneficence itself obscures the particular nature of the ways that we do good for our friends, and encourages the false picture that what we do for our friends we could as well be doing for others, and thus that we choose against others when we choose to do good for our friends.

VI

It might be thought that I have left out an important aspect of friendship which would lend support to the Kantian view, and that is that friendship involves duties to the friend, duties which have a greater degree of stringency than duties to strangers. For cases in which the good of friends is given precedence over the good of others could be explained and justified by the stronger duties to one's friends, and so the acts of benefiting one's friend would not lie outside the Kantian moral perspective, as I have claimed that they do.

I will grant that there can be duties to friends, but I do not think this will help the Kantian view. For there are surely many situations in which we aid, comfort, support, or benefit our friends which, while integral to the friendship, are not actually morally required by it; they are not covered by the actual duties of friendship. It would be a poor friendship in which the only actions of benefit to the friend performed by his friend were those which he was required to perform. But if there are many actions not covered by the duties of friendship, these, in accordance with our argument so far, cannot be accommodated within the Kantian framework.

A second point is that it is not even clear that the duties which do exist within friendship can be accommodated by a Kantian framework, in particular whether they can be vindicated from a perspective of impartiality. For, it can be argued, duties within particular friendships have a dimension which is particular to the friendship — in being dependent on mutual understandings particular to the friendship — and cannot be accounted for from an impersonal perspective.[10]

One more line of thought might be open to the Kantian here, which does not abandon the perspective of impartiality as definitive of the moral point of view but rather attempts to encompass friendship within that perspective. Granting that many of our particular acts of friendship violate a stance of impartiality, in that often when we act for the benefit of our friends we could, even taking into account the trouble and effort involved, find others more worthy and warranting of our beneficence, and granting that nevertheless it seems improper to condemn such acts of friendship; still it might be argued that if we looked not to individual acts of friendship but to friendship as a whole, friendship could be seen to be morally acceptable from an impartial point of view. Such an argument could be that it is in general a good thing, or conducive to the interests of everyone, that there be a practice according to which people act beneficently towards their friends without in every case considering whether there is not someone else who could be better served by their beneficence. This argument could draw on the considerations that we are in a better position to know what our friends need and to help them than we are to do the same for others. Such a view would admit that this practice would in particular cases lead to benefiting someone who is less warranting of it than someone else. But in the long run, it would claim, the interests of humanity are best served by our having such a practice; and so friendship will have been justified from an impartial perspective.

In order for such an argument actually to show that friendship as we understand it can be encompassed within an impartial perspective, it is necessary that the argument take a 'rule-utilitarian' form.[11] That is, it must show that friendship as a practice promotes the general welfare better than any comparable practice. It would not be enough to show that under our present practice of friendship some long-term benefit is gained by violation of impartiality in particular situations. The argument must yield that practice which actually maximizes that benefit. For if it fails to maximize then some other practice would better promote the general welfare, which the impartial perspective compels us to take as our standard for assessing a general practice. To put this another way, if the practice of friendship fails to maximize welfare, this means that some aspect of the moral foundation of friendship cannot be encompassed within the impartialist framework.

But friendship cannot be given the required rule-utilitarian justification. For one could imagine another practice which was the same as friendship except that one helped the other in preference to one's friend in situations in which one did in fact know what another needed, in which one was equally able to meet that need, and in which that need was manifestly greater than one's friend's need. Such a practice is only one among many alternatives to friendship which if generally practiced would bring about more total benefit than friendship.

To this it could be replied, to draw on on the argument of a previous section, that there are certain goods internal to friendship itself, and our interest in them must be taken into account and allowed in some cases to outweigh more impersonally defined interests. But this is not a vindication of friendship from an impartial point of view. For to accept the goods internal to friendship is to accept friendship itself, including the feature of benefiting the friend for his own sake and independent of any impartialist justification.[12] So the non-impartialist nature of friendship is really acknowledged in the premise of the argument itself. It is no doubt true that we do in fact prefer the present practice of friendship to any practice which detracts in any substantial way from our benefiting our friends in favor of benefiting others who, according to impersonal criteria, are more deserving or more worthy. But this is simply to say that we prefer a world in which the impartial perspective is not always required of us to one in which it is. This truth does not help the Kantian.

The attempt at an impartialist vindication of friendship is caught in a dilemma. If it appeals to interests only contingently connected with friendship, it will turn out that friendship as we understand it will not be the practice which maximally promotes those interests. But to the extent that it acknowledges the value of goods internal to friendship, it implicitly abandons an impartialist perspective.

A deeper issue which the failure of an impartialist vindication of friendship points to is the conception of friendship as a practice, on the model of a game or institution involving rules, defined roles, positions, and responsibilities, etc. This model, which when applicable may well lend itself to rule-utilitarian justifications (baseball is a better game on the whole if only three strikes are allowed rather than four), applies very poorly to large areas of our personal moral lives and experience. The illumination which this game- or institution-model provided within moral philosophy — seeming to preserve the insights of both act-utilitarianism and intuitionism while avoiding their defects[13] — has diminished as the model has gotten stretched and distorted in being applied across the board.[14]

Even if an impartialist argument were able to justify benefiting friends rather than others in situations in which we regard it as appropriate, it would not give us what we want. For what friendship requires is acting for the sake of the friend as such, rather than because, as it (contingently) turns out, such a practice serves the general interest, or is otherwise amenable to an impartialist justification.[15]

It is not merely that an impartialist justification does not work. In addition, actually taking up such a perspective of impartiality regarding one's own friendships would signify a distorted relationship with one's friends. It would belie the emotional importance which the friendship had for one. For that importance involves (among other things) benefiting the friend simply because he is one's friend and purely for his own sake. Yet this is precisely what the perspective of impartiality forbids. According to it one benefits one's friend only because, from an impersonal point of view, one's friend most warrants benefiting, among all those whom one could benefit. Such an attitude evidences an emotional detachment not compatible with true friendship.

VII

A challenge could be made to the view I have put forth of the relations between friendship and impartiality which would make that view compatible with a Kantian perspective.[16]

I have admitted that in some situations it is morally incumbent on a person to take into account the interests of others as well as those of one's friends and loved ones, and that, in a subset of those situations, one is required to treat these interests on a plane of strict equality or impartiality. But if this is so then a person who fosters the good of a friend and regards himself as morally permitted to do so might be thought of as operating from a moral principle which tells him that the given situation is one in which he is permitted not to give equal weight to the interests of others (who are in the range of his potential beneficence). And so he would be applying a moral principle to or taking up a Kantian moral standpoint towards his relationships.

There are two ways the person could be portrayed as applying such a principle, or operating from it. One is to picture him as motivated by the thought, 'Action X will foster my friend's good, and in circumstances such as these it is permissible to ignore the interests of others in order to foster my friend's good.' The second is to picture him as testing his proposed action against the principle in question and, finding it morally permissible, performing it with the thought that it will promote his friend's good. The difference here is that in the second case the principle is regarded not so much as the directly motivating thought, but as something against which the directly motivating thought is tested for its acceptability. But the substance of the two pictures is the same. For in both cases the alleged principle is seen as central to the considerations on the basis of which the agent acts.

In confronting this line of thought I aim to say something about the moral epistemology of impartiality in relation to acting in regard to the friend's good. In what way does the principle of impartiality bear on action done from friendship? More precisely, how are we to understand or portray the fact (for which I have argued) that impartiality fails to apply to normal contexts of friendship? What is the correct conceptualization of the way that someone acting out of regard for his friend's good takes account of this fact of the limit of impartiality?

First, in general, even if the moral principle in question is envisaged to play some role in the agent's action, the role is not that of a consideration on the basis of which the agent acts. It is evident that in most normal situations of acting from friendship the agent neither acts from the thought, 'My friend needs help and in situations such as this one it is morally permissible to offer that help'; nor does he normally test the proposed action against a principle which specifies when it is permissible to ignore, or to fail to give equal weight to, the interests of those in the range of his beneficence. (Nor, as I have been arguing, is it morally appropriate for him to do either of these things.)

The most that can be claimed here is that the fact that the given circumstances are ones in which it is morally permitted to act without taking into account the interests of others whom one might help forms a sort of background condition to the conscientious person's acting from friendship. That is, if the person contemplating an act of friendship believed that there were considerations of an impartial nature which needed to be taken into account, then he would not act until he had taken account of those considerations. The agent must therefore believe that there are not such considerations, in order for him to act from the direct thought of his friend's need. In this sense the absence of considerations of impartiality forms a background condition for his action – a necessary condition of his being motivated in the way he is – but is not part of the considerations which he actually brings to bear on the situation or proposed action.

A non-moral analogy here would be that it is a necessary or background condition of my playing a certain record which I want to hear on my record player that I do not believe that doing so will harm my record or my record player. But this does not mean that in contemplating whether to play the record I ask myself or investigate whether playing it will have these effects.

Thus the most that can be claimed about the alleged higher-order moral principle is that it be a necessary condition of the morally conscientious agent acting directly and solely from friendship that he not regard the principle as forbidding his action. But this is much weaker than saying that the agent does, or should, bring the principle to bear on his situation or that it is a consideration on the basis of which he acts.

A second point is that the alleged principle involved here cannot be a principle of impartiality. For it is a principle whose function is to specify the range of application of the principle of impartiality. It is not so much a higher-order principle than the principle of impartiality itself, but rather is simply a specification of the types of situation to which that principle applies.

It is even misleading to regard such a principle as one of 'moral permissibility' (specifying that in such-and-such circumstances it is morally permissible to give preference to the wants and needs of one's friends); for this implies that there is some question or doubt regarding the morality of acting out of friendship, a question to which the principle provides a response. But in most cases of acting out of friendship there is no such question at all. This is the point I have been concerned to emphasize: normal situations of giving support, help, or comfort to a friend are simply ones to which the only morally relevant consideration is a regard to the friend's good.

One can imagine situations in which there does seem some moral question regarding the permissibility of acting for the benefit of one's friend and ignoring or giving less consideration to the interests of others. In such situations it makes sense to speak of consulting a principle which helps to decide whether it is morally permissible to benefit our friends. But these are not typical of the normal circumstances of friendship. (Even if the principle were pictured as a principle specifying moral permissibility, it would still not be a principle of impartiality itself. Rather, it would say that actions of a certain sort failed to contravene a principle of impartiality.)

Further, not only are we not dealing here with a principle of impartiality (hence not a Kantian principle), but it is even misleading to portray what one knows, when one knows (as a background condition of one's action) that a given situation is not one in which impartiality is demanded of one, as a moral principle at all, e.g., one of a higher order than impartiality. It is rather knowledge of how a particular moral principle is to be applied, of what its range of application is. This knowledge is presupposed in knowing how to apply the principle at all. If a specification of the range of applicability of a principle were itself a moral principle, we would be caught in an infinite regress, for then this principle would in turn have its range of applicability whose specification would constitute another moral principle, and so on.

If it is granted that the principle of impartiality is limited in its range of application to certain sorts of situations (and then to persons who hold only certain positions within those situations); and if it is granted that these situations do not normally comprise the usual contexts of friendship; then it can readily be granted that to believe that one's situation is not one in which impartiality is applicable is not to believe something on the basis of application of a moral principle. In fact it is a form of understanding which, in being presupposed in knowing how to apply the principle of impartiality at all, is part of what it is to be a competent moral agent.[17]

Thus, to summarize, the Kantian view is unable to accommodate the fact that in normal contexts of friendship it is appropriate to act for the friend's benefit without having to vindicate that action from a perspective of impartiality. For the fact that one need not vindicate one's action is not a consideration which one acts from, consults, or brings to bear on one's action; nor, in any case, is this consideration a moral principle itself, much less one having the character of impartiality.

VIII

What does morality demand of us? The upshot of this chapter is that it does not demand of us that we regard all our proposed actions from an impartial perspective. In this sense Kantianism fails to define 'the moral point of view.' For in areas of life in which impartiality is not applicable, other considerations will from a moral point of view be appropriate and valid. So it will be proper to act for the sake of one's friend's good simply as such, independent of the vindication of such action from an impartial point of view.

This means also that friendship as a central human endeavor does not require a moral vindication, in the sense of a justification according to impersonal and universal principles. The personal importance which friendship has to us lies outside of this moral framework. In my argument I have focused primarily on one particular aspect of friendship, namely acting for the good of one's friend. But that aspect is central to (though hardly exhaustive of) the full significance which friendship has for us personally.

The argument made here about friendship could in fact have been made with regard to many personal projects or involvements of ours. Since, if my argument is right, impartiality is limited to particular sorts of contexts, we do not violate its strictures in many situations in which we simply pursue an endeavour of importance to us which does not involve benefiting others. In this way my argument is meant to counter a sort of overmoralized view of human life in general which is implicit in some aspects of the Kantian view – that we ought to determine that all our endeavours are justifiable by appeal to an impartial standard.

With regard to friendship itself, what we have seen is that Kantianism is not able to accommodate it within its moral viewpoint, and on the other hand is not able to produce valid objections to it as the human endeavor which friendship is. In addition, since friendship does have a moral aspect, namely the concern for the friend's good and the beneficent disposition towards him, Kantianism is unable to give articulation to all aspects of morality itself. That is, the beneficence of friendship is entirely morally appropriate and good; but this moral appropriateness cannot be expressed from within a Kantian perspective.

The claims made in this chapter for the limitations of impartiality, and the inappropriateness of making sure that one's actions can be vindicated from an impartial perspective, may perhaps seem a bit too pat. For in many cases it will not be obvious whether considerations of impartiality need to be taken into account. People sometimes act unthinkingly from friendship, in neglect of a broader perspective which bids them to take account of others in the potential range of their beneficence. Or they may rationalize and convince themselves that a rule of justice or impartiality which in some way they recognize to be applicable yet can be ignored.

My argument is not meant to deny any of this. The existence of friendship does in a way pose a range of anti-moral temptations. Nevertheless the central thesis of this chapter is not touched by such considerations, namely that in normal situations of comforting, helping, advising, sympathizing with, being concerned for, supporting, being glad for a friend, the impartial perspective is neither required nor appropriate.

On the other hand, and this point will be taken up at greater length in the next chapter, our sense that it is improper to neglect the interests of others because of a too-exclusive focus on one's friends is not properly accounted for wholly, or even primarily, by impartiality; rather it has to do with proper, or even obligatory, levels of beneficence towards others. The moral proprieties here do not in themselves have anything to do with friendship, but exist as a range of moral considerations in their own right. That is, it is improper or wrong to pay too little attention, or to give too little of one's concern, to the good of strangers, whether or not one fails to do so because of paying overmuch attention to the good of one's friends.

Finally, my argument is not meant to deny the fundamental moral truth in the notion that each person's good is as worthy of pursuits as is any other's. For example, in the area of social arrangements it would be wrong to favor a policy which promoted only one's own or one's friends' interests, unless doing so could be vindicated by impersonal criteria, such as, e.g., the considerations that one's own group had in the past been unduly neglected in other comparable policies. The question is only how this truth is to be reflected in the actions and deliberations of an individual moral agent. What I have argued is only that it is not properly reflected by the demand that the agent himself be equally concerned with the fostering of everyone's good.

IV

FRIENDSHIP AS
A MORAL PHENOMENON

I

It is entirely appropriate, as we have seen, that a friend act for the benefit of his friend for his own sake and without apprising himself of other possibilities for his beneficence. Not only is this appropriate but, I will argue in this chapter, it is also morally good. Clearing out of the way the concern with impartiality opens up a realm of moral inquiry which includes the altruistic emotions in general, and friendship as a particular relationship which embodies them. In this chapter I will examine friendship as a moral phenomenon in its own right, and will discuss conceptions of friendship which would deny its moral significance.

Friendship is a largely unfamiliar territory for modern moral philosophy, dominated as it has been by Kantian concerns or with utilitarianism, neither of which is hospitable to particular relationships which are both personally and morally significant. For example, contemporary emphasis on conduct which is morally required of us, or on considerations which we are required to take into account, does not easily allow for a focus on friendship as an arena for morally good, yet not morally obligatory, behavior and sentiments.

Let me begin with two central claims. The first is that, other things being equal, acts of friendship are morally good insofar as they involve acting from regard for another person for his own sake. This does not mean that every altruistic act within a friendship is morally admirable or praiseworthy. Some forms of considerateness towards one's friend, or willingness to help, are such that their absence would constitute a moral failure, and their presence merely something which is to be expected of a friend. So acts can be morally significant though not morally praiseworthy, and this is what I mean by saying that any action done out of regard for the friend for his own sake is morally good. It is analogous to saying that every dutiful act is morally good although some are such that performing them is only what is to be expected, whereas failure to perform them is blameworthy.

Second, the deeper and stronger the concern for the friend – the stronger the desire and willingness to act on behalf of the friend's good – the greater the degree of moral worth (again, other things being equal). Thus a friendship which involves a very deep and genuine regard for the friend's good is a morally excellent relationship.

The argument that friendship is, or can be, a source of moral excellence begins best with an example of what such a friendship might look like. Kate and Sue are friends. Both are clerical workers in the same large insurance firm. Sue is a quiet, thoughtful and somewhat moody person; Kate is cheery and outgoing.

Sue and Kate enjoy each other's company. They enjoy talking about people they know and events that take place in the office. They appreciate and value qualities they see in each other. Kate feels she learns a lot from Sue.

Kate cares very much for Sue. Sue has a tendency to get depressed quite often. Kate has learned how to make Sue feel better when she is in such moods. Sue is not naturally or readily open about what is bothering her; but Kate has learned how to draw her out when she feels that Sue wants to talk. Sometimes she pushes Sue too hard and is rebuffed by her, in a not especially sensitive way. Kate is hurt by such rebuffs. But more often Sue is glad to have such a good friend to talk to, and is grateful for Kate's concern for her, and for Kate's initiative in getting her to talk. Sometimes Kate can cheer Sue up just by being cheerful herself (as she naturally is anyway), but she often senses when such a mood would not be appropriate.

Kate and Sue are comfortable with each other. They feel able to 'be themselves' with each other, more so than with most other people. They trust each other and do not feel that they need to 'keep up a good front' with one another. The women trust each other with personal matters which they do not usually discuss with their husbands. They know that the other will treat the matter seriously, and will not breach the confidence involved. They know each other well and know how to be helpful to the other in discussing intimate personal matters. They care deeply for each other, and they know this about each other, though they do not express it to each other explicitly. Each one appreciates the care and concern which she knows the other has for her. This is part of what enables them to be so open with each other — the knowledge that the response will be a caring one, even when it is not directly helpful in a practical sense.

Kate and Sue are willing to go to great lengths to help each other out. They readily do favors for each other — helping shop, picking up something at the cleaners, making excuses and covering for each other at work, taking care of each other's children.

When Kate is troubled about something Sue is concerned too; and vice versa. Sue thinks about how to help Kate out. For example, she helps her to think about how to deal with her horrible boss.

The relationship between Sue and Kate was not always so close. They came to know each other gradually. Their different temperaments kept them from taking to each other immediately. In addition, Kate often felt, and still sometimes feels, shut out by Sue's reserve, and her rebuffs. She was anxious to please Sue, to have Sue like her, and this often made her forget her own desires and needs. In her insecurities in the relationship she would also not be able to focus attention on Sue's own needs, feelings, and situation. In struggling with Sue, and with herself, to reach a deeper level of commitment, she worked through these insecurities. She was thereby enabled to distinguish more clearly Sue's needs and feelings from her own, to overcome tendencies to distort.

I have attempted here to describe a friendship which is both realistic (i.e., not involving saints) and yet which has reached a high degree of moral excellence. I mean to have brought out the following features: the concern, care, sympathy, and the willingness to give of oneself to the friend which goes far beyond what is characteristic and expected of people generally. The caring within a friendship is built up on a basis of knowledge, trust, and intimacy. One understands one's friend's good through knowing him well, much better than one knows non-friends, hence much better and more deeply than one knows their good. One is more sensitive to one's friend's needs and wants than one is to non-friends. In genuine friendship one comes to have a close identification with the good of the other person, an occurrence which is generally much rarer and at a much shallower level with other people.

In addition one gives much of oneself, unselfishly, to one's friend, as part of caring for him. One takes this for granted and does not typically regard it as a sacrifice; this is because one does care about the friend, and not because one is motivated by self-interest. The level of self-giving is generally much greater, though also of a different nature, than with non-friends. All these aspects of friendship are of great moral worth and significance. I will refer to these aspects generally as 'deep caring and identification with the good of the other.'

The caring in such a friendship ranges over a period of time and involves a commitment into the future. Kate and Sue know that neither one will simply drift away from the other. They will stick by each other. Their caring means that if trouble arises between them, they will try to work it through. Of course they know that, human existence being what it is, there is always a possibility of some kind of breach that would drive them apart. But this possibility is not translated into any actual distancing of themselves from one another, or into self-protection through 'lowering one's expectations.' In fact, each expects the other's care, concern, and commitment to extend into the foreseeable future; this is a source of deep comfort and joy to both of them, though they are seldom aware of it explicitly.

It is not the willing self-giving which is by itself the ground of the moral excellence of friendship, but only the self-giving which takes place within a relationship in which one genuinely understands and knows the other person, and understands one's separateness from him. For under the influence of a romantic passion one might be willing to do all sorts of things for the other person, to sacrifice for him. But this passion, and its associated disposition to act for the sake of the other, might be superficial, though very intense. It is not grounded in a real knowledge and understanding of the other, and of one's relationship to the other, such as exists in the example of Kate and Sue. In such a passion one not only gives of oneself – which is morally meritorious – but one, as it were, gives oneself away. And, as many writers have pointed out, this giving oneself away – failing to retain a clear sense of the other's otherness and of one's own separateness and integrity as a person – can stem not only from romantic passion or infatuation, but can be an integral part of long-standing and stable relationships, and can be a settled tendency within an individual's way of relating to others.[1]

We can say, in summary, that the moral excellence of friendship involves a high level of development and expression of the altruistic emotions of sympathy, concern, and care – a deep caring for and identification with the good of another from whom one knows oneself clearly to be other.

II

Let us consider some conceptions of friendship which would deny its moral significance.

On the first conception, friendship is pictured as a sort of natural process, as something which merely happens to one. In one's life one runs across certain people whom one likes and is drawn to, and some of these people become one's friends. This happens to virtually everyone. There is nothing special about it, rather it is simply a natural part of human life, not a particular achievement or a matter of something which one works at.

Moreover, the course of friendship is largely a matter of the vagaries of our emotions. It is thus not really something over which we have control.

> Personal relations cannot be controlled by morality because they cannot be controlled at all. . . . they are not the sort of thing of which it makes sense to speak of making them different. They exist or occur; they are lived, experienced, and they change; but they are not controlled.[2]

Thus friendship cannot be a moral excellence, because it is not the sort of thing on which we exercise moral control and agency.

There are several things deeply wrong with this picture of friendship and of personal relationships generally. Most fundamentally, not everyone does have friends in the same way. People have very different relationships to their friends and treat their friends differently, and some of these differences are morally significant. In particular the levels of caring for and giving of oneself to one's friends are very different among different people (and within the same person's friendships).

I might have a genuine friend, someone whom I genuinely like to be with and to do certain kinds of things with, yet I might not care for and about him very deeply. I wish him well, hope for good things for him, and am willing to do some things for him, even if they inconvenience me to some extent. But I do not give much of myself to him. Perhaps I do not even know him very well, and do not make an effort to do so. I do not in any very significant way identify with his goals and aspirations, nor substantially desire his good for its own sake.

There is not necessarily anything wrong with this friendship. Perhaps, even if I could care more about my friend, I do not wish to do so. We understand each other's feelings and neither would want the relationship to be more than it is. There is nothing blameworthy here.

Nevertheless, this friendship is evidently not at the personal and moral level of Kate and Sue's friendship. It involves much less in the way of caring, of the giving of oneself to the other; of the transcendence of self involved in the deep identification with the other's good; of the level of considerateness, sympathy, and concern involved in Kate and Sue's friendship.

We all, I would think, can recognize that we have friendships at differing levels of commitment, care, and concern. Though all genuine human caring has moral worth and significance, is it not evident that a deeper level of caring involves greater moral worth? Such caring, far from being a natural process, is difficult to achieve, and is not really so common. It involves getting outside oneself, being able to focus clearly on and to know another person. It involves being willing to give of oneself, and in a way which is not simply experienced as self-sacrifice or self-denial. It involves overcoming within oneself obstacles, defenses, or distortions which prevent the deep caring for the other. (And this will generally involve some kind of shared process with the other person.)

Not only are there variations of moral level within one's own friendships; but it is also true that people may vary greatly among themselves in this regard. Some people are generally more caring, giving, helpful, and considerate towards their friends than are others.

III

Thus some people may have no friendships of a high level of moral excellence. And, as Aristotle recognized, some people may actually be incapable of such friendships. A truly selfish person could not have friends in the fullest sense. If he were genuinely able to care for another person for his own sake, if he were able to give much of himself to the other freely and for his own sake, based on a genuine understanding of him, then he would not be selfish.

It is true that selfish people can be very attached to one or another person, e.g., a spouse or friend. But it seems that such a friendship could not be a friendship of the most morally excellent kind. The attachment or friendship would be too grounded in self-centred considerations. Thus a selfish man could be very attached to his wife, dote on her, and in some ways do a lot for her. But this does not mean that he really cares for her for her own sake. His behavior would be compatible with his caring for her, so to speak, for her willingness to serve him, to be at his command, to flatter his ego. His giving could be either a minor concession for her serving him or even a further expression or assertion of his power over her and of her dependence on him. If he were truly selfish then something like this would be the most likely explanation of his 'beneficent' behavior. That a person should care very genuinely and fully for only one person while basically being very selfish seems an impossibility.[3]

Nevertheless, it would be wrong to say that a selfish person cannot really have friends at all, in any sense of the term. For first of all there are important aspects of friendship besides caring for the other, i.e., enjoying being with the other person or sharing certain kinds of activities with him, liking the other person. So a selfish man can have friends, in that there are people whom he likes and enjoys sharing certain activities with. Second, even a selfish person can wish another well, be well-disposed towards another. (Here we have to keep in mind the difference between a humanly selfish person and a sociopath.) It is only caring in the full sense which is incompatible with selfishness.[4]

Thus there are very different levels of friendship, levels which are understood in moral terms, in terms of how fully one cares for the other. If this is so then there is something wrong with the conception that friendships happen, so to speak, naturally, without our moral intervention, and that friendships are of a uniform moral type. Friendship always involves a giving of self to the other and a valuing of the other for his own sake. Friendship thus involves an orientation of our (moral) selves towards another person, rather than a process which merely happens to us and which (in Mayo's word) cannot be 'controlled.' On a more general level, personal relations are not merely 'lived' and 'experienced,' nor is their 'change' a merely natural process unrelated to moral aspects of ourselves, as Mayo implies. Rather friendship is an expression of moral activity on our part — of a type of regard for another person, a giving of oneself, and a caring for another for his own sake.

IV

In the case of Kate and Sue, the 'moral activity' involved in the friendship is especially evident. For I have described the deep level of caring between the women as an outcome of effort and struggle, and hence as a kind of moral achievement. Certainly, attaining a deep level of friendship, in which the parties mean a great deal to one another and care deeply for one another, often involves obstacles and difficulties, the overcoming of which requires effort. One friend disappoints the other, or feels let down by him; they misunderstand each other; they quarrel and feel that there are insuperable barriers between them. Such happenings within the history of a friendship can lead to a distancing and weakening of the bonds between the friends. Or they can constitute tests of the relationship, which ultimately strengthen the ties and deepen the meaning of the friendship. The friends can make the effort to rectify or to correct a misunderstanding, to struggle to achieve the greater mutual understanding which will prevent such disappointments and misunderstandings in the future.

It is difficult to conceive of a deep friendship which does not involve some such effort and struggle. Nevertheless, it is not such effort and struggle in its own right which grounds the moral significance of friendship. For one thing, friendships which involve something like the same level of caring do differ in the amount of effort and struggle which has gone into them, and, I would argue, it is not the effort and struggle but the level of caring itself which primarily determines the level of moral value in the friendship. It is the genuine care for another person which constitutes a moral activity of the self, not primarily the exertion of will or effort which might have gone into the development of that caring. In caring we as it were go out from ourselves to another person; we give of ourselves; we affirm the friend in his own right. These processes cannot be portrayed as something which merely happens to us, or which we simply experience, as is, e.g., finding ourselves attracted to someone. And so effort and will are not required for the activity essential to morality.[5] This is not to exclude the possibility, however, that effort and will could be a further source of moral value in a friendship beyond (though also requiring as a condition of this moral value) the caring involved.

Thus in a friendship in which the parties care deeply for each other but in which the relationship has developed without much pain, difficulty, effort, and struggle, there is still great moral merit in the caring.[6]

V

Another conception of friendship which conduces to failing to see its moral significance pictures friendship, or rather doing good for one's friends, as a kind of extension of the self, so that when one acts for the other one is simply promoting what is in a sense one's own good. This self-centredness would exclude friendship from being a moral good, much less a moral excellence.

Our discussion can help us to see what is wrong with this conception as a general characterization of friendship. For a genuine friend truly cares for the other for his own sake. He is willing to give of himself to promote the other's good; he understands the other in his own being and interests, and can distinguish the other's interests from his own, even while he is able to care deeply for their realization and in that sense identify with the friend and his good. He grieves for the friend's sorrows. He is happy for him at his good fortune or successes in valued endeavors; he is sad for him at his losses and disappointments. It is his human growth and happiness which he desires — and for the friend's own sake, not his own.[7]

Thus the sense of identification involved in genuine friendship is not a matter of self-interest at all, and caring for the friend is not simply an extension of caring for oneself. This mistaken conception of friendship trades on an ambiguity within the notion of 'identification,' which can have either an egoistic or a non-egoistic sense. Even in the non-egoistic sense described above, the one who identifies gets pleasure from the good accruing to the one with whom he identifies. But this pleasure is not the motive of his beneficent action; in fact it is a sign of the degree to which he cares for the other as other than himself and in his own right.

The conception of friendship as extended self-interest is more appropriate to a kind of symbiotic attachment to another person (in which one has no clear sense of a self separate from the other, and in which one lives through the other so that, in that sense, his pleasures are one's own). Such an attachment can be of great importance to the person, of great emotional intensity, and can take on some of the forms of friendship — but is not at all friendship in the fullest sense.[8]

In arguing that Kate cares for her friend Sue for Sue's sake and not for Kate's own, that Kate is aware of Sue in her otherness from herself, and that Kate gives of herself to Sue, I am not arguing that Kate sacrifices herself for Sue. Nor am I arguing that when she acts for Kate's good, she acts in a manner unconnected with her own interests. She acts altruistically in the sense that her actions are motivated by genuine concern for her friend's weal and woe for its own sake; but not in the (more familiar) sense in which it implies acting in disregard of or contrary to one's own interests (see p. 10). But this is, partly, to say that the terms 'egoism' and 'altruism' as usually understood serve us ill in describing acting from friendship. Let us explore this further.

Friendship involves persons being bound up with one another. The different sorts of emotions and feelings which the friends have towards one another get their meaning and significance from the entire relationship of which they are a part.[9] In caring about the weal and woe of my friend Dave it is integral to the nature of this caring that it be for someone whom I like, whom I know likes me, who cares about my weal and woe, whom I trust, who is personally important to me, who cares about our friendship, etc. In acting from friendship towards Dave I express my acknowledgment of a relationship which includes all these feelings and attitudes. This is why the caring and the acts of beneficence in friendship are not separate from my own interests, from what is personally a good to me; it is not, in that sense, 'disinterested.' In fact friendship is a context in which the division between self-interest and other-interest is often not applicable. The friendship itself defines what is of importance to me, and in that sense what is in my interest. In that sense I do not generally sacrifice my own interest in acting for the good of my friend. I act with a sense of the friendship's importance to me, even though it is the friend whose benefit I directly aim at (i.e., which is my motive for acting), and not my own.

It is not that in acting for the friend's good I am acting from a combination of altruistic and egoistic motives, e.g., that I am both disinterestedly concerned with my friend's good, yet I also enjoy acting to help him. Nor am I acting from the former motive in combination with acting in order to preserve the friendship (which I am conceiving to be of benefit to me), nor in combination with the thought that my friend will be led to be more likely to benefit me in the future. These latter three portrayals involve possible motivations, which can be seen as a combination of an egoistic and an altruistic motive; but they are not accurate portrayals of our typical beneficent acts of friendship.

The way in which the value to me of my friendship with Dave figures into my acting for his good is not as a consideration for the sake of which I act. Nor is my liking of Dave a liking to do or enjoy doing every action which promotes his good. Rather, these figure in as a context of meaning of my action. They are background conditions of my being motivated to act for the sake of Dave's good. I am not doing less than acting fully for the sake of his good, and in that sense altruistically.

The notion of sacrifice implies an interest which the agent forgoes in order to promote something which is not an interest of his. It implies a clear separation between the interest he forgoes and the one for the sake of which he acts. It is the absence of such a separation in the case of friendship which means that it is not true as a general characterization of acting from friendship that in acting for the good of one's friend one is sacrificing for him. (Nevertheless in some particular actions it would be true to say that we sacrificed something of what we wanted in order to help our friend.)[10]

VI

Even if the notion that friendship is a kind of extended self-interest is abandoned, the previous discussion indicates what might be thought to be a moral deficiency in the kind of concern involved in friendship, namely that one would not have the concern if the other were not one's friend. The friendship, with all it involves, is a necessary condition for the concern, even if the concern is granted to be directed genuinely towards the friend for his own sake. Let us call this 'conditional altruism.'

Conditional altruism might be thought to be deficient precisely because it is not a universal form of concern. It is not directed towards the friend simply in virtue of his humanity but rather only in virtue of some relationship in which he stands towards oneself. This line of thinking, which I will call 'universalist,' is given a particularly stringent expression in Kierkegaard's *Works of Love*. He says that love of one's friend (one's beloved) has no moral value except insofar as it stems from a love which one would have for 'one's neighbor,' i.e., for any human being; and so, for example, if one saves a drowning person because he is one's friend — i.e., one would not do so if he were not one's friend — one's act would not have moral significance. Kierkegaard does not say there is anything wrong with loving one's friend and acting out of love for him; he says only that such love has no moral significance.[11]

A weaker view would be that love or concern for one's friend, though not without moral significance altogether, is yet in important ways deficient as a moral attitude towards another person. Though Kant himself does not say this in his own discussions of friendship (which are generally sensitive and sensible),[12] it can be seen as an extension of some themes within the Kantian outlook, in particular the focus on universality and impartiality in the moral attitudes we take towards others. On this view conditional altruism would be, though not without value, yet without the full moral value that a universalistic altruism would have.

The consequences of this challenge to conditional altruism go far beyond the moral significance of friendship itself. For there are many sorts of special attachments, connections, and relationships between people – such as family member, neighbor (in the non-Christian sense), fellow worker, comrade, fellow member (of various organizations), member of same ethnic group of community, regular frequenter of the same pub, fellow citizen or countryman – which can be sources of a stronger sympathy, concern, and willingness to help one another than might exist in their absence.[13] The special connection or relationship is a condition of the altruism, which is therefore not purely universalistic.

Thus the issue here is at the core of the moral significance of the altruistic emotions themselves. For these special connections give rise to sympathy, compassion, and concern, and on the view which I am putting forth here these are morally good, independent of how they have arisen and whether they would exist towards the person in question in the absence of those special circumstances or relationships.

VII

Let us then examine the universalist challenge to all conditional altruism, or altruism based on special relationships. On my view, such conditional altruism does involve concern for the other for his own sake. The fact that if he were not our friend we would not have this concern for him does not mean that it is not for his own sake that we care about him. What detracts from such concern is only if the regard to the other's good stems primarily from self-concern. One could be concerned about one's friend Joe primarily because how Joe is doing reflects on oneself in the eyes of others. One could be involved in helping poor persons who are members of one's ethnic group primarily because one feels that the existence of such persons reflects badly on the group as a whole, and therefore on oneself. These examples would be excluded by my own formulation, of caring for the good of the other for his own sake, for they involve a primary concern with oneself rather than with the other.

On the other hand, if an Italian is dedicated to helping poor Italians, and is genuinely concerned for their welfare, then, even if he would not be so concerned if the persons were not Italians, he is still concerned genuinely for them for their own sakes; and, on my view, that attitude (and the actions stemming from it) have moral value.

Conditional altruism might be thought to be defective because concern with those in special relationships to oneself often takes the form primarily of hating, being opposed to, or denying the legitimacy of the interests of those outside the relationship in question. These are the familiar phenomena of chauvinism and provincialism. (It is less clear how this would work in regard to friendship; perhaps jealousy is an analogous phenomenon in that one's energies are directed against someone outside the relationship rather than towards one's friend or towards strengthening or enriching the relationship itself.)

There are two negative aspects of this chauvinism, which can exist independently of one another. The first is the opposition to those outside the relationship, an attitude bad in itself. The second is that the outside focus may mean a deficiency in one's concern for those within the relationship; one may be not so much genuinely concerned with their good as with hating or opposing those outside it. (Yet this connection is not an invariable one. It is quite possible for someone to be genuinely concerned with a group to which he is attached — to really care about their well-being — and yet also to have despicable attitudes towards those outside of his group.)

These are deficiencies within conditional altruism. But my view allows for the condemning of the despicable attitude towards those outside the special relationship, and also accords no moral value to the attitude towards those within it which does not consist in a genuine regard for the weal and woe of the persons in question. My view does, however, say that if the concern is genuine then it is *ceteris paribus* morally good; and if it is accompanied by a despicable attitude towards those outside then it is this accompanying attitude which is condemned and not the conditional altruism itself.

There may be some tendency on the part of a universalist outlook to think that conditional altruism always involves a negative attitude towards those who do not satisfy the condition. If this were true it would be a reason for regarding conditional altruism as a whole as fundamentally defective. But it clearly is not true. A person may be deeply devoted to the welfare of the Italian community without being suspicious of, or wishing the harm of, non-Italians. He may even wish well for non-Italian communities and recognize the worthiness of their aspirations, though he does not have the actual concern for them which he has for his own community. Sympathy for the interests of other groups could fairly naturally grow from concern for the interests of one group. Conditional altruism merely implies not being as concerned about the good of those who do not satisfy the condition as one is about those who do. It does not necessarily involve having an attitude towards those who do not which is in itself morally deficient.

It is important to recognize that genuine devotion to a particular group — family, neighborhood, ethnic community, ethnic group, club — is in itself morally good, and becomes morally suspect only when it involves a deficient stance towards others. It is morally good in that it involves (among other things) an admirable degree of sympathy, compassion, and concern for others. Moral philosophy ought to be able to give expression to the moral value of such an attitude, and an exclusively universalist perspective cannot do so.

On the other hand, the pitfalls of such conditional altruism should not be ignored. The connection between concern for those who satisfy the condition and opposition to those who do not is often no mere coincidence. For example, in a situation of scarce resources, devotion to one group competing for those resources can well mean opposition to others, and this can easily involve blameworthy attitudes towards these other people. (It should be noted, however, that merely competing against other groups for resources which one desires for one's own is not in itself reprehensible. It becomes so only if one either competes in an unfair or despicable way, or if, as is unfortunately too natural, one comes to develop unjustified and negative attitudes towards the other group.) Moreover, in some situations alleged devotion to the welfare of one group can, as things stand, mean little more than hatred or opposition to groups outside. Devotion to the welfare of whites as whites in America would be an example of this; there is virtually no room for this to be a genuinely altruistic attitude, or for it really to be other than opposition to non-whites.

VIII

On the universalist view, one cares for the other in a fully morally appropriate manner only when one cares for him simply as a human being, i.e., independent of any special connection or attachment one has with him. On my view one's concern need only be genuinely for the other and not, directly or indirectly, for the sake of oneself. Whether one would care about the other in the absence of the special connections does not detract from its full moral value.

This is in no way to deny that it is morally good to have altruistic attitudes towards those with whom one has no special relationship; indeed such attitudes must be central to any moral view which places emphasis on the altruistic emotions. But it is to say that whatever factors encourage the development of genuinely altruistic attitudes are themselves to be regarded favorably, from a moral point of view. In addition, this is to be realistic in our moral outlook; for in general we do care more about those to whom we stand in some special relationship than about those to whom we do not. These relationships involve a deeper identification with the other's good than is customary in their absence; and it is entirely proper that they do so. It is true that some persons can develop a quite deep sense of identification with the good of others, or of particular groups of others (e.g., oppressed Chileans, people suffering from a certain disease) to whom they stand in no (prior) special relationship; and such an attitude does seem more morally admirable than conditional altruism of (if we might speak this way) the same strength. But such attitudes are too rare for a moral outlook to be built entirely around them (although in my view their moral value is still able to be given full articulation), and, in any case, their exceptional moral value is not a reflection of a deficiency in the moral value of conditional altruism.

The tradition of which Kierkegaard is a representative places sole emphasis on altruistic attitudes towards strangers, or towards others in abstraction from the special relationships in which we stand to them. This must be an incomplete conception of love or concern for others, though a conception (such as Aristotle's or those of Greek philosophers generally) which gives little or no place to the notion of concern for others simply as human beings is similarly incomplete. For both are significant forms of our concern for others for their own sake, and it is this which has moral value.[14]

This chapter has investigated friendship as a moral phenomenon. The full moral dimensions of friendship are difficult, if not impossible, to focus on within a Kantian framework, with its emphasis on obligatory conduct, on impersonal considerations, on universal attitudes. I have been particularly concerned to show that friendship can be morally excellent and not merely, as argued in chapter III, morally legitimate, But, in addition, all friendships are morally good to the extent that they involve a genuine concern with the good of another for his own sake (and, in that sense, involve self-transcendence).

In emphasizing, in contrast to the Kantian view, the moral dimensions of friendship, I want to avoid on the other side an overmoralized view of friendship, and of its personal and human significance. One such view sees the concern for the friend's good as the central element in friendship, downplaying or neglecting the liking of the friend, the desire to be with him, the enjoyment of shared activities, etc.[15]

A second overmoralized view sees friendship, or at least the highest forms of it, as having its grounds, its object, or the source of connection between the friends primarily in the friend's moral qualities and character; Aristotle, for example, seems to hold this view in his discussion in *Nichomachean Ethics*.

I argued in chapter II that it is no defect of personal feelings that they fail to have such moral grounding. The same argument holds for friendships. To make the friend's moral character the central feature of friendship is to neglect too much the shared liking and caring (and mutual recognition of these by the friends) and the shared activities in which these are expressed. These features, though not unrelated to a person's moral character, are not primarily grounded in them either.

One does not need to regard someone as a virtuous person in order to care for him as a friend; nor, in caring for him for his own sake need one focus primarily on whatever morally virtuous qualities he has.[16]

The arguments of this chapter and the previous one have also borne, directly and indirectly, on the altruistic emotions in general. Most obviously, friendship is a relationship in which sympathy and concern flourish, and an argument that beneficence prompted by friendship is morally good is an argument that beneficence prompted by altruistic emotion is morally good. Related to this, the argument that conditional altruism or altruism stemming from special relationships is morally good bears directly on many, though by no means all, forms of altruistic emotion. In the background of these arguments is the argument of chapter III, refuting the Kantian view that the impartial perspective is required of us in all our actions. Clearing this argument out of the way is a necessary condition for building towards a positive view of the moral value of altruistic emotions.

In addition to providing a context for the altruistic emotions, friendship also can serve as a metaphor for them, in relation to the Kantian view. For the two conceptions of friendship which I have discussed as contradicting the view that friendship involves moral excellence have direct analogies to Kantian views of altruistic emotions. Analogous to the 'natural process' view of friendship (pp. 71-4) is the Kantian view that altruistic emotions, and emotions in general, are like natural processes over which we, as moral beings, have no control, and for which we cannot be blamed, praised, or morally assessed. Analogous to the 'extended self-interest' conception of friendship (pp. 75-7) is the Kantian view that acting from altruistic emotion — or, rather, acting from feeling or emotion in general — is acting out of a kind of self-interest, in that it involves acting to gratify an inclination or desire.

In chapter VIII I counter the former view of altruistic emotions and feelings. There I argue that we are not passive with respect to our feelings and emotions. They cannot be regarded as natural processes external to our moral agency, for which we cannot be morally assessed. Rather they are an expression of our moral being, just as the quality of a person's friendships is partly an expression of his moral being or character.

I do not counter the 'egoist' view of altruistic emotions directly in this book, partly because so much philosophic argument has gone into showing that this fairly crude form of psychological egoism is false.[17] If one accepts that acting from altruistic emotion involves acting genuinely altruistically then these well-known arguments will support my viewpoint here. In addition, in chapter II, I have tried to show that acting from altruistic emotions does not necessarily involve acting from inclination, but on the contrary can involve acting contrary to it; and that in fact it is a necessary feature of the altruistic emotions that they involve a willingness to sacrifice some of our own interests, comfort, or convenience, for the sake of another's good.

V

DIRECT ALTRUISM, UNIVERSALIZABILITY, AND CONSISTENCY

I

The next three chapters articulate a view of the nature of morality which brings out and explicates the moral value of altruistic emotions. The present chapter focuses on the nature of moral action and of altruistic emotions as motives to action.

Let us begin with the 'direct altruism' view, which states one way in which an action can have moral worth, or be morally good. According to this view an action is morally good (other things being equal) insofar as it is motivated by a regard for the good of others. (To simplify matters let us assume that the act succeeds in bringing about the good which the agent intends.) A shorthand statement of the direct altruism view is that an action is morally good if it is altruistic (other things being equal).

The direct altruism view is not intended as a full account of right action, but rather as a partial view of morally good action. Other features of altruistically motivated acts can count against their moral goodness. So direct altruism claims to articulate only a prima facie or *ceteris paribus* aspect of moral worthy action. Nevertheless this aspect forms the basis of the moral value of a wide range of (altruistic) virtues: compassion, kindness, sympathy, thoughtfulness, generosity, benevolence, considerateness.

To say that a directly altruistic action is morally good is not to say that the agent is necessarily praiseworthy or admirable for performing it. Directly altruistic actions include those which it is blameworthy, indecent, inconsiderate, or reprehensible to fail to perform. The direct altruism schema operates at a very general level of abstraction. It describes how an action can have moral significance, without telling us how to assess that significance in particular cases. It encompasses actions ranging from the noblest acts of selfless altruism to those which can be expected of any decent human being.

The direct altruism view draws on an intuition which, it seems fair to say, has played a fundamental role in demarcating the domain of the moral at least since the advent of Christianity: namely that it is morally good to act from regard for the good of others. I do not claim that the direct altruism view states the only way that an action can have moral value (the position taken by Schopenhauer in *On the Basis of Morality*), but only that it states *a* way. In particular I would reject the view that action done out of regard for one's own good can never have moral value. (Standing up for one's rights, for example, can be morally good.)

As it stands, the direct altruism view may seem not too different from Kantianism itself, and even to be encompassed within it. For both views firmly reject ethical egoism — the view that our only reasons for action lie in the promotion of our own interests, however broadly construed. Both portray morality as bidding us to take the interests of others into account. Yet, I will argue in this chapter, the structure of moral action is different on the two views, and following out the implications of the direct altruism view leads in quite different, and in some ways incompatible, directions from the Kantian view. I will argue further that to the extent that Kantianism fails to assimilate the direct altruism view, it seeks to produce arguments to undermine it; but these arguments are not successful.

Let us turn then to the Kantian view of moral action. On the Kantian view moral action is grounded in rational and universal principles. In order for an action to be a moral one it must be capable of being generalized or universalized. The action must be right not only for the particular agent who performs it but for any agent in a situation which is similar in all essentials to the given one. It betokens a fundamental inconsistency, and hence irrationality and immorality, for an agent acting on a certain principle to regard that principle as applying to himself alone, and not to others (situated in positions essentially like his own). Morality demands of an agent's principles, and actions which are based on them, that they be applicable to all agents, including himself in the future.

This line of thought places the notions of *generality*, *universality* or *universalizability*, *consistency*, and a certain conception of *rationality* connected with these, at the center of the conception of moral action.

On the Kantian view all action has a certain kind of structure, which it is worth spelling out explicitly. When an agent acts, he acts according to a principle (or maxim). The same act can have different principles, and the same principle can lead to different acts. So for the purposes of assessing the morality of an action, we must include the action together with its principle. Either implicitly or explicitly the principle specifies the description under which the act is performed, and the intention in, and/or reason for, performing the act. The principle also specifies (again, this may be implicit only) the circumstances in which that action is to be performed, i.e., in which the principle itself is applicable. This entails a specification of the general features of the situation which are the operative ones for determining the applicability of the principle.

On the direct altruism view, action also has a particular kind of structure. The agent acts with a certain conception of his action which includes a certain intention. The intention is to foster the good of another person; and his conception of the act includes its being one which aims to achieve this end. The agent can also be said to act from certain considerations which are features of the given situation and which relate to the weal and woe of other persons.

The direct altruism structure contrasts with the Kantian structure, in that intentional action performed for altruistic considerations does not, according to that view, necessarily involve acting according to principles or maxims. This divergence concerns not so much the nature of moral action as the nature of action itself. On the Kantian view all action must have, or can be viewed as having, a particular structure; on the direct altruism view some action (in particular, directly altruistic action) does not have this structure.

Regarding the nature of moral action, the direct altruism view differs from the Kantian view in two ways. First, it denies that in order to be morally good an action must be (or be regarded by the agent as) universalizable. Second, it denies that in order to be morally good an action must be (or be regarded by the agent as) morally obligatory or morally incumbent on the agent.

Before proceeding it is worth making explicit the implication of this argument for the altruistic emotions. Action prompted by altruistic emotion conforms to the direct altruism structure. Acting from sympathy, compassion, concern, kindness, generosity all involve acting out of regard for the good of others. They are different forms of regard for the good of others. In acting from compassion my reason for acting is that I am able to relieve the woe of another. Action prompted by altruistic emotion then is a subset of altruistic action; it is not the whole of it since an act can be directly altruistic yet not prompted by emotion.

The direct altruism view is intended to help articulate what is morally good about the altruistic virtues (kindness, compassion, etc.). The Kantian view either denies that these are genuine virtues, or misinterprets their nature by assimilating them to the Kantian conception of virtue.

If the direct altruism view is correct then action from altruistic emotion is morally good (other things being equal). It is therefore necessary, in order to vindicate the moral significance of altruistic emotions, to rebut the Kantian view, which imposes conditions on moral action which most action from altruistic emotions fails to meet.

II

Let us begin with an example of an altruistic action as a point of reference.

John does not own a car, primarily because he would find it inconvenient to have one in the city, where he lives. He would prefer to make do with public transportation. Let us imagine that John has often passed by people digging their cars out of the snow, and has not offered to help.

Then John gets a job for which he needs a car. Like others he now faces the problem of getting his car out of the snow. He wishes people would be more willing to volunteer their help. This situation makes him more sympathetic to persons trying to dig their cars out. One day he is passing by someone digging his car out, in the sort of situation which in the past he would have just passed by without thinking much about the person's situation — without really taking it in. He stops to help. On the direct altruism view John's action of stopping to help is a morally good one.

Let us begin with the issue of universalizability. A person acting altruistically is motivated by a direct concern for the good of another person (or other persons). But he does not necessarily regard the action he performs as one which anyone in a situation similar to his ought to perform. That is, he does not necessarily regard his action, or the grounds on which it is based, as universalizable. He does not necessarily regard the action as generalizable to others.

The point here is not that someone acting altruistically regards his action as right or appropriate for himself alone, denying its appropriateness or rightness for others; for he does not typically judge the action to be inappropriate, or not right, for others. It is rather that he typically makes no judgment at all regarding the rightness or appropriateness of the action for others. So it is not that the person motivated by sympathy typically denies that his action is universalizable. It is rather that he does not (necessarily or typically) think of his action one way or the other in terms of universalizability.

We can see this in the case of John. Though he stops to help the man because the man needs help, he does not necessarily hold the view that anyone in a situation similar to his own ought to perform an act of this sort. For example he need not hold the universal principle that people ought whenever possible to stop to help others dig their cars out of the snow. He may not have thought about whether others ought to do this. He may simply have responded to the present situation without having held, and without coming to hold, a principle about what others ought to do in such situations or what it would be wrong of them not to do.

It is true that he might come to hold such a principle. It may be that he regards this act of help as morally required of anyone in a situation such as his own (passing by, with nothing pressing to do at the time, etc.). His own frustration at having to dig his own car out may have impelled him to the moral reflection which would lead to the adopting of such a principle. He would then regard his action as conforming to a universal principle.

The fact that there can be an altruistic act which is grounded in a universal principle actually confirms the direct altruism view; for such a case stands in contrast to the many situations in which an altruistic act is not so grounded. Surely one can imagine many cases in which the agent acts altruistically, but in which he does not regard his act as morally binding on anyone situated analogously to himself; he does not regard others as wrong for failing to perform such an act. He may simply fail to give thought to whether his action has this sort of universal validity. It seems to me that, typically, our acts of compassion, sympathy, kindness, and concern are performed without our having a view whether the particular act is universalizable. But my argument requires only that it is perfectly intelligible that an agent act out of a direct regard for the good of another person, without having a belief that his action either is or is not generalizable to others.

Direct Altruism, Universalizability, and Consistency

The point of the direct altruism view is that the altruistic action (under the description and with the intention with which he performs it) is morally good whether or not it is universalizable or is regarded as such. The value is derived from the act's involving a direct response to or regard for the good of another person. There is not a further requirement, such as the Kantian view imposes, that the action be, or be regarded as, universalizable.

But could it not be claimed that the point of the Kantian view is not that every agent who acts altruistically actually does regard his action as universalizable, but rather that he is committed to holding such a view, whether he realizes this or not?

What would it mean to say that the agent is committed to such a conception of his act, if it is admitted that it is perfectly intelligible that he not be so committed? Let us suppose it means that the agent must agree that his act is universalizable, on pain of inconsistency.

Suppose I perform an altruistic act in a certain situation. Someone who sees me perform this act is later faced with a situation which seems to him analogous to the one in which I have acted. He fails to perform the analogous act to mine. He tells me of this. Am I committed to regarding what he has done as wrong? Surely not. For one thing even if the other person regards our situations as analogous, I myself might not. It might seem to me that there are important differences. Am I, then, committed to the view that he acted wrongly, unless I believe that there are significant differences? It seems not. I might resist making a judgment about this person's action, without either granting or denying the existence of particular relevant differences. I might simply fail to hold the belief that the situations are entirely analogous. Nothing compels me to have any belief about this matter. But if I lack such a belief then I am not compelled by logic to hold any view of the rightness or wrongness of the man's action. Thus I am not compelled, on pain of inconsistency, to agree that the other man ought to have done what I did. In this sense I am not committed to regarding my act as universalizable.

Perhaps it would be regarded as odd for someone who, having acted altruistically in a particular situation and being pressed to say how someone else ought to act in an essentially similar situation, to take no view on this matter. But I am not (at this point) denying that it is odd; I am denying only that the person is logically required, in order for his act to be genuinely altruistic, to regard his action as universalizable.

Even if it were odd for the agent not to take a position on the other person's action, the significance of this for the moral status of the agent's own act is questionable. Yet it is the status of that act which is at issue. On the direct altruism view, that action is morally good because it is genuinely altruistic. The Kantian arguments I have so far considered do not challenge the moral value of the act, but address only whether in some way the altruistic agent must regard his act as universalizable, whether it be unintelligible for him not to do so. These arguments have not been successful. The import of the possible oddness of the agent's failing to take a position on the rightness of another person's action in a comparable situation does not really bear on the intelligibility of the agent's acting altruistically without having a view on the universalizability of his action.

This point becomes clearer if we recognize that the altruistic agent is not necessarily (or typically) viewing his act as the morally right one to perform in the circumstances. He acts with some thought such as, 'X seems as if he needs help,' but not necessarily with the further thought, 'Helping X is the morally right thing for me to do.' The step from acting out of a direct regard for the good of the other to acting out of a sense that it is morally right to act beneficently is one which incorporates an element of universalizability. For to regard the act as right is, at least, to regard the considerations on which one acts as valid for everyone, as ones which anyone in a comparable situation ought to take into account. To regard an act as right generally carries the implication that anyone similarly situated ought to perform it, that it is right not only for me but for any agent in my situation (taking into account relevant differences between the agents, etc.).[1] But to act merely out of a direct regard for another's good does not carry this implication and does not require taking up the stance of 'any moral agent.' One is simply moved by another's suffering to help him; one need not, in addition, hold the belief that this consideration which has moved one is binding on others as well.

The punch of this argument lies in the fact that we can perform an altruistic act without being required to believe that what we have done is morally right. Not that we believe our act *not* to be morally right; rather our conception of our action simply does not include anything about its moral rightness. It includes only its being an action in which we help another person. In this regard, such an act is not different from an act motivated by self-interested considerations. I might perform a certain act with the thought that I will in the long run profit from it (although, let us say, I have no present desire to perform the act). I need not, in addition, hold a view as to whether my action is morally right or wrong, or even morally permissible. That is, it is intelligible that I perform the act for the self-interested reason, without being committed to holding any view as to the moral propriety of my act. Similarly, an agent may act for an altruistic reason without having a view as to the moral status of his action (its rightness, or wrongness).

Of course there is an important difference between the altruistic action and the self-interested action; namely, in the first case the action (according to the direct altruism view) is, *ceteris paribus*, a morally good one, whereas in the second it is not. (In the latter case it is, let us say, morally indifferent.) But the fact that it is morally good does not mean that the agent, in performing it, is committed to a view of its moral status. He is not compelled to think of it as morally right.

<h2 style="text-align:center">IV</h2>

A second dimension on which action having the structure of directly altruistic action differs from moral action on the Kantian scheme concerns *obligation*. In acting out of regard for the good of others one does not necessarily, or typically, regard oneself as obliged or in any way morally bound to perform the act in question. Nor, in general, is such altruism in fact a matter of obligation or duty. In helping the man dig his car out of the snow, John does not necessarily regard his action as morally incumbent upon him. Certainly he in fact has no obligation or duty to help the man.

We respond to others' needs, do favors, listen sympathetically, comfort friends — all for the sake of another's good. But we are not typically morally required to perform such acts. These acts are not typically mediated through a judgment that the situation is one in which a certain action is morally incumbent upon us.

There are three points here. One is that in acting altruistically we are not motivated by obligation or duty; this is true by definition since acting altruistically means acting simply out of a direct regard for the good of another. But an altruistic agent could still regard himself as under an obligation to perform the beneficent act, even if that sense of obligation plays no part in his actual motivation (e.g., acting out of concern for a friend when one's action is also required by one's duty to one's friend). So the second point is that the altruistic agent does not typically regard himself as under such an obligation, even if that fact were to play no role in his motivation to perform the act.

A third point is that, independent of what the agent believes to be the case, most altruistic acts are not in fact duties nor morally incumbent on their agents. This is not because such acts necessarily involve doing more than duty commands, where this carries the implication of doing more of the same kind of thing than duty commands. Many altruistic acts are quite trivial — e.g., giving someone directions, letting someone with few groceries in front of you in the check-out line — and, while not covered by duty, are not usefully seen as going beyond it in the way that does, for example, a teacher's devoting much more time to helping his students than his duties as a teacher call for. Rather, most altruistic acts are best regarded as within a different domain than dutiful acts.

But failure to perform altruistic acts is not necessarily a minor moral failure, compared, for example, to failure to do one's duty; it is just that the failure will be expressed in different terms. For example, in many cases failure to act altruistically will signify failure to do what can be expected of a decent human being (e.g., failing to press the desired floor button for a blind person in an elevator). In other cases it will simply mean failure to do what it would have been good to do, and what a kind, or compassionate, person would do (e.g., failure to guide the blind person to the precise area of the building which he is looking for).

V

It seems, to summarize, that altruistic action does not conform to the Kantian conception of action grounded in universal moral principles. It is action with a different sort of structure. Since, on the Kantian view, action in order to be moral must stem from universalizable principles, it is open to the Kantian to make the claim that altruistic action's failure to so conform deprives it of moral worth, or at least renders it seriously deficient as moral action. I mention this argument here in order to put it aside for now; it will be taken up in a later section.

Let us grant for the moment that directly altruistic action is morally good. What does this say about the Kantian view? The direct altruism view does not make the same criticism of action which conforms to the Kantian schema that the Kantian view makes of directly altruistic action. Rather the direct altruism view allows that it is, often, morally good to act from universal principle, or from a sense of duty. In many situations it would be wrong of us to fail to act in a way which can be generalized to others; we ought, or are obliged, to take up the perspective of any moral agent, and to act from considerations which we regard as binding for anyone. (We saw in chapter III that one important domain of such action concerns our institutional roles and responsibilities, though the area in which Kantian requirements on action are appropriate do go beyond this domain.)

What the direct altruism view asserts is only that the domain in which Kantian requirements on action are appropriate is limited, or, to say the same thing, that the domain in which morally good action takes the form of universalizable principles of obligation does not exhaust the area of morally good action.

Another useful way of putting this point is that there are different kinds of virtues. What makes some of these virtues virtues − i.e., what makes them morally good traits of character − is articulated by the Kantian view, while what makes others of them morally good is expressed by the direct altruism view. Examples of the former are justice, impartiality, conscientiousness; of the latter are kindness, concern, compassion. To try to see Kantianism as articulating the foundation of all virtue is inevitably either to deny what is of value in altruistic virtues, or to distort the nature of those virtues.

The contrast between justice, understood as 'giving each his due,' and kindness illustrates the difference in moral foundation between the different kinds of virtues. Justice, unlike kindness, really does involve universal principles. It is concerned with the right rather than the good. Justice plays a role in situations of conflicting claims and interests. The just person gives each of these its due and acts accordingly. For it to be just, his action must be guided by principles which are objectively valid. They must be universalizable. A just man honors the valid claims of another, even if doing so means sacrificing some of his own desires; but the point of view from which those claims are assessed as valid is an impersonal and objective one.

So the virtue of justice requires an objective and universal standpoint (as I argued in chapter III). But the virtue of kindness or compassion does not require this; its moral value derives from a different source. Justice is a Kantian virtue, kindness is not. What makes the latter morally good is the fact that the agent, in doing it, has responded to a certain consideration. There is no further requirement that the agent regard it as morally incumbent upon others to take that consideration into account. It is not even necessary that the altruistic agent regard himself as doing something which is morally good. The kind or compassionate person need not think of his act *as* kind or compassionate, and he certainly does not necessarily act for the sake of being kind or compassionate. What the kindness or compassion consists in (among other things), and what the grounds of its moral value are, is a direct desire for the good of another.

Some form of universalizability condition is required only when an agent makes some moral judgment regarding his (or other's) action. If he merely acts altruistically, without making a moral judgment, then such a condition is not required. In that case what is relevant to a moral assessment of his beneficient act is only whether it is directly altruistic.

VI

In setting up direct regard for the good of others as an alternative to universality it is necessary to guard against a possible misunderstanding. It would be possible to hold a view of morality according to which it is a requirement of morally appropriate action that it involve an appreciation of the uniqueness of each particular individual. I do not know of someone who actually holds such a view, but it is one with which the direct altruism view could be confused. Such a view is regarded as existentialist by Bernard Mayo, who states it (in order to reject it in favor of a Kantian-like view) in the following way:

> the situation in which [the moral agent] finds himself is itself a
> unique situation, involving other unique individuals different from
> himself and each other, and in fact an infinite assemblage of
> individualising factors. A genuine moral decision, it is argued, must
> be a response to the uniqueness of the total situation, and not an
> application of a rule which takes account of only a limited number
> of general features.[2]

According to this view, each individual is unique, and what constitutes his good will be unique; morally adequate action will have to involve an appreciation of this. This will mean at least that morally appropriate action cannot be grounded in universal principles, which abstract from the uniqueness of the individual.

The direct altruism view differs from this 'uniqueness' view. On the direct altruism view, morally appropriate action concerns itself with the good of other persons; it need not concern itself with persons' uniqueness or unique good. Thus the particular good which one is concerned about could be a good shared by or common to a group of persons. One could, for example, be concerned with persons who had a certain disease, or who suffered from a common condition of oppression. The object of one's concern in these cases will be a good, or a condition relating to the good, shared by certain particular individuals. Action to foster this good will not necessarily be regarded as universalizable; but nor, on the other hand, will the concern necessarily be with a unique good of the individuals in question.

The direct altruism view need not deny that in some perhaps deep sense every individual is unique and his good is unique. It denies only that a morally worthy concern must be directed to this unique good. On the direct altruism view, concern has moral value whether it is directed to the unique good of particular individuals or the shared good of particular individuals. The uniqueness view tends to downplay or even to deny the shared and common sources of weal and woe among people.

The uniqueness view rejects the possibility of action grounded in universal principles as ever being morally appropriate. The direct altruism view does not reject this possibility, but only the notion that universalizability is necessary for an action to have moral worth.

Thus the direct altruism view of moral action differs from both the Kantian view (grounded in universality) and the uniqueness view. It is important to see this third alternative, since a rejection of the uniqueness view is sometimes thought to leave some form of Kantianism as the only alternative.[3]

VII

Granted that there is a difference between the Kantian and the direct altruism views of moral action, what exactly does this difference come to? What is its moral import? Consider a statement by W.D. Ross articulating this difference between a direct desire or concern for the good of another, and a universalizable principle to the effect that one ought, or is obliged, to do a certain act of beneficence:

Direct Altruism, Universalizability, and Consistency

> The conscientious attitude is one which involves the thought of good or of pleasure for someone else, but it is a more reflective attitude than that in which we aim directly at the production of some good or some pleasure for another, since in it the mere thought of some particular good, or of a particular pleasure for another does not immediately incite us to action, but we stop to think whether in all the circumstances the bringing of that good or pleasure into existence is what is really incumbent on us.[4]

Ross seems to imply that we are dealing here with the same range of beneficent acts (bringing about good or pleasure to another), and are simply talking about two different kinds of motive or attitude which produce those acts. But many actions of direct altruism are ones which it is not morally incumbent upon us to perform (above, pp.91f.), and so the occasions on which we act from duty regarding the bringing about of good or pleasure to another are actually a subset of those in which we act from direct altruism. So if we accept Ross's characterization of the difference between the two types of action, many more morally good acts of beneficence will be performed from direct altruism than from Kantian motivation. So, at the very least, one contrast within the area of beneficence between action on the Kantian schema and action on the direct altruism schema is that there is more of the latter than the former — not only more actual beneficent acts, but more acts which are morally good, that is, motivated by a morally good motive.

Ross's account draws on one strand of thought within the Kantian insistence on universalizable principles, namely that acts performed must be regarded as morally incumbent or obligatory. But there is an important ambiguity within the notion of universalizability (or, as I sometimes refer to it, universality) which allows for a second way to understand the Kantian view. The ambiguity is between universality as meaning that one must regard one's act as something which everyone ought to perform, or which it would be wrong not to perform; and universality as meaning that one's act must be such that one can regard everyone as morally permitted to pursue it. Let us call these the 'strong' and the 'weak' interpretations of universality as a condition on moral action. To take a simple example: suppose I wish to buy a car. In one sense my action is universalizable; I can regard it as acceptable that anyone in a similar situation should buy a car. This is 'weak universalizability.' But in another sense the action is not universalizable, in that I do not regard it as morally required for anyone in my situation

96

to buy a car. This is 'strong universalizability.' All actions which are strongly universal (i.e., obligatory actions) are weakly universal, but the converse is not the case.

This ambiguity in the concept of universalizability yields two distinct interpretations of what it means for an action to conform to the Kantian schema — that is, for it to have moral value in a Kantian way. On the weak interpretation, an action conforms to the Kantian schema if the agent regards the action as permissible for anyone in his sort of situation to perform. On the strong interpretation, an action conforms to the Kantian schema if it is regarded as required for anyone in the agent's situation to perform.

This ambiguity affects how Kant's views are to be understood. Are the formulations of the moral law or the categorical imperative meant to generate principles of morally obligatory conduct? Or is the categorical imperative best understood as a test or condition which maxims of action must pass or fulfil in order to be morally acceptable, but which is not capable by itself of actually generating principles binding on all moral agents?

This ambiguity does not always show itself, since often the maxims (such as, lying to gain advantage for oneself) which the categorical imperative is used to test are found not to be permissible. And there is a natural act-category corresponding to such maxims which it is plausible to regard as a component of the moral principles generated by strong universality — e.g., 'Do not lie for the purposes of securing advantage.' In other words, the focus of discussion of the weak universality criterion in discussions of Kant is on maxims (and actions or omissions) forbidden by that criterion, rather than those permitted by it; and the non-performance of those actions or omissions is precisely what conforms to the strong universality interpretation of the Kantian schema. Overlooked in such discussions is the moral status of that wide range of actions permissible by the weak criterion yet not conforming to the strong one, because not morally obligatory.

Nevertheless the difference between the two interpretations is significant for what is meant by saying that actions must be universalizable, and that they must be grounded in universal rational principles. Is this meant weakly: that the action is acceptable to a universalization test or criterion? Or is it meant strongly: that universalization so to speak compels its performance?[5]

When comparing direct altruism as an account of moral action with the Kantian account, the ambiguity yields two distinct Kantian accounts.

On the weak view, a beneficent act is universalizable if the agent can regard it as permissible for anyone in his circumstances to perform. On the strong interpretation, a beneficent act is universalizable if the agent can regard it as obligatory for anyone in his circumstances to perform.

The nature and significance of the contrast between the Kantian schema of moral action and the direct altruism schema depends on which interpretation one uses. We have already, in the discussion of Ross's views, seen the weakness of the strong interpretation in regard to beneficent action. Only a minor part of the range of beneficent actions which could be altruistically motivated can actually be regarded as obligatory or incumbent on any moral agent. It seems arbitrary to restrict morally valuable beneficent acts to those which are morally required and could conceivably be prompted by a sense of duty. It thus seems evident that the strong universality interpretation of the Kantian schema cannot accommodate the full range of morally virtuous acts of kindness, sympathy, compassion, etc.

VIII

The weak universality interpretation of the Kantian view does not suffer the deficiency which the strong does. For many more beneficent acts accord with the weak universality schema than with the strong, namely all those acts of kindness, compassion, etc., which, while not being duties, are nevertheless not prohibited by universalizability considerations. These constitute a substantial subgroup of the class of beneficent acts motivated by altruistic considerations. So weak but not strong universality allows for the bulk of altruistic actions to be accorded moral value. Therefore, unlike strong universality, weak universality appears to provide, with regard to beneficent action, a viable alternative theory of morally valuable action to that of direct altruism.

What exactly is the difference, then, between the two views? Weak universality excludes some actions which direct altruism would allow as having moral value. For direct altruism accords prima facie moral value to any action which is intended to bring about good to another and is motivated by a desire to bring about that good. Weak universalizability imposes a further condition, namely that the agent regard the action as permissible for anyone to perform in the circumstances. This condition would exclude actions such as the following: X is prompted to help Y but upon reflection decides that it would not be right for any agent in his circumstances to help Y, because help in such circumstances tends ultimately to undermine the recipient's self-respect.

The direct altruism view does not actually deny the moral deficiency in non-universalizable beneficent and altruistic acts such as these. For it is a theory only of prima facie or *ceteris paribus* moral value. It allows for the possibility that other negative factors regarding an altruistic action weigh in an overall moral assessment of the act, so that an altruistic act might on balance be a morally bad one. Thus the direct altruism view does not say that an altruistic action has overall moral value independent of its universalizability, i.e., even if it is not universalizable. It does not recommend actions in spite of their non-universality. What it says is only that an agent need not actually take account of an altruistic act's universalizability in order for it to have prima facie moral value; and it allows (which the Kantian view does not) that an action can have some moral value in virtue of being directly altruistic while having disvalue in virtue of being non-universalizable.

What the direct altruism view does fail to do, in contrast to weak universality, is to offer a positive account of how a failure to be (weakly) universalizable detracts from the moral value of an act.

IX

Another important difference between direct altruism and weak universality (and, by implication, strong universality as well) has to do with the greater role of reflectiveness in the Kantian view. (Cf. Ross's statement that conscientiousness is a 'more reflective attitude' than direct altruism.) For the Kantian, morally good acts are always mediated by judgments as to their moral appropriateness — whether they are morally right or permissible — which in turn requires giving thought to their universalizability.

Direct altruism does not require these sorts of judgments and processes of thought, and does not by its nature necessarily involve moral reflectiveness. To act from kindness or compassion involves only that one respond to certain features in one's situation — that is, recognizing that someone else is in need and being moved by this consideration to help him. The link between the perception of need and the action is a direct one. One does not step back to reflect whether one is doing the right thing, or whether one could will everyone to act similarly.

Iris Murdoch notes a tendency in much modern Anglo-American

moral philosophy to overemphasize the role of moral self-awareness, of consciously striving to act in accordance with the demands of morality. Against this she says that moral philosophy must be able to give expression to the fact that 'the unexamined life can be virtuous.' 'Philosophers have often connected consciousness with virtue,' Murdoch says, but 'it must be possible to do justice both to Socrates and to the virtuous peasant.'[6]

The direct altruism view means to express a kind of virtue which does not depend on moral reflectiveness or self-consciousness. It depends only on being responsive to the weal and woe of others. In acting virtuously the Kantian agent is striving to be virtuous; he acts for the sake of moral rightness. But the compassionate or kind person does not necessarily or typically act in order to be virtuous. So, for example, if Jones stops to help a lost child find her parent his action is kind or compassionate if he is motivated directly by concern for the child and sympathy for the parent. He need not *aim at* being kind or compassionate. He need not even — in order to be kind or compassionate — have a conception of himself, or of his action, as being kind or compassionate. What is necessary is only that he aim to meet the other's need, relieve her suffering, etc. He need not even have a conception of himself as acting well or virtuously. The only requirement, in the way of moral self-awareness, is that (as Sidgwick points out) he not think of himself as acting *badly*.[7]

Not only is it not necessary, in order to be virtuous, that one act for the sake of virtue; but such a form of motivation, though not incompatible with virtue, leads away from it and thus introduces a potentially corrupting influence. For it is not such a large step from acting for the sake of compassion to acting in order to maintain one's image of oneself as compassionate (and from there perhaps to acting in order to maintain others' image of oneself as compassionate). Each of these motivations moves further away from the genuinely altruistic concern which compassion requires, and the last has nothing whatever to do with it.[8]

The argument here is not meant to impugn the knowledge of oneself as compassionate or otherwise virtuous. It is meant to correct the overemphasis on moral self-awareness in Kantian and much other moral philosophy.

The moral nonreflectiveness of this directly altruistic person does not imply a random or haphazard quality to his (beneficent) action. The directly altruistic person must be genuinely moved by the other's weal and woe rather than, for example, by whim or ulterior motive. In many cases one cannot be certain whether the consideration which moved someone was genuinely altruistic (nor of the extent to which an altruistic consideration was a component in a complex of motives). But there are ways to attempt to discern motives, in oneself as well as others, and problems discerning altruistic motivation are no different in degree or kind from any morally significant motivation.

X

So far, weak universality seems a more attractive interpretation of the Kantian view than strong universality; for it encompasses within its framework a much larger range of morally valuable altruistic action. In addition it may seem to have an advantage over the direct altruism view in excluding those actions which, while motivated by direct altruism, are not universalizable. Thus interpreted, the Kantian view may seem to preserve the positive features of direct altruism and yet to go it one better.

But this advantage is illusory. For, unlike strong universality, weak universality is not a full alternative to direct altruism. It does not actually provide an alternative account of the grounds of all morally valuable altruistic action.

Weak and strong universality constitute two distinct ways in which moral action conforms to a Kantian schema. On strong universality, moral action is actually generated by the schema. The Kantian standpoint commands the performance of the actions in question, e.g., acts of beneficence. The agent recognizes that universalizability requires him to perform the beneficent act (i.e., omitting to do so could not be universalized). Moreover, the Kantian standpoint provides the motive to the act or, to put it more generally, the understanding the agent has of his action. It is because the agent recognizes that considerations of universalizability require him to perform the act that he does so; he performs it because it is obligatory. It is in this sense that strong universality generates those actions (or principles) which conform to it, and offers an account of the source of moral worth in those actions.

Direct altruism shares this latter feature. It purports to give an account of one source of moral worth in beneficent actions, namely that they stem from a direct regard for the good of others.

By contrast, actions which conform to the weak universality

101

interpretation of the Kantian schema are not actually generated by the schema but merely accord with it or are countenanced by it; i.e., they do not violate its strictures.[9] Because of this, weak universality does not constitute a full theory of the source of moral value of those actions which conform to it; rather it merely imposes a condition which actions must meet in order to be moral, namely that they be able to be universalized. Hence, though weak universality does accommodate (most) altruistic action — i.e., allows for it to have moral value — it does not account for that moral value. The universality condition does not by itself exclude the possibility of other sources of moral value in the motive which prompts the action in the first place. (By contrast, strong universality provides the motive and the sole source of moral merit in actions which conform to it.)

Suppose that one intends to perform a certain beneficent action, motivated by altruism; one determines that one can weakly universalize one's action, and so one performs it. The motive to the action is still a direct concern with the good of the other. One has simply determined that in this situation it is morally permissible to act from this motive.

Although the universalizability of this action is certainly a factor in its moral value, nevertheless the dominant factor is the altruism. For suppose one were motivated by self-interest to pursue a certain course of action, yet one was morally conscientious and wanted to determine if one's action was morally permissible. So one determines that it is (weakly) universalizable, and one performs it. The act does not thereby acquire significant moral value, for it is motivated by self-interest; though it is certainly better that one tested the act for moral permissibility than that one did not, and in this sense one can say that the act itself is better than the same one not tested for universalizability but just motivated directly by self-interest. Thus, even if the direct motive is not the only factor in the moral value of an action, it is the dominant factor.

The universalizability is only what makes the act morally permissible. It is not what makes it positively morally good. The Kantian may still claim that the act is *not* morally good precisely because it is merely permissible rather than obligatory. But this claim cannot be based merely on the act's failure to be (weakly) universalizable.

This point is obscured by a moral psychology which essentially groups all motives in categories of 'duty' or 'inclination' and then tends (though not unambiguously) to see the latter as primarily egoistic. For then an action which is weakly (but not strongly) universalizable (and therefore permissible but not obligatory) will have whatever moral value it does have in the fact of its universalizability, since there is no conception of a direct motive which itself has even conditional moral value, all such motives being seen as forms of inclination. But if it is proposed that some such direct motives do have prima facie moral value, we see that weak universality has no way to deny this. To put it another way, the weak universality interpretation of moral action does not lend any support to the duty/inclination moral psychology scheme; the latter, on that interpretation, becomes a separate component of the Kantian view, and both would need to be assumed to be true in order to refute the direct altruism view.

As a criticism of the Kantian view this argument has ramifications beyond that view's failure to undercut the moral value of direct altruism. For any good motive which is weakly universalizable will have to be countenanced by the weak universality interpretation. This would include, for example, the disinterested desire that a beautiful forest not be cleared for a highway (not so much because of people's enjoyment of the forest but simply because one regards it as a good thing that such natural beauty exists).

XI

One point needs clearing up. It might be thought that in my interpretation of the Kantian view I have placed too much emphasis on the agent's believing that his action is universalizable, whereas the point of the Kantian view is that the action actually be universalizable; it is this which makes the action morally right. It is a matter, that is, of justification, not motivation.

But the act's universalizability is not what determines whether the agent has acted well in performing the act; and yet it is this — the action's moral value — that we are concerned with. If an act turns out, as it happens, to conform to the requirements of universalizability, but this fact comprises no part of the agent's own understanding of his action — so that, in relation to this agent, it is merely an accident that the act is Kantianly justifiable — then the action does not, on the Kantian view, have moral worth. Kantianism as a whole may well also involve a theory of agent-independent justification of acts;[10] but it is not this which competes with the direct altruism view. It is rather the view of the moral worth of action, which must include the understanding which the agent has of his action. So when I speak of an action's being universalizable I mean that the agent regards it as universalizable, and that this belief forms part of the considerations for which he performs the action.

So weak universality, in contrast to direct altruism and to strong universality, does not offer a self-contained theory of moral action. An action which is weakly universalizable may still be morally good on grounds other than its universality. In particular, unlike strong universality, weak universality does not by itself exclude acts motivated directly by altruism from having moral value.

Also while weak universality does differ from direct altruism as a theory of moral action, it does not differ by excluding altruism as a source of moral worth, and yet neither does it account for that source. A weaker version of weak universality is that altruistic actions have some moral merit if they are not weakly universalizable, but have less than if they were universalizable.

The difference between this view and the direct altruism view is that, according to direct altruism an altruistic action's moral worth is not diminished merely by the agent's failure to give consideration to whether it can be (weakly) universalized. If, out of kindness or compassion, an agent acts directly for the sake of someone's good without thinking about whether it is morally permissible for anyone in such a situation to do so, his action has full moral value (*ceteris paribus*). It is diminished in moral value only if the action is in fact not universalizable and the agent could have recognized this. Whereas weak universality deprives the action of some of its value solely because the agent has failed to test for universalizability.

Let us then consider as a Kantian position, that weak universality on this interpretation is superior to direct altruism, as a view of the moral worth of beneficent action. Is beneficence grounded in universal principles (understood as weak universality) superior to beneficence grounded in direct altruism? That is, is it morally essential, or anyway morally preferable, to make certain that one's intended altruistic beneficent action is (weakly) universalizable, rather than to act directly from sympathy, compassion, kindness, etc.?

One argument in support of weak universality is that action prompted by direct altruism, because it is not grounded in universalizable principles, is liable to conflict with principles which are strongly universal and thus morally binding. For example, if I act unreflectively from compassion I might forget certain obligations I have to other persons. I get so carried away by my compassion that I neglect commitments and obligations which should take precedence in my actions. So a morality in which we allow free rein to our altruistic emotions in guiding our actions is inherently deficient.

In response to this, our actual duties to others comprise only a restricted portion of the occasions of our interaction with others. We have duties and obligations to others regarding institutional relations in which we stand to them, and regarding specific commitments made to particular people (e.g., promises, commitments to friends); and perhaps we have a 'duty of beneficence' to persons in general, independent of any special relationships to them. (But if the latter exists, the occasions of such a duty are quite restricted.) But occasions on which such duties are applicable comprise only a small portion of our interaction with others. Thus most occasions on which, out of sympathy, compassion, or concern, we pursue the good of another person are ones in which our action will not conflict with a duty to someone else. As argued in chapter III, this holds as well for the duty of impartiality, which requires us to give equal consideration to the interests of those to whom the duty is owed.

If we think of the many ways we help others – friends, acquaintances, strangers – out of sympathy, compassion, concern, we realize that in most such situations we violate no moral demands in doing so. I respond to an acquaintance's difficult situation by doing something helpful; John helps the man dig his car out of the snow; Kate acts out of friendship for Sue – in these acts the agent is typically not running up against any moral demands which performing these beneficent acts violate.

If the restricted nature of our actual duties to others is granted, the fact that action from altruistic emotion can on occasion conflict with such duties and obligations will not seem so disturbing; for on most occasions directly altruistic actions will not conflict with them.

Yet it may still seem somewhat disturbing, for if we give free rein to our feelings and let them guide our actions entirely, will we not be blinded to the other moral demands (connected with duty and obligation) in cases where they do arise? So will it not still be at least somewhat better to act from universal principles of beneficence than from direct altruism?

But the person acting from altruistic emotion is capable of acknowledging these other considerations; and is capable of acknowledging that in cases in which his duty would lead him to perform act A, while his sympathy would lead him to perform act B rather than A, he ought to perform A. That he generally (i.e., in the normal situation in which direct altruism violates no moral stricture) gives free rein to his concern and sympathy does not necessarily blind him to these other moral considerations. The picture of altruistic emotions as blind, irrational, or as overwhelming us and preventing any other considerations from weighing with us is not accurate.

But how is it possible for altruistic emotions which are not grounded in moral principles to allow for the acknowledgment of moral principles which limit their morally proper scope of activity? To put it another way: if I restrain from acting from altruistic emotion because doing so would conflict with a moral principle, does this not show that my compassion is not without principle, but on the contrary is grounded in general principles regarding when it is permissible or not permissible to act from compassion?

The answer to this is analogous to the argument given in chapter III, regarding the functioning of impartiality *vis-à-vis* friendship (see pp. 61-4). If it is acknowledged that our duties and obligations are restricted in their application, then when someone acts from altruistic emotion in a situation which he knows not to be covered by duties and obligations, he is not acting from universal principle. For what he knows is not itself a moral principle but is rather simply that his situation is one to which certain moral principles are inapplicable. Thus John, in helping the man dig his car out, could rightly believe that he is not thereby violating any duties to others. In acting out of sympathy to help an acquaintance I can already know that I am not acting in conflict with any other duties which I have. But what John and I know in these situations is not something grounded in universal principles. Rather, it is knowing that no universal principles apply to our situation.

Every universal principle of duty or obligation applies to certain situations and not to others. So, in order to be able to apply such a principle, one will have to be able to identify when one is in a situation to which the principle applies and when one is not. But such knowledge

106

of the situation is not something which one can know on the basis of the principle; for it is a precondition of knowing how to apply the principle. Such knowledge cannot be assimilated to a further moral principle without infinite regress.

One can know, or justifiably believe, that one's altruistic action does not violate universality, without actually having to test the act for universality, simply by being justified in believing that there are no moral requirements within one's situation (with which acting altruistically might conflict). In such situations weak universality has no advantage over direct altruism.

And so altruistic emotions need not be grounded in moral principles in order for us to act on them freely and spontaneously in situations in which no moral demands are made on us, while yet *not* acting on them freely and spontaneously in situations in which moral demands are made on us (and in which acting from altruistic emotions would or might fail to honor the demands). This is the sense in which we can give 'free rein' to our sympathy, compassion, etc. – i.e., we can do so when we are not in situations in which we violate any moral demands by doing so. Our actions in such cases will have moral worth, insofar as they involve acting out of a genuine regard for the good of other persons.

XIII

A concern related to whether action not grounded in principle is liable to conflict with morality is that, unless our beneficent acts are grounded in some principle, we are liable to be beneficent towards persons who do not deserve it; and in that way our 'non-principled' altruistic emotions will lead us morally astray. It might seem that this could hardly be a particularly serious or central problem, since whether someone is, so to speak, an appropriate object for beneficence seems to have less to do with whether he deserves the help than whether he needs it or could use it. The notion of desert seems out of place in most contexts of possible beneficence. Concern with it stems at least partly from taking charity – i.e., beneficence from the financially secure towards the disadvantaged and dependent – as one's general model of beneficence (on this subject, see chapter III, p. 57), together with the concern generally attached to the social ideology of charity, that one not act charitably towards those who are undeserving of it,

107

e.g., those who are slothful or who have brought their unfortunate condition on themselves. Thus, in illustrating the general Kantian notion of action on principle, C.D. Broad gives as an example

> the case of a member of a Charity Organisation Society giving relief to a complete stranger. He analyses the situation to see whether it does or does not come under a certain rule or principle of action which he has accepted. If it does he gives relief; if it does not, he refuses it. And he would treat in exactly the same way any other man whose case had the same features.[11]

W.D. Ross also, in illustrating the distinction noted previously between an action in which we aim directly at the good of another person and one in which we aim at doing the right thing, sees the difference as illustrated well by that between the discriminate and indiscriminate charity.[12]

But charity is only a very special case among the entire range of forms of doing good for others. It implies a situation in which the giver is very much better off than the recipient; in which the recipient is regarded as essentially powerless and dependent, unable in a fairly permanent way to get along without the charity contribution; and finally, in which what is given by the giver is some form of money or material goods which in giving he gives up or gives away (though, it is also implied, he can well afford to do so).

But most forms of action from sympathy, compassion, or concern lack at least some if not all of these features. Often what we give when we give to others out of altruistic emotion is our time, energy, efforts, advice, comfort — things which we have not thereby lost to ourselves in giving them (anyway not in the sense in which money which we give away is lost to ourselves). Also, very often when we help friends and acquaintances, and even strangers, their general life situations are not regarded as so hopeless that they are permanently dependent on the resources of others to be able to take care of themselves; rather they are simply temporarily in need of some kind of help. The person is basically regarded as an equal who happens to be in a jam; whereas in the case of charity the recipient is always regarded as unequal to oneself (the giver). Finally, the agent in usual acts of direct altruism is better off than the recipient only within the situation at hand, but not necessarily in any other (temporary or permanent) way. One can appropriately have sympathy for a person who is financially or socially better off than oneself.

108

Furthermore, the worry that one's charity might be 'indiscriminate' is not necessarily a morally admirable concern, much less a morally fundamental one, and stems from a view of poor people which is connected with a certain social and political outlook — namely, that poor people are basically divided into those whose poverty is a reflection of their own inabilities (or, even more, their own laziness) and those whose poverty is due to circumstances not of their own making. The view that the former group is a large one, that such persons are undeserving of charity, and that therefore we must be on our guard with principles which discriminate clearly between the deserving and the undeserving, is a questionable one.[13]

So the case of charity does not show that we need to be especially concerned about the issue of doing good to persons who do not deserve it. From a moral point of view this is one of the least of our concerns. In the normal round of our day-to-day lives it is quite evident that many persons' situations warrant sympathy, compassion, concern. A direct concern with the weal and woe of others, unmediated by principle, is all that is generally necessary, in order for us to do what it is morally good to do. An overconcern with the deservingness of persons who are potential objects of our actions of sympathy, compassion, etc. betokens a kind of meanness of spirit and an unwarranted distrustfulness, as well as the above-mentioned questionable social views.

XIV

Another Kantian concern can be put this way: just because we desire the good of others does not mean that we will achieve it, and acting directly from our altruistic emotions might well be less likely to lead to that end than acting from reasoned general principles grounded in reflection and relevant information.

This objection is unfairly framed. We have to assume that the compassionate or sympathetic agent is genuinely concerned with fostering the good of those to whom his emotions are directed, rather than simply acting impulsively on the basis of a superficial reading of situations. He will understand that there is a distinction between fostering the other person's good and doing what the other wants one to do.[14] And he will be no less likely than the Kantian agent to make himself as well-informed as he thinks necessary to achieve his desired aim.

This is not to say that the altruistic person necessarily possesses the intelligence, insight, and knowledgeability sometimes necessary to give effect to his genuinely good intentions. A person can be compassionate yet blind, shortsighted, or unrealistic. But if he is to be genuinely compassionate we must assume a genuine concern with others' good, and not merely with superficial indications of their wants or needs.

Moreover, the Kantian agent himself does not necessarily possess the intellectual virtues mentioned, nor necessarily avoid the deficiencies. He too can be stupid and unrealistic about how to accomplish what he takes to be his duty. He can, because of ignorance, apply his principles badly. He can misperceive his obligations, wrongly working out what reason bids him to do.

Granted that knowledge and certain intellectual qualities make it much more likely that the person with altruistic intent will succeed in acting beneficently, it might be thought that Kantianism must have some advantage over a morality of altruistic emotions, since it is a view which by its nature requires more reflection. But this is not so. The reflection required by Kantianism takes place only at the stage of attempting to determine one's duty given how one already understands one's situation. It does not itself produce a more informed grasp of one's situation. On the other side, sympathy and compassion themselves impel, or can impel, the necessary reflection when the situation presents elements of complexity, when it is not evident how best to carry out one's beneficent intent.

The point here is that it is unfair to compare a poorly functioning directly altruistic agent with an ideally functioning Kantian one.

XV

A final issue in the alleged superiority of weak universality to direct altruism is *consistency*, and the agent's commitment to acting in the same (morally good) way in the future.[15] In acting from universal principle on a certain occasion one commits oneself to acting the same way in similar situations in the future; whereas acting from direct altruistic emotion, insofar as it is not action on principle, involves no such commitment. Hence action from altruistic emotion is liable to inconsistency in a way that principled action is not. Philip Mercer, expounding a Kantian view, puts this objection in the following way:

110

to be generously disposed towards someone one day merely because I happen to be in high spirits is not morally commendable if the next day I don't care a damn about him. . . . These kinds of emotionally based behavior do not commit the agent to similar behavior in the future. We must admit then that insofar as it is correct to say that some emotionally motivated conduct cannot be backed by justifying reasons it cannot provide us with any grounds for expecting, or requiring, its repetition in the future when circumstances are appropriate; and that insofar as this is so it cannot possess moral worth.[16]

But the contrast implied here between action on principle and action grounded in altruistic emotion is neither very great nor very significant. It is not clear that action from altruistic feeling is any more liable to lead to inconsistent behavior than action from principle. First, merely invoking moral principle in one's behavior is no guarantee of consistency of behavior, nor even of consistency of principle. One might be prone to citing various principles to rationalize (or even genuinely to explain) one's actions, and yet it be the case that the principles which one cites on different occasions are incompatible with one another.

Still, invoking principles is not synonymous with actually holding them and acting from them. Nevertheless, even if a person genuinely possesses certain moral principles and attempts to live according to them, this is no guarantee that he will necessarily do so. It might be that he simply fails to live up to his genuinely held principles, or lives up to them in an inconstant fashion. (However, there must be a sufficiently genuine attempt to guide one's conduct according to the principles in order to say that the person holds them.) Thus, having principles is no guarantee of consistency in action.

On the other side, let us consider a person who we would say is a sympathetic or compassionate person. Such a person would be prone to acting out of compassion or sympathy in certain situations (situations which 'warrant' sympathy or compassion). It seems that by saying that he is a compassionate or sympathetic person — in contrast to someone who occasionally or inconstantly shows signs of compassion or sympathy — we are attributing a measure of consistency to his behavior. He tends to be moved by certain sorts of considerations. But this is not to say that he acts from universal principles.

Therefore, that a person does not explicitly guide his conduct by universal principles does not mean that he is not likely to act consistently

111

in a sympathetic and compassionate way. The fact that there is no guarantee that he so acts does not mean that he is *not likely* to. And, as we have seen, acting from principle is no guarantee of consistency in any case.

Thus, acting from altruistic feeling does not necessarily or even typically involve acting inconsistently. Acting from principles may have some advantage on this score, but not nearly so much as the original contrast implied. Therefore universal principle is not required for consistency regarding the kind of behavior prompted by altruistic feeling.

And so Mercer is wrong when he says that 'emotionally motivated conduct . . . cannot provide us with any grounds for expecting, or requiring, its repetition in the future when circumstances are appropriate' (see above, p. 111). For an established pattern of sympathetic or compassionate action in someone does give us grounds to expect such action in the future. It does not give us grounds to require such action in the future; but neither does someone's adhering to a principle in one situation give us grounds for requiring him to do so in the future. Adherence to universal principles does give us grounds to appeal to the person to do a beneficent act on some future occasion; but we have grounds of appeal in the case of altruistic emotion — namely the considerations (relating to another person's good) to which the person has shown himself in the past to be responsive.

XVI

None of this is to deny that a person who acts from altruistic emotion can act inconsistently. An example of this can help us to gain a clearer picture of the moral significance of consistency.

Sal is a genuinely kind and sympathetic person, but is so in a particularly inconstant way, in that she is especially moody and her kindness seems to depend very much on her moods. When she is not feeling 'down' she is available to others, willing to give of herself to help them out, responsive to other people's needs and concerns. But when Sal is in a depressed state she is not open to others, not very responsive to them, not so willing to be helpful. Her sympathy and kindness are inconstant and her behavior, in that sense, inconsistent.

What exactly is the moral defectiveness involved in this sort of inconsistency? To help explore this question let us imagine that Sharon is an acquaintance of Sal's, who has had the benefit of Sal's kindness but has not yet been made aware of the change in her altruistic behavior when she is in a bad mood. Then let us suppose that Sharon is in a situation in which it would be possible for Sal to be helpful to her. Because Sal happens on that occasion to be in a foul mood, she is curt and unresponsive to Sharon. Sharon is disappointed, surprised, and taken aback by this.

One clear deficiency in Sal is her unreliability in the area of helpfulness to others. One cannot count on her to be helpful, though often she is helpful. Also, as the situation of Sharon brings out, Sal in a way raises expectations which she then disappoints. Besides the unreliability, what exactly is wrong with this? The fact of raising expectations in others does not give those others any special claim on Sal. It does not constitute a commitment to them. Thus, when she fails to be kind she does not necessarily violate commitments to others or fail to honor their claims.

It is true that we are sometimes angrier and more resentful towards people who, though generally sympathetic and available to us for help, do not come through on some particular occasion, than we are at others whom we know to be self-centred and whom we would never even expect to go out of their way for us. This says something interesting about anger and resentment, but it does not signify any greater claim against the kind person simply because he has raised expectations which he disappoints.

But perhaps, even though the raised expectations do not give others a claim on the person's beneficence, nevertheless they do constitute some legitimate expectation, hence some moral defect if that expectation is not met, though a less serious one than violation of commitment. I think there is something in this, but its force depends to some extent on how we are picturing the way the expectations are raised. Such a defect is not identical with one in which a person, so to speak, gives it out to be understood that he can be relied on or counted on to be kind or helpful, perhaps in order to be thought well of by others. In such a case there is perhaps a kind of deceit involved.

Certainly in some particular situations this inconstancy of feeling for others might involve a serious moral failure; for example, if Sharon were in a really desperate situation and Sal were able to help her out yet did not do so because she was in one of her depressed moods. This might constitute a breach of the 'natural duty of beneficence' (see chapter III, p. 45). Still, it would be compatible with the kind of inconstancy described in Sal for Sal when in a bad mood to be available to people in truly desperate situations, even while her moodiness keeps her from being available to people who are worthy of sympathy and help though not desperately in need of it. In fact, if this were not true of Sal she would seem almost schizophrenic rather than just exceptionally moody.

Another thought might be that if a person is inconsistent then he will not follow through on actions undertaken on others' behalf when he is in his accessible moods. This is a charge made against capricious feelings which carries some weight. However, many acts of kindness or sympathy do not involve action over time as subject to such moods. Moreover, if an inconsistently kind person did, out of kindness, undertake something on another's behalf, he might still be capable of recognizing that this constituted some sort of commitment to carry through on the undertaking, despite change of mood. The commitment to follow through is of a different moral status than the original undertaking itself (which involves no such commitment), and the inconsistently kind person would be capable of appreciating and acting on this difference. (The contrast with the consistently kind person might be that his following through would be done in a somewhat different, less positive spirit.)

One might think that another serious moral deficiency is involved here, namely that the discovery of the inconstancy of feeling would lead us to question the genuineness of the sympathy and kindness shown when Sal is in a good mood. If she were really sympathetic then how could she be unresponsive on so many occasions when she was in a bad mood? We might begin to search for some ulterior motive which Sal might have had in being helpful; or we might begin wondering if we had not read more sympathy and kindness into her behavior than was really there.

This is a real possibility; yet it is also important to recognize that it is possible for sympathy and kindness to be both inconstant and yet perfectly genuine. Failing to be sympathetic when one is in a bad mood does not necessarily indicate an inadequacy or ungenuineness in the sympathy one shows on other appropriate occasions.

Unreliability, possibility of lack of genuineness of altruistic feeling, potential for failing to follow through on beneficent action undertaken — these are the moral defects we have noted in the failure of behavior stemming from altruistic feeling to be consistent, at least in the way portrayed in our particular example. Thus what is morally deficient about inconsistency in action is not just one kind of thing. It can be different things on different occasions.

Such defects and potential defects must be taken into account in an overall moral assessment of Sal's character. And there is room here for disagreement regarding the weight of these defects and hence regarding the overall moral assessment. The point remains that the defects are not so fundamental as to undermine all moral value in the inconsistently kind person's behavior. Sal is still capable of kindness and sympathy and these qualities do have moral value.

In particular the kind of inconsistency noted here involves less serious moral deficiency than the capriciousness discussed in chapter II. For a capricious person is one who is, so to speak, totally unreliable about acting in a beneficent way; Sal on the other hand is *partially* responsive, sympathetic and kind.

On the Kantian view consistency is a *sine qua non* of morality. The above argument suggests that the only consistency which is actually required is the consistency involved in holding universal principles at all; i.e., in applying the principles consistently, to all who come within their scope, and in particular not making an exception of oneself. But consistency in behavior, though generally (not always) morally desirable, is not a necessary condition of the moral worth of action or character.

In summary: failure of action to be grounded in universal principles does not necessarily lead to inconsistency in action. For a compassionate or sympathetic person can be entirely consistent in his behavior. Thus consistency is not as closely tied to universality and principle as the Kantian view implies. But further, consistency in behavior is not a *sine qua non* of moral value. It is one virtue among others.

These considerations mitigate whatever superiority, up to this point, weak universality has to direct altruism. They should in any case make it clear that the failure to test one's beneficent acts for (weak) universality is not typically a serious moral defect.

XVII

We began this chapter by counterposing two seemingly entirely divergent views of the structure of moral action and the sources of moral worth in actions — namely the Kantian view and the direct altruism view. Subsequent argument has uncovered several versions of the Kantian view, which seems caught on the horns of a dilemma. To the extent that Kantianism presents a comprehensive view of moral action (e.g., in its strong universality version), and thus presents a full alternative to direct altruism, it cannot plausibly aspire to encompass the full range of morally good beneficent action which direct altruism purports to encompass. Whereas to the extent that it (e.g., as the weaker version of weak universality) is able plausibly to encompass this range it increasingly forfeits its character as a full alternative to direct altruism as a theory of moral action; for it is parasitic on other motivations to action than are provided by the Kantian schema itself, and is unable to exclude the possibility that some of these (e.g., altruism) may have moral value. So, while direct altruism is clearly a distinct view from all forms of Kantianism, the Kantian view cannot produce arguments which undermine the direct altruism view.

Thus we were left in the previous sections with considering a Kantian view which was really little more than Kantian window-dressing on the basic direct altruism view, namely the claim that it is morally desirable to test proposed altruistic actions for weak universality. (And even here the argument for the moral superiority of the Kantian view was not compelling.)

As for the role of universality or universalizability in morality, this depends on the concerns one is addressing. It may be that universalizability is a valid requirement for acceptable moral principles. I have been concerned, however, with a different issue, namely whether universalizability is a valid requirement for moral (i.e., morally good) action. It is only the latter role for universalizability which I have denied.

VI

ALTRUISTIC EMOTION, REASON, AND PERCEPTION

Direct altruism, I have argued, is a form of motivation distinct from Kantian-type motivation. It is, moreover, meant to be the kind of motivation involved in the altruistic emotions. That is, sympathy, compassion, and concern are forms of direct altruism. And so, vindicating the moral value of direct altruism as a motive entails a vindication of the altruistic emotions as motives.

But the connection drawn here needs explanation. For it might be thought that direct altruism has nothing specifically emotional about it and that, in fact, it can be understood in purely rationalist terms. For example, Thomas Nagel argues in *The Possibility of Altruism* that the good of another always constitutes a reason for an agent to foster that other's good. Thus we always have a reason to act altruistically, and *qua* rational we are compelled to acknowledge this reason as applicable to us. Moreover, what makes it a reason has nothing to do with emotional factors in our make-up, but only with structural aspects of us as rational beings (in a world of other rational beings). Altruism grounded in such considerations would be direct altruism, yet would be purely rational.

The mere existence of such purely rational altruistic motivation does not by itself undercut the moral value of altruistic emotions, so long as the latter are genuine forms of direct altruism. If so, then direct altruism would simply take different forms, of which pure rational altruism would be one, and sympathy, compassion, etc. would be others.

It would be useful then to be clear on the ways that (acting from) altruistic emotion differs from (acting from) pure rational altruism, and at the same time to show that altruistic emotions are a genuine form of direct altruism and are no less direct (and in that sense 'pure') than is purely rational altruism (if there is such a thing).

I

We can best bring out this difference by first contrasting acting from sympathy or concern with acting from duty (of beneficence). (Although Nagel's pure rational altruism cannot by any means be equated with duty, it shares the feature of being a motive which is in no way grounded in emotion but is purely rational.) I have an acquaintance, Becker, who is in a jam. I have concern for Becker, and out of that concern I help him. Cathcart, who cares nothing for Becker, nevertheless regards himself as under an obligation to help him, out of a duty of beneficence. Both of us, in helping Becker, intend that Becker be relieved of his difficulty. But our ways of regarding this aim are different. My motive in helping Becker is my direct desire or concern for his good. Cathcart does not have a direct desire or concern for Becker's good, though he acts with the intention of bringing about Becker's good.

Suppose both Cathcart and I perform acts to help out Becker. And let us suppose, first, that the actions do serve to help Becker out of the jam he is in. What would our respective feelings, attitudes, etc. be towards the resultant situation? Since I am concerned about Becker and care about him, I am greatly relieved that he is out of the jam. I am pleased for him. What I am pleased about is not primarily that it was I who was able to help him out of the jam (though I may be pleased about this also), but that he is out of the jam. What would Cathcart feel? It seems that what Cathcart would mainly be pleased about is that he has discharged his duty, that he did the right thing. He would have 'moral satisfaction,' or satisfaction at having done his duty.[1] But we have hypothesized that Cathcart cares nothing personally for Becker, nor has he any emotional responses to his situation (his weal and woe). And so he is not particularly pleased for Becker at his being out of the jam (which is not to say that he is displeased). This is not a thing which makes Cathcart happy, or relieved, as it does me. If we imagine Cathcart to be pleased for Becker (as I am) then we are imagining that he feels something more than a sense of duty towards Becker. He would then have some altruistic emotion towards him.

We can see this more clearly if we imagine a situation in which both Cathcart and I perform the acts of beneficence, but, through absolutely no fault of our own, these acts fail to help Becker (e.g., we lend him some money but then the money is stolen). How would we each respond to this outcome? I would naturally be upset, both that my action had failed to help, and that Becker was still in the state which originally prompted my concern. I would naturally continue to be concerned about Becker, since the grounds of that concern would still exist. (In fact I might be more concerned, or at least discouraged, at the failure of a reasonable attempt to help.)

But if Cathcart had acted purely out of duty he would not feel these things. We are assuming here that he regards himself as doing what was his duty to do, and that he regards it as entirely a matter of bad luck, no fault of his own, that it did not work out. So he would feel that he had done what was his duty, or that he had done all that could have been expected of him in attempting to discharge the duty. If he were really emotionally indifferent to Becker, then, having done what he regarded as all that is required of him, he would have no more feelings about the situation or towards Becker. He would not be concerned about Becker, or distressed at the turn of events. Were he to do so this would show that his emotional attitude towards Becker included more than regarding him simply as someone towards whom he had a duty.

Finally, let us consider the situation where Cathcart and I are prepared to do the appropriate beneficent act, but Becker gets himself out of the jam without our efforts. I am pleased about this. I no longer need to be concerned about Becker. I am happy he is no longer in a jam. I feel relief, perhaps also joy for Becker. But Cathcart has nothing to feel in this situation, except that he no longer has a duty to Becker. The situation which gave rise to his duty no longer exists. (Perhaps he is glad that he does not have to discharge the duty; but this would be another matter, not inherent in acknowledging the duty itself.)

Someone might take issue with the way I have treated this example. For, one might say, if Cathcart regards himself as having a duty of beneficence to Becker, then in acting from this duty his aim or goal is that Becker be benefited, i.e., that he be out of the jam. If this aim were not met would Cathcart not therefore feel frustrated, unhappy, etc.? And similarly, if this goal did come about (by whatever means), would he not have reason to rejoice, feel happy, feel relieved, etc.?

There are two things to be said in response to this. First, even if one grants (which I do not) that the man acting from duty has the goal that Becker be benefited, still the feelings associated with the realization and frustration of this aim are different than with acting from concern or sympathy. For if the dutiful man is unhappy when his aim is unrealized, what he is unhappy about is that-his-aim-is-unrealized. But what the concerned man is unhappy about is that-Becker-is-still-in-a-jam (and/or that-an-effort-to-help-Becker-is-unsuccessful). The dutiful man's feelings are not directed at Becker's situation for its own sake, but only insofar as it involved something at which he was aiming. The second point is that if it is genuinely out of duty that someone acts, then his aim is, strictly, not that a certain state of affairs should come about but that he should do the right thing. Of course these will generally coincide – his doing the right thing will bring about the desired state of affairs. But when they do not coincide – i.e., when his performing the dutiful act fails, because of fortuitous circumstance, to bring about the desired state of affairs – then the person acting purely from duty is satisfied when he has done the right thing.

A person acting from duty might well have a wish that the other person be benefited. And this wish can generate the emotions mentioned. But such a wish is separable from the duty. It constitutes a different motive, which can operate separately from or together with the sense of duty.

The concerned person's emotions are focused directly on Becker in a way that the duty-motivated person's are not. Thus his reactions to various different outcomes in the situation are conditioned by what happens to Becker, regarding his weal and woe. But the dutiful person's reactions are directed not to Becker directly, but to Becker's situation as it relates to the performance of his duty towards Becker.

Thus there is a significant difference between acting out of concern for someone and acting out of a duty of beneficence. Different attitudes towards the person and the action are involved, which involve differences in emotional response. Acting from concern is constituted, in part, by a readiness to have feelings of pleasure, joy, sadness, frustration, and hope regarding various outcomes of the situation one is in. Acting from duty is entirely separable from such emotional reactions, though in practice they might well go together. (This latter point would suggest the unnaturalness of a theory of moral motivation grounded in duty alone.)

Insofar as Nagel's purely rational altruism can be regarded as a genuine motive, most of what has been said regarding the contrast between acting from duty and acting from altruistic feeling can be applied to it. For Nagel's pure rational altruism contrasts with the duty of beneficence only in that the action which the agent has a purely rational altruistic reason for performing is not (necessarily) a morally required one. But my account of the contrast between altruistic emotion and acting from duty depends not on this feature of the latter, but merely on its being a purely rational motivation not involving any emotional attitude towards the person to be benefited. So, if it is merely a purely rational reason for which I act, then the feelings associated with acting out of altruistic emotion will not be associated with it.

II

The differences between pure rational altruistic motivation and emotionally grounded altruistic motivation do not render the latter any less direct or pure as altruism.

This point can be brought out by focusing on some passages from Nagel's *The Possibility of Altruism*, which contain a certain familiar picture, one which denies this point, concerning what it is to act from altruistic emotions or sentiments. That picture is, roughly, that to act from emotion is for the grounds of one's action to be the emotion rather than some consideration in the situation itself. This picture can be seen in some passages from Nagel:

A defense of altruism in terms of self-interest is unlikely to be successful. But there are other interests to which appeal may be made, including the indiscriminate general sentiments of sympathy and benevolence. . . . I prefer to concentrate instead on trying to provide a better account, thereby showing that an appeal to our interests or sentiments, to account for altruism, is superfluous. My general reply to such suggestions is that without question people may be moved by sympathy, benevolence, and love . . . on some of the occasions of which they pursue the interests of others, but that there is also something else, a motivation available when none of these are, and also operative when they are present, which has genuinely the status of a rational requirement of human conduct. There is in other words such a thing as pure altruism (though it may never occur in isolation from other motives). It is the direct influence of one person's interest on the actions of another, simply because in itself the interest of the former provides the latter with a reason to act.[2]

121

The general thesis to be defended concerning altruism is that one has a direct reason to promote the interests of others — a reason which does not depend on intermediate factors such as one's own interests or one's antecedent sentiments of sympathy and benevolence.[3]

The view presented here is opposed . . . to any demand that the claims of ethics appeal to our interests: either self-interest or the interest we may happen to take in other things or other persons. The altruism which in my view underlies ethics is not to be confused with generalized affection for the human race. It is not a feeling.[4]

What I am interested in here is not Nagel's view that there is a kind of altruism grounded in reason alone, apart from any element of sentiment or emotion; but rather the contrast which Nagel draws between this pure rational altruism and altruism which is grounded in emotion or sentiment (such as sympathy, love, benevolence). Nagel implies that these differ in that, whereas the former involves a direct influence of one person's interests on the action of another, the latter does not. Nagel's conception of the way that the interests of one person influence the action of a person acting from altruistic sentiment or emotion is that the emotion or sentiment is some kind of factor ('intermediate' or 'antecedent') which mediates between the interest of the other and the action of the agent, making the influence of the former on the latter an indirect rather than a direct one.[5]

Another way to state Nagel's view seems to be this: there is a reason which an agent always has to promote the interests of another person. When one acts from a pure (rational) altruism one is acting solely and directly on this reason. But when one acts from sympathy or benevolence (or compassion, concern, etc.) one is not acting directly on this reason but is rather acting from the emotion (sympathy, benevolence, etc.). This in turn can be interpreted (quasi-egoistically) to mean that one acts beneficently only because one happens to have the feeling or desire in question, with the implied contrast to acting genuinely in response to the other's situation.

All this involves a false picture of the altruistic emotions and of what it is to act from them. For sympathy, compassion, etc. do involve a direct influence of the interests (or good) of one person on the actions of the agent. The altruistic emotions are not intermediate entities between the good of others and the actions of the agent. Rather, in acting from altruistic emotions, one's reason for or consideration in acting *just is* the good of the other. In that sense action from altruistic

122

emotion is rational. But Nagel's view of altruistic emotions does not allow for this. (Altruistic emotions are less purely rational than pure rational altruism, if this means that they involve an emotional dimension. But this does not make their motivational component less than fully rational, in the sense of involving the other's good as providing a direct reason for the agent to act.)

The picture of acting beneficently only because one happens to have a desire or feeling for another's good does apply to some forms of altruism, or pseudo-altruism. For example, because of guilt one may have a sort of compulsion to give money away to those whom one regards as needing it. In the absence of such feelings of guilt one would not, let us suppose, be concerned with others' welfare. This situation seems to fit the quasi-egoistic description of acting beneficently primarily because one happens to have a certain desire. (But such situations do present real difficulties in classification in terms of egoistic and altruistic motivation.) Yet clearly altruistic motivation need not conform to this pattern.

Thus, if there is such a thing as pure rational altruism, it does not contrast with altruistic emotion in involving a direct influence of the interests of the other on the actions of the agent. Rather, this is a feature which these phenomena share; they are both forms of direct altruism. The contrast lies rather in the attitude, the associated feelings, the way the other person and his situation are viewed by the agent (as spelled out in the previous section).

Nagel appears to regard the possibility of such direct influence as in need of some explanation, except when the altruism is grounded in feeling or sentiment. And he appears to find the explanation for such direct influence within reason alone, expressed as 'the recognition of the reality of other persons, and on the equivalent capacity to regard oneself as merely one individual among many.'[6] Giving such an explanation appears to be one of the main tasks of Nagel's book.

But why is altruism grounded in altruistic emotion not equally in need of some explanation? For in acting from compassion the good of another moves me directly. I am recognizing the reality of another person when I feel concern, compassion, care for him. Nagel appears to regard the human capacity for sympathy, compassion, benevolence, etc., as perfectly intelligible, in a way that acting from pure rational altruism is not. He regards taking an interest in another's weal and woe as very much like taking an interest in one's own weal and woe, except with a different object. And so, for Nagel, as for adherents of Kantian views in general, the significant division is between acting from interests, feelings, sentiments on the one hand, and acting from purely rational considerations on the other. But this way of portraying the situation fails to take seriously that in acting directly for the good of another, whether I do so for purely rational considerations or from altruistic emotion or sentiment, I recognize the reality of another person and take account of his good for its own sake in a way in which I do not when I act only for the sake of my own good. Thus, as I have tried to argue throughout this book, the crucial moral distinction is between concern for one's own good and concern for the good of others, rather than between emotional (or interested) considerations and rational considerations. Because of his focus on altruism, Nagel, despite failing to see this, provides us with at least some of the perspective from which this point can be appreciated.

III

For Kantianism, morality is primarily a matter of reason and rationality; these in turn are understood as exclusive of emotion. What implications does the theory of direct altruism have for the relation between morality and reason? In particular, in what ways is morally good, directly altruistic action rational or non-rational?

Directly altruistic action is grounded in certain considerations, namely altruistic ones, which move the agent to perform beneficent acts. He is aware that the other is in need or is suffering, and he acts in order to relieve the other's woe. In these ways the directly altruistic agent is not acting blindly, randomly, or irrationally. He understands the other's situation and his own response to it — in the sense that he understands that the other is in a state of woe, and he regards his intended act as being intelligibly related to the relief of that woe. Altruistic action has a certain structure, in that the altruistic agent acts in order to bring about a good, namely the good of the other person.

One can say that in so acting the altruistic agent acts for a reason, that the consideration which moves him is the reason for which he acts. It is particularly worth saying this to make clear that directly altruistic action such as acting from compassion or sympathy is not irrational, non-rational, contrary to reason, unrelated to reason, and the like.

IV

On the other hand, there are certain implications which some philosophers have thought acting 'for a reason' to carry, which directly
altruistic action seems to me not, or at least not necessarily, to involve.
Most obviously, there is no essential contrast, much less a conflict,
between the action being prompted by emotion (at least in the sense
in which altruistic emotions are emotions) and its being done for a
reason. For, in this sense, acting from sympathy, compassion, or
concern involves acting for a reason. Appreciating this point requires
abandoning the picture, discussed in previous sections, of an emotion
as a non-rational force which, so to speak, goads us into action (in
contrast to a reason conceived as a rational force which leads us into
action). In addition, working out its implications would undercut the
reason/emotion dichotomy which is a central part of Kantian moral
psychology.

On the other hand, that acting from altruistic emotion might be said
to involve acting for a reason in no way implies that such action is in
some way grounded in reason, as if the rational element were somehow
what was fundamental, and the emotional merely secondary or epi-
phenomenal, an 'affect' added on but unrelated to the emotion's essential nature or moral significance.

A second common implication of 'reason,' which I would want to
deny, involves universality. We have already seen (pp. 87-92) that acting
altruistically does not commit the agent to the view that everyone
ought to act as he has done in the situation. And so it does not commit
him to the view that the reason or consideration which prompted him
to act is one which is equally binding on all (similarly situated) agents.

But there is a weaker sense of the universality of reasons which
might be thought to obtain, namely that to act for a reason implies
regarding one's reason as a reason for anyone (similarly situated), if not
actually as having to carry the same weight for everyone. The distinction is this: one might regard one's reason as a consideration which
everyone ought to take account of in the situation at hand — which it
would be wrong to ignore entirely — without thinking that the consideration ought necessarily to carry the exact same force or weight
with other agents as it has done with oneself. The stronger position
here is really tantamount to the universalizability-of-actions position
discussed earlier (in chapter V), for if the different reasons were to
carry the same weight with any agent as they did for the agent in

question, the same overall balance of reasons in favor of the action which the agent actually performed would be the result. So not only the reason but the action itself would be universalizable.

The weaker position here is in fact much weaker, in that it allows for different agents to be differently influenced by the same reason. One agent might be willing to be late for a job interview in order to help an injured person; whereas another might, while acknowledging a reason to help the injured person, decide that his desire to be on time for a film outweighs this consideration. The weaker position requires only that other agents take account of the consideration − that it not completely fail to weigh with them. It puts no constraints on what that weight is to be. This sense of universality of reasons might be thought to have strayed far from the spirit of Kantianism; it has certainly abandoned most of the notion that our actions are to be grounded in or derived from universal or rational principles or considerations.

It may be, in any case, that reasons are universal in this weaker sense. But I do not think that directly altruistic considerations are; and if this is correct it would be grounds for not saying that the altruistic agent acts 'for a reason.' The fact that X acts for the sake of Y's good does not mean that X necessarily regards Y's good (or the good of someone situated analogously to Y) as a consideration which everyone in X's sort of situation ought to take account of. Though he may do so, he need not, by the mere fact of his own acting for the sake of a particular person's good, hold any general view about what others ought to take account of in their actions. (And the reason for this is not that the agent regards the consideration as one which applies to himself alone.)

Let us consider someone who, though generally quite selfish and narrow in spirit, is, because of some unusual combination of circumstances, deeply moved by another's plight, and shows an uncommon considerateness and generosity of spirit towards that person.[7] He shows a regard to the other's weal and woe which he does not customarily show. We can suppose also that after this incident he returns to his accustomed way of responding to others and is not again so touched by the plight of another. Having acted altruistically on that one occasion, is he necessarily committed to the view that others ought to be similarly motivated, that, at least, they ought to take account of that particular sort of consideration in their own actions? Certainly he gives no evidence of actually holding such a view.

It may be the case that through being moved in one particular case to give consideration to another's welfare − in a manner which is unexpected and out of character — one is awakened to a deeper sense of concern for others. One may then come to regard others' weal and woe as a general reason which everyone ought to take account of.

On the other hand, as in the example above, one may very well not come to hold this view, but may instead return to one's former narrow and self-centered view of the world. And even if one does come to hold the view in question, this would not show that simply by acting altruistically one must have thereby held, or was committed to holding, the view that such-and-such altruistic consideration constituted a general reason for anyone (in the weak sense described).

It may also be that if one is forced to think about — or if one simply does think about — an altruistic action which one has performed, one might naturally come, at least while one is thinking about it, to regard the given altruistic consideration as a general reason. But, first, one might *not* come to so regard it. Second, and perhaps more important, that one does acknowledge something as a general reason, while one is thinking about it, means neither that one was already committed to that view, nor that one actually comes to hold the view. Whether one does hold that view is shown by what one actually does, and by how one actually regards others and their actions, not simply by what one assents to in one's mind.

This argument has proceeded on an extremely abstract level. Suppose in a particular case X helps Y, with the thought, 'Y is suffering.' I am arguing that X need not hold the view that someone's suffering constitutes a general reason which anyone must take account of in acting. But certainly X *will* hold that view; hardly anyone is going not to regard someone's suffering as a reason to act to help him. By contrast, that someone could use some help, or that it would be in someone's interest to do such-and-such, though genuinely altruistic considerations capable of moving someone to act, are not so compelling that an altruistic agent would necessarily regard others as having to take them into account. Here the factor of level of importance of someone's weal and woe is significant (see chapter II, p. 12). So, while there are many altruistic considerations which an agent, in acting from, will likely regard as generalizable to others (at least in the weak sense which does not involve generalizing the weight or force of the consideration) there are other altruistic considerations which are not so generalizable.

In addition, the appropriate specification of someone's reason (or of the consideration motivating him to act) is not necessarily identical with what he says when asked why he acted. There will be qualifying situational factors (e.g., how much cost, inconvenience, or sacrifice to the agent is involved) in any full specification of the considerations. And it is this full specification which, I am arguing, is not necessarily generalizable to others, even in the weak sense involved here. If this is right then the considerations for which the altruist acts ought not to be called 'reasons.'

A possible source of confusion regarding whether altruistic considerations are reasons lies in the fact that the altruistic agent regards himself as bringing about a good, in the sense of a good for another. The intentional and motivational structure of this action may seem to be acting for a reason. But this does not necessitate that the agent view the state of affairs at which he aims as, impersonally regarded, a good thing, which anyone has a reason to promote; such a view would involve some universality of reasons. (It should be noted however that such a view, if it is interpreted to mean merely that it would be a good thing for other agents to take account of the consideration in question, may be even weaker than the weak view described above. For such a view seems weaker than saying that others ought to take account of the considerations in question. But I do not mean to pin too much on this distinction.)

The altruistic agent is no more required to regard the state of affairs at which he aims as impersonally a good thing than is a self-interested agent to so regard the state of affairs at which he aims. The situations are analogous: the self-interested agent aims at a good for himself, the altruistic agent at a good for another. Only in this sense do the agents in question necessarily aim at a good, though the self-interested agent may, just as the altruistic may, in addition regard the good in question as one which everyone has reason to promote (e.g., his piano playing, which he regards as in itself a good thing, and not merely a good to him).

This point may be difficult to see because of the moral difference in the two cases, namely that (on my view anyway) to aim at another's good is to do something morally good, whereas to aim at one's own good is (generally) to do something morally indifferent. Still, as I have argued, this moral difference is constituted simply by the difference in object (and motivation) and does not require the agent's further view as to the objective moral worthiness of his aim. For this reason, even if one were to say that the altruistic agent acted for a reason, it might be misleading to say that he acted for a moral reason, if this is taken to imply that the agent necessarily regards his act as morally good or right and his reason as a moral reason. (This would still allow us to say that altruistic reasons *are* moral reasons, in order to emphasize that it is morally good to act from them.)

Finally, whatever sense of 'reason' is involved in altruistic emotions, it does not carry the intellectualist connotations of involving moral reflection and judgment which it does in the Kantian scheme. It requires only a certain kind of understanding or apprehension of others, and of what one aims to do, which might not involve moral reflectiveness and judgment.

So, in summary, there are reasons for and against saying that directly altruistic considerations are 'reasons' (or 'moral reasons'). What is important is only that we know what we do and do not mean in saying this, and that, in any case, acting from altruistic emotion is not acting irrationally or contrary to reason.

V

The argument of chapter V focused on moral action and motivation — on the understanding which the moral agent has of the acts which he performs. I argued that direct altruism as a theory of moral action is superior in certain respects to Kantianism. Here I bring in a further issue — namely perception of situations — which is essential in a theory of morals, and in regard to which the Kantian view, in comparison to a moral view grounded in altruistic emotions and virtues, is deficient.

The way we act in a given situation depends on how we perceive or apprehend the situation. We can speak of 'the description (or descriptions) under which a situation is apprehended,' referring thereby to the description of a situation which is most salient or operative for an agent in setting the context for his response to that situation. Can we say anything general about the sorts of descriptions of situations relevant to altruistically motivated action? It seems that a condition of a person being motivated to act altruistically (to act for the good of another) is that he apprehend the weal and woe of the other person as at stake in the situation. For example, one apprehends the weal and woe of B as at stake when one apprehends B as suffering, in need, uncomfortable, having a potentiality of being greatly benefited, etc. Another's weal and woe may be at stake in a situation, but if the agent in question does not perceive it to be, he will lack a condition of being motivated to respond to it.

What does it mean, in practice, for an agent to apprehend a situation under a description relating to someone's weal and woe? (I am going to make a simplifying stipulation by referring to 'the' description under which a situation is apprehended. Obviously there is often more than one such operative description for a given agent.) We can best illustrate this with some examples:

1   I am riding seated on a subway train. I see other people standing. One of them is a woman holding a shopping bag. She is somewhat uncomfortable. Let us say that the description under which I apprehended this situation is 'A woman standing holding a shopping bag.' This description is neutral in relation to the woman's weal and woe. On the other hand I could perceive the situation under the description 'A woman who is uncomfortable standing, because she has to hold her shopping bag.' This description makes reference to the woman's weal and woe – i.e., her discomfort.

2   I walk past a man digging his car out of the snow. I can apprehend the situation as 'A man digging his car out of the snow'; or I can apprehend it as 'A man who is having a bit of a hard time digging his car out of the snow.' The second description makes reference to the man's weal and woe (his having a hard time); the first does not.

3   A man comes to my house and asks if this is the residence of the Morelli family. I can apprehend this situation as the man's asking a question (to which the answer is no). Or I can apprehend it as the man's looking for something or someone, wanting to know something. The latter characterization is more related to his weal and woe. If I apprehend the situation in the former way I simply answer, 'No.' If I apprehend it in the latter way I might try to give him some help in what he is looking for. I know, for example, that the Morelli family does not live in such-and-such houses on my block, so the man can avoid going to them. Perhaps he can say some more about the Morelli family, which might help to jog my memory, or give me a further clue as to where they might live, or at least where they certainly do not live. I could share my knowledge and suppositions with the man, thereby helping him to find what he wants.

To say that someone apprehends a situation under a certain description is not to say that he necessarily or typically completely fails to be aware of any features of the situation which do not figure in that description. It is only to say that the description in question is the operative one for him. It represents his 'take' on the situation, the main way in which he apprehends it. For example, in case 1, that I apprehend

130

the situation under the description 'A woman standing holding a shopping bag' does not mean that I am entirely unaware that she is also uncomfortable. For instance, if someone asked me, 'Does that woman seem uncomfortable?' I might say yes, and realize that at some level I had been aware of her discomfort all along. But I had not, as it were, taken this discomfort in. It had not been salient in the way I had apprehended the situation. All I had been fully consciously aware of was that she was standing holding a shopping bag. This is why the given description is the one under which I apprehended the situation. (The person's asking me the question might have the effect of changing my apprehension of the situation, so that I now apprehend it under a description which involves the woman's discomfort.)

In distinguishing the description under which a person apprehends a situation from other aspects which the person is at some level aware of, could readily become aware of, or is not at all aware of, I want to avoid two sorts of portrayals of the matter:

First, I am not envisaging that it requires particular intelligence, sensitivity, or perceptiveness for the person to apprehend the features of the situation which relate to the other person's weal and woe. Thus, in the subway train example, I am not envisaging it as requiring special sensitivity to see that the woman is uncomfortable; but rather that this can readily be realized by a person of normal sensitivity or perceptiveness. One could, for a contrast, imagine a case in which special perceptiveness would need to be involved in seeing that the woman was uncomfortable, e.g., where there were no normal or readily perceptible signs of it but only subtle ones (a slight rigidity in the way the woman is standing, a slightly tight look on her face, her shifting position a bit too often, etc.).

Similarly, in examples 2 and 3, it does not require great sensitivity, intelligence, or perceptiveness to realize that the man is having a bit of a hard time digging his car out, and that he could do with some help; or that the man asking about the Morelli family wants to know something (about which one might be able to be of some help).

On the other side, I mean to exclude cases in which it is so obvious that the other person's weal and woe is at stake that it would be virtually impossible for someone in the situation not to realize this in a way which figured into his conscious apprehension of the situation (e.g., if the person is being beaten).

I am aiming to describe situations in which, though a person could quite readily, in the ordinary course of day-to-day life, fail to take in the weal and woe as part of his apprehension of the situation, it is not a failure to be especially perceptive or sensitive which accounts for this.

Having said something about what it means for someone to apprehend a situation under a description, and for the description to relate to another person's weal and woe, let us now discuss the relation between apprehending the situation and responding to it altruistically. Apprehending a situation as relating to another person's weal and woe is an essential prerequisite for acting out of regard for their weal and woe. (Again I am making an oversimplification in my focus here. I am contrasting descriptions which do not relate to the other's weal and woe to those which do. But the contrast will typically be a matter of degree (e.g., of how important an aspect of the weal and woe is at stake — suffering, mere discomfort, inconvenience, pain, etc.) rather than an absolute one. Still, this simplification avoids some complexities which are not, I think, central to the argument.) So a person who is beneficently disposed (either from altruistic emotion or principles of beneficence) is more likely to so act if he perceives weal and woe at stake than if he does not. In example 1, unless I perceive the woman as uncomfortable, I lack a reason to get up and give her my seat. In example 2, there is less of a reason for me to help the man if I merely apprehend him as digging his car out of the snow than if I apprehend him as needing help. In the third example, as described, I am more likely to offer some help to the man if I perceive him as wanting something or looking for something than if I merely apprehend him as asking me a question.[8]

VI

Let us now consider the relationship between altruistic emotion and apprehension of the situation in terms of weal and woe. My general contention is that part of what characterizes a person as caring, compassionate, sympathetic, or concerned is that he is more likely than other persons to apprehend situations in terms of the weal and woe of others. Someone who tends to view others 'through the eyes of sympathy' (who tends to have sympathy for others) is more likely to apprehend the woman in example 1 as uncomfortable, the man in example 2 as having a bit of a hard time digging his car out, the man in example 3 as being able to use some help in looking for the Morellis.

It is evident that a sympathetic, compassionate person is more likely to act to foster the good of others. This is part of what it means to be sympathetic and compassionate, insofar as these involve dispositions to have certain emotions, and these emotions involve a disposition to act for the sake of the other's good (see chapter II). What I am arguing here is that this difference between the sympathetic, compassionate person and the unsympathetic, uncompassionate person should be seen as having two components: the first is apprehending the situation as involving weal and woe, and the second is responding to that apprehending with altruistic action.

The model to be avoided here is that of all persons as having the same apprehension of situations, and differing only in how they act in response to such apprehension — the compassionate person acting to relieve the perceived suffering and the uncompassionate person not doing so. This model misrepresents both the complexity of what is involved in having altruistic emotions (and their associated traits of character), and also yields a false picture of the uncompassionate person's failure to act to help others.

Often the uncompassionate or unsympathetic person simply fails to see that another's weal or woe is at stake (or, a similar point, fails to apprehend its level of importance; see chapter II, p. 12). This is not to deny that the uncompassionate or unsympathetic person sometimes does perceive the weal and woe yet does not act out of regard for it. An intentional ignoring of another's perceived woe constitutes callousness, but not all absence of sympathetic action involves it. The point is that an unconcerned or unsympathetic person is characterized as either failing to apprehend (or take in) others' weal and woe, or failing to be sufficiently motivated to do anything about it, or both.

That there are two parts to what is involved in moral action (apprehension and acting) — and in the differences between possessing and failing to possess certain virtues — is often not appreciated in moral philosophy. Rather, the apprehension, and hence the description, of the situation is taken for granted, and the focus placed solely on how the person acts in the situation (and on the considerations or reasons for which he acts).

These points can be illustrated in the teacher/student example discussed in chapter II (p. 36). As I portrayed the original situation, the student Clifford evidences in his talking to his teacher, Jones, pain and distress regarding his situation with his family. But this portrayal of Clifford, though accurate, is, so to speak, a description from the point of a sympathetic person perceiving the situation. It is the way that

133

Brown (the sympathetic teacher) apprehends the situation (with Casey in the place of Clifford) (see pp. 40-1). But it is not the way that simply anyone would apprehend the situation. Another teacher might apprehend it under the description, 'Clifford bellyaching about his family,' or 'Clifford talking about his problems' (where this carries the implication, '... which are no concern of mine'). This does not mean that such teachers would not in some way be aware of Clifford's pain and distress; but it may not register with them, they may not take it in so that it becomes part of the descriptions under which they apprehended the situation.[9]

Evidently a teacher who apprehends Clifford's pain and distress is much more likely to act to help, e.g., by forgoing the talk he had planned to attend, than is a teacher who does not apprehend that pain and distress. (The case originally described of Jones and Clifford presents a sort of intermediate situation, in which Jones at some level perceives the pain and distress in his apprehension of the situation, for originally he feels some sympathy for Clifford; but the implication is that this pain and distress are not particularly salient for him in his apprehension of the situation. He does not fully take them in. This is part of why his sympathy is weak.)

Of course a teacher could apprehend the pain and distress and yet choose not to respond to it, for any one of a number of reasons. But he is much more likely to do so if it is part of the primary way that he apprehends the situation than if it is not.

The kind, compassionate, sympathetic, or concerned person perceives people differently from someone lacking these qualities. The latter, for example, is more likely to perceive them in terms of categories relating to their effect on his own pleasure or advantage — e.g., as boring, fascinating, obnoxious. While the sympathetic person is by no means immune to such categories, they will generally play a less central or anyway less exclusive role in his 'take' on people. For example, if A is acting obnoxiously, B, a sympathetic person, is more likely to perceive, behind A's obnoxiousness, that (and if) A is hurting, wanting to communicate, needing friendly gesture, etc. (This is not to deny that A may simply be obnoxious, with nothing 'behind' it, and B need not fail to recognize this.) One can say, in a Wittgensteinian spirit, 'The world of the kind person is different from the world of the unkind.'

In a way, the sympathetic person will understand more about people than will the unsympathetic, at least in regard to their weal and woe. He is more likely to see someone's pain, frustration, disappointment.

This is connected with his having more empathy, and therefore seeing the other more from the point of view of how he is experiencing things rather than, as the sympathy-less person does, in terms of the other's effect on him. And so it is not merely that the sympathetic person perceives things differently from the sympathy-less person, but also that he sees things more accurately, with more insight. But this point should not be overstated; there is much about other persons (e.g., rel ting to their less-than-honourable motives) which the sympathetic person can, perfectly compatibly with his sympathy, fail to perceive.

VII

An agent's response to a situation — the action he takes — is conditioned by what he takes that situation to be, by the description under which the situation presents itself to him. So an adequate moral theory must deal not only with action and with motive but with perception, with how situations come to present themselves in particular ways to moral agents. A theory grounded in altruistic emotions and altruistic virtues can accommodate this requirement. For it recognizes that a full characterization of what it is to possess an altruistic virtue involves not only the actions performed and the motives from which they are performed, but also the fact that the agent perceives others' weal and woe as at stake in situations. Similarly the altruistic emotions are not merely motives to altruistic actions, but involve perceiving situations as involving the weal and woe of others. Part of what it is to have a certain emotion is that the situation which one apprehends presents itself to one in a certain way.

Let us now see how perception of the situation, as a feature of moral life, figures into the Kantian view. Consider a well-known passage from Kant's *Foundations of the Metaphysics of Morals*, in which Kant is discussing the moral value of acting from duty in contrast to acting from sympathy.[10] He is considering persons faced with a situation in which they have 'the power to benefit others in distress.' First he considers a basically sympathetic person who in this particular situation is unable to be touched by, to care about, the needs of others in distress, because of a personal sorrow.[11]

What I am interested in here is the man Kant next considers, namely a man lacking in sympathy for others, indifferent to their sufferings. Kant imagines such a man coming to the aid of others in distress not out of sympathy but out of duty; and he sees such motivations as morally superior to acting from sympathy.

As Kant sets up the example the man of sympathy and the unsympathetic (indifferent) man of duty are faced with the same or equivalent situations — persons who are in distress whom it is in each of their power to help. But this omits the fact that the indifferent man of duty is much less likely than the man of sympathy to apprehend the other persons as in distress in the first place. This is part (though only part) of what is involved in saying that he lacks sympathy for others (or is indifferent to their weal and woe).

If we are to make sense of the Kantian notion of a person without emotional response to the sufferings of others, nevertheless acting out of a duty of beneficence towards them, I submit that we must envisage the person in the following way: when he is convinced that others are in distress, suffering, etc., then he is conscientious in doing what he regards as his duty to help them. But such a person will not naturally perceive others as in distress to the extent that the sympathetic person does. Thus he will less often actually be convinced of the need, pain, suffering, distress of others than will the sympathetic person. Therefore, he will not perform beneficent acts in every instance in which the sympathetic person does.

It is thus misleading of Kant to imply, as he seems to, that the unsympathetic man of duty and the man of sympathy differ only in the motives for which they perform beneficent acts; for they differ also in the scope of their beneficent activity, and this stems from or is connected with differences in the ways that they apprehend situations in terms of weal and woe. All these differences (motives, scope of beneficence, apprehension of weal and woe) are, or should be, taken into account in an overall moral assessment of the two types of person. Such an assessment cannot be limited, as Kant's view would have it, merely to the sorts of motives from which the person acts.

It should also be noted that if we are to conceive the unsympathetic man of duty as really being motivated by duty, then we can hardly envisage him as regarding every situation in which he is convinced that the weal and woe of others is at stake as one in which he regards himself as having a duty to help. I have suggested earlier that the duty of beneficence, if it exists, must be regarded as encompassing only a small area of our potential beneficence to others (e.g., that area in which we can avoid great harm to others at little or no cost to ourselves). If this is so then the scope of beneficent activity of the unsympathetic man of duty is even further limited than the previous argument implies.[12] For it is limited not only by the unsympathetic man of duty's failure to perceive weal and woe as at stake; but also by his failure to consider many occasions on which he does perceive weal and woe, and in which a man of sympathy would act beneficently, as ones in which duty requires him to act beneficently.

Thus Kant's failure to see the importance of apprehension of the situation leads him to a false view of the full differences — and the moral significance of these differences — between the man of sympathy and the unsympathetic man of duty.

VIII

The problem in the passage from Kant is endemic to Kantian moral theory in general. That view emphasizes the importance of universal and rational principles for guiding action; but it does not take sufficiently seriously the problem of the application of those principles to actual situations. One feature of that problem is how situations present themselves to the moral agent. Kantian principles specify, at least theoretically, what action to take in a situation of a certain type of specification. So the actions which the Kantian agent actually takes depend on how he perceives the situations before him. His perception will determine which principles he regards as applicable, and hence which actions he is to perform.

But the view does not, as it stands, address the issue of how situations do present themselves to the agent in the first place. It is easy to fail to notice that the issue is being avoided. For in writing moral philosophy the author presents situations in which the moral choice is to be made and the principles applied. So the situation as presented to the hypothetical moral agent already has a certain character. But that it has the character for any given moral agent cannot be taken for granted; and, more important, that it is to particular agents (and under certain descriptions) that situations must present themselves is ignored by the theory.

Suppose, to take a very general example, that a Kantian agent holds the principle, 'Help those who are in pain.' This principle is properly applied in situations in which others are in pain. But the mere fact of holding the principle will not tell an agent when someone is in pain. And whether he perceives people as in pain will depend on many different factors. Because of a failure of empathy he may often fail to perceive that people are in pain, or may take what is actually pain to be something less serious, such as discomfort, difficulty, or unease. It is a weakness in Kantian theory, in comparison to theories of altruistic emotion and virtue, that it fails to deal with this issue.

This failure is connected with a weakness in much contemporary moral theory, which Iris Murdoch has been concerned to emphasize, and that is an overemphasis on choice and decision.[13] The Kantian theory emphasizes having the appropriate principles to guide us in the choices we make. But equally significant from a moral point of view is what an agent regards his options to be, among which he must choose; and, in the same spirit, whether he regards himself as facing a choice at all. A morally insensitive person may not regard a certain situation as presenting a moral issue, and so will fail to work out which principle ought to govern his action in that situation. A person insensitive to others' weal and woe will not see acting in regard for that weal and woe as one of his choices.

As Murdoch points out, much of our moral nature is shown in the situations in which we regard ourselves as having morally problematic or morally significant choices to make, and in the options we see as the viable ones. And so much of our 'moral activity' — here construed very broadly — will consist not only in choosing principles and actions but in regarding others and ourselves in certain ways, so that we perceive certain dimensions of situations which present themselves to us. For example, learning to be a more sympathetic person might involve coming to terms with certain prejudices, fears, or disappointments which stand in the way of perceiving others — or certain groups of others — sympathetically. In doing this one will see certain actions (e.g., beneficent ones) as options for oneself which one had not considered to be real choices before. Changes in our ways of perceiving will be part of the process of our moral growth.

We have already seen, in the discussion of weak and strong universality, the impossibility of carrying through on a certain ideal or fantasy which Kantianism involves, namely to ground a theory of morals in reason alone. For, at most, such a view would yield only actions which were actually morally obligatory on an agent; it would thus leave out the much greater range of actions which are from a moral point of view admirable, decent, desirable, good, exceptional, praiseworthy, noble, etc.

The issue of 'perception of the situation' exposes another flaw in that fantasy, namely this: from reason alone one can at most generate the correct set of principles. What one cannot do is ensure that they are correctly applied, for (to raise only one of the possible problems here) possessing the right set of principles does not ensure correctly perceiving the situations in which they are to be applied. This perception cannot be assured, so to speak, by reason alone. Hence, what cannot be gotten from reason alone is the full-blooded moral agent, with his perception as well as his principles; all one can get (to follow out the fantasy some of the way) is the principles themselves.

The point here is closely related to that made in the argument in chapter II, that Kantian theory cannot provide a moral motive which ensures its own availability, for it cannot ensure that an agent will be moved by that motive on occasions on which it is appropriate.

What has to be given up is the goal of a morality grounded solely in rational and universal principles — not given up as an ideal of what our moral principles should be like, but given up as a conception of what it is to be a morally good or admirable person (or even, I might add, actually to possess any particular non-Kantian virtue).

I should clear up one point here. I am not arguing that because the Kantian theory does not take account of perception of the situation the truly Kantian moral agent can never perform acts, that Kantianism is not a philosophy which one could live by. What I am saying is that whatever perceptions of situations are involved in the Kantian agent's actions are not accounted for by Kantianism itself. It might be thought that Kantianism does not really need a theory of situation-perception, that it is best construed only as setting conditions and criteria for moral principles and actions. This is essentially the weak universality view. If so, it should then be acknowledged that Kantianism can no longer compete on the same level with the theory of altruistic emotions or virtues, which does involve a view of situation-perception. It will be a theory about something different — not what it is to be a morally good person, but only part of that, namely what the conditions are for morally acceptable principles and actions.

139

VII

THE INTRINSIC VALUE OF ALTRUISTIC EMOTIONS

A major aim of this work is to show that altruistic emotions have moral value. The arguments of previous chapters, especially II and V, have accomplished part of this aim, namely to show that altruistic emotions have moral value as motives to beneficent action.

In chapter II I argued that altruistic emotions are capable of being reliable incentives to beneficent acts. In chapter V I said why it is that action motivated by altruistic emotion is morally good, namely that it involves a regard for the good of others.

But to focus on sympathy, compassion, and concern solely as motivation to perform beneficent acts is to limit their significance as moral phenomena. In the previous chapter the perceptual aspect of altruistic emotions was discussed, but its moral significance was portrayed primarily in terms of its contribution to motivation: perception of someone's weal and woe is a condition of acting out of regard for his good. In this chapter I will show that the full moral value of altruistic emotions is expressed non-motivationally as well as motivationally. In chapter II, when giving a preliminary sketch of some important aspects of altruistic emotions, I argued against a view which obscures their non-motivational dimension and thus makes it difficult to see the value of that dimension; the view was that having sympathy, compassion, or concern necessarily involved being motivated to help the person who is their object (pp. 14-15). I argued that this is true only of situations in which the agent could readily help the other, but is not true of situations in which the agent is in no position to help (without extraordinary sacrifice on his part or wholesale rearrangement of his priorities).

A focus on motivation as the sole locus of moral value characterizes

Kantianism as well as the view just stated. Although Kant is rightly noted for emphasizing not the actions which an agent actually produces but his inner psychological state in attempting them, it is only *qua* motive-to-action that Kant is interested in that psychological state. Kant does not see idle wishes, emotions, desires, or even intentions as having in their own right any moral significance; what counts are our motives for endeavoring to bring about certain states of affairs (even though the success of those endeavors is not regarded as significant). And so, despite Kantianism's concern with the 'inner,' it is concerned with only those aspects of the inner which constitute motives to action. By contrast, I argue that morality encompasses a much wider scope of our inner life than this.

I

The emphasis on motive, in moral theory, goes along with conceiving of human action in a particular way for the purposes of moral assessment — namely (what I will call) 'the schema of motive and act.' A central feature of this schema is the distinction between the rightness of the act and the moral goodness of the motive. A certain act (e.g., keeping a promise) can be the right act to perform in a certain situation independent of the motive for which the agent performs it; he might perform it simply because he has promised to do so, or he might perform it because he expects to gain some advantage thereby. What makes the act the right one to perform will be independent of the motive to perform it.

On the other side, the moral goodness, or moral worth, of the motive to the act is a separate matter from the rightness of the act. A person can, from a morally good motive — say, sense of duty — perform what is in fact a wrong act, because he is mistaken as to the moral requirements of the situation or is mistaken about some bit of information crucial to determining what is the right action. In any case, what makes something a morally good motive is grounded in considerations other than what makes the act itself a right one, though it is generally thought to be a necessary condition of a motive's being morally good that in acting from it we mean to be performing a right act.

On this schema, what makes the act the particular act that it is — what constitutes its morally relevant description(s) — can have nothing to do with the motive which prompts it. For if it did then considerations regarding its rightness would be involved with its motivational aspects, contrary to the assumptions. The act must be one which could be prompted by any one of a number of motives, while still remaining the same act that it is.

Applying this schema to beneficence, we would say that what makes an act a beneficent one is that it brings about some good to the recipient of the action (and that it be intended to do so, for whatever reason).* A beneficent act can be motivated by an altruistic motive, that is, one in which the agent's ultimate purpose in performing the action is to bring about a good to the recipient of the action. But it can as well be performed for other (e.g., self-interested) reasons.

The schema allows, but also compels, us to assess the act separately from the motive. My argument will be, not that there is a general deficiency in this schema itself, but only that it is inadequate to most situations in which we act from altruistic emotion. In particular, I will argue with regard to some of the examples already discussed that the emotion itself is often part of what makes the act the morally right or appropriate one in a given situation; for essential to how the act brings about a good to its recipient — hence essential to its being the act of beneficence which it is — is that it is motivated by an altruistic emotion. I will not deny, however, that in many cases the schema of motive and act is entirely appropriate for the moral assessment of action.

For example: in the case of the hospital visit (chapter II, p. 37), an integral part of the good to Sue in Bob's act of visiting her in the hospital is that he is thereby showing concern for her. We cannot envisage the act of visiting prompted by some other motive, while still preserving the good to Sue of that act. Suppose that Bob's motivation in visiting Sue is not concern for her but a sense of duty towards her. His attitude is not one of concern for how she is doing, or of making her feel better by his visit. There is no direct desire to see her. Rather, Bob regards her condition as constituting a morally binding reason for him to visit her, and his motivation is this sense of obligation.

Let us assume that Sue realizes that Bob's motivation in visiting her is duty rather than concern. Would Bob's visit then bring about a good to Sue? Would it bring about the good to Sue which was originally envisaged when we described the situation in chapter II? It seems that

---

*I will refer to the person who is benefited by the action, and who, when the action is intended to benefit, is intended to be benefited by it, as the recipient of the action.

the visit would probably bring about *some* good to Sue — a familiar face when she has seen only heretofore unknown medical personnel, someone with the time to talk to her, someone she knows with whom she can presume to talk about certain things. But it would not bring about the full good brought about by a visit done out of concern. For one thing, even the good to her of the dutiful visit will be mitigated by her discomfort, anger, or disappointment, attendant upon her recognition that it is not concern which Bob shows by his visit, but that he feels compelled to visit her and is in that sense not doing so fully wholeheartedly.

Thus, when we examine our original presumption that the (morally) appropriate thing for Bob to do in this situation is to visit Sue in the hospital, we see that part of this appropriateness involves his having certain emotions (concern) and his acting from these emotions. But this means that the motive of the action cannot be separated from the action itself, when one is considering the act as the morally appropriate act of beneficence which it is. In this situation there can be no sharp separation between assessment of motive and assessment of act.[1]

We can see the same point in the case of the teacher listening to the student (chapter II, pp.36-7, 40). In order for the student to be made to feel better in this situation it is not sufficient that the teacher merely continue listening to him. The student must also not feel that his confessing his troubles to his instructor is improper. If he does feel this, he may well feel shame and perhaps humiliation (as well, perhaps, as some fear that this will lessen his esteem, and perhaps his grade, in the mind of the instructor). In order for this not to happen, therefore, the student must understand that he has some sympathy and understanding from the instructor. Thus the act which the instructor performs must involve more than simply listening; it must be listening-sympathetically, listening which is motivated by and expressive of sympathy.

So the emotion which prompts the act of beneficence has significance beyond its merely producing or being the motive for that act. For the beneficence which is appropriate to the situation will require more than an overt act, externally described; it will also require certain emotions accompanying the act, or, rather, emotions as integral parts of the action as a whole.

II

Beyond the fact that an emotion is sometimes required for the act to be a morally right or appropriate one, is the more general point that emotions which an action expresses are often part of the good which the action brings about to the recipient. I will illustrate this in two examples which, in contrast to the two discussed above, do not involve a previously existing relation (e.g., of teacher/student, friend/friend) between the parties involved. The two examples differ in that the first involves some kind of interaction between the parties, the second does not.

Suppose I have a flat tire by the side of the highway, my jack is broken, and there is no phone nearby. I am dependent on a passing car to stop. When, eventually, Manero stops to help me, I am greatly relieved that my tire is changed so I can get on the road again, and I value Manero's act of beneficence for this reason. But, in addition, I would naturally value Manero's act as expressive of the human sympathy and compassion it showed in Manero's taking the trouble to stop and help me. If I had reason to believe that the act was not expressive of such sympathy and compassion — e.g., if Manero had a kind of minor business connected with his auto repair shop, in which he carried tire-fixing equipment around with him and offered for a fee to fix the tires of persons in my sort of situation — then I would regard, and value, the act differently. Though it would still have the substantial value to me of relieving my helpless situation and enabling me to drive my car (and for this I am quite happy to pay the fee), it would lack the element of human sympathy or compassion. For Manero would be doing the act purely (let us assume) as a business proposition. The good to me of the two different acts would differ.

A final example: in a strike of farmworkers against California fruit growers, citizens sympathetic to the strike may support the strike through boycotts, sympathy strikes, support picketing, donations, etc. This support will be of concrete aid to the strikers, helping to put economic pressure on the growers, enabling the strike to continue longer, and perhaps more generally influencing the general political climate in ways which pressure the growers to make a settlement desired by the workers. But, in addition, at least some of the striking workers will value and appreciate the support, not only for this concrete assistance, but also for the human sympathy which they take it to express. For it shows that other citizens, unknown to them personally and remote from their situation, support them and their cause, agree with their position in the dispute, care enough to give something of themselves even though they themselves do not (typically) benefit, etc. Thus the support given the strikers is valued not only for its concrete assistance in their struggle, but also for the sympathy and human support (i.e., 'moral support') which it expresses.

In all four of the examples discussed, the good to the recipient of the beneficent act done from a certain kind of emotion, or expressive of that emotion, is greater than if the act were done from certain other motives. So, altruistic emotions are essential to bringing about the specific good which they do bring about when they motivate certain acts.

One consequence of this is that the moral significance of altruistic emotions transcends their being motives (conceived as described on pp. 141-3) to acts of beneficence.

A second consequence is that the schema of motive and act is sometimes not adequate to conceptualize our moral assessment of situations in which altruistic emotions prompt acts of beneficence. For in such situations the morally appropriate or morally right act to perform is not independent of the emotion which prompts it. If the friend and the instructor are to do the right thing — if they are to respond appropriately to their situation — then they must have certain emotions and must act from them. The emotion is integral to what makes these actions or responses the right ones.

I have so far expressed the inadequacy of the motive/act schema by saying that the emotion is part of the action itself. Other philosophers have made a similar point by saying that in order to give a proper moral assessment of action it is necessary to know under what description the action is being considered. Thus in the case of Bob and Sue the action described as Bob-visiting-Sue-out-of-concern is different, from the point of view of beneficence, from Bob-visiting-Sue-out-of-duty. In the case of helping to fix the tire, Manero-stopping-to-help-as-part-of-his-business is different — from the point of view of the good to the man with the flat tire — from Manero-stopping-to-help-out-of-sympathy.

In this terminology, what I have argued is that the relevant act-description in these cases will involve the fact that the act is done from, or is expressive of, a certain emotional response to the recipient's situation. I think it is most useful, however, if we do not press the notion of act — even act-under-a-certain-description — to help articulate what is going on in these situations. The act together with, and expressive of, the emotion constitutes a kind of totality which is the bearer of the good to the recipient. I will refer to that totality as the agent's 'response' to the situation. So I will say that it is Bob's response to Sue, Jones's response to Clifford, etc. which bring about a certain good to the recipients of those acts. The response will then be what is morally appropriate to the situation, and the emotion will be morally appropriate as an inextricable part of that total response. Let us say that the response 'conveys' a good to the recipient.

I have said so far that the emotional element in the response which is morally appropriate is essential to the beneficence. But the concept of beneficence is really out of place here, when we are referring to a good conveyed by a response with an emotional aspect. Beneficence more properly refers to good brought about by overt, or what I will call 'behavioral,' acts, i.e., acts considered independently of emotions which they might express.

III

A related deficiency in the exclusive focus on motivation, and in the schema of motive and act, is their obscuring the fact that altruistic emotions can be of value to — can convey good to — their recipient even when they do not lead to any act towards that person. Let us consider an example.

Joan is an astronaut, circling the moon. Something goes wrong with her life support system. She signals control headquarters. After some attempts by them and by herself it becomes clear that nothing can be done. In a matter of about an hour Joan will be dead. Let us imagine two friends of Joan — Dave and Manny. They both learn of Joan's situation. They take different but entirely characteristic attitudes towards the situation.

Manny considers that he has an obligation to Joan to make certain that everything possible be done to try to save her. He is thorough, dedicated, and conscientious in exploring every possibility — double-checking on the indicators and on their interpretation with the scientists and technicians involved, etc. Finally he is convinced that nothing whatever can be done to help Joan. Though perhaps sorry about this, Manny feels that he has done what he could and so has lived up to his obligation to his friend. With no more scope for helpful action on his part, Manny turns his energies and attention to other matters.

Dave, on the other hand, is very distressed about the situation, both for Joan's sake and because he is losing a friend who is dear to him. His concern for Joan leads him to attempt to do everything possible to save Joan's life. Let us imagine that in doing so he engages in all the same actions as Manny does; and that eventually he comes to the same conclusion, that nothing can be done. But throughout the inquiry he is fervently hoping that the life support mechanism can be fixed. He is picturing Joan's situation, pained by her likely suffering, hoping that she is not suffering too horribly, hoping that she can find consoling thoughts, wanting her to know how much she has meant to him, and lamenting his own loss. When he reaches the conclusion that nothing can be done, he does so with anguish in his heart. He continues to be taken up with thoughts and feelings for Joan. Yet he does not engage in fruitless and hopeless activity. He recognizes the situation for what it is.

The contrast between Manny and Dave is not meant to be a contrast between two different ways of expressing an equal care and concern about a friend — an unemotional way and an emotional showy way. For one thing we need not picture Dave as particularly showy, as the 'heart on his sleeve' type; this is not the point. The contrast is rather between two different responses to a friend's plight, yet both involving the same beneficent (or attempted beneficent) acts. Manny acts from obligation, and his response encompasses only the scope of his possibly helpful actions; it is meant to exclude other motives and emotions. Dave acts from care and concern. He performs the same behavioral acts as does Manny (though from different motives) but in addition he has a range of emotional responses which Manny lacks, evidencing concern and care for Joan.

Let us assume that Joan, in her last hour, is able to think about some of her friends, and that because Manny's and Dave's reactions in the situation are so characteristic of them, Joan believes, even knows, that they are reacting in the way they in fact are. A good to Joan which both Dave and Manny's responses involve is the help which they attempt to get for her. But beyond that, Dave's response to the situation involves a certain good to Joan which Manny's does not, namely the good of the emotions of care and concern from a friend. This good, then, is a good not connected with beneficent action, but is involved simply in the emotional reaction itself.

This example rests on a certain absurdity, namely that Manny, imagined as a friend of Joan, would not respond to the situation with emotions connected with concern and care for Joan, but rather that he would act in her behalf only out of duty (the duty of a friend). Such a response would show that Manny was not truly a friend of Joan at all. But this absurdity really helps to confirm my point here; for what is integral to being a friend, and integral to what we want from our friends, is not only the help they can render, but their concern and care for us.

And so it is, or can be, a good to us that someone be concerned for our weal and woe even when the person cannot help us. Hence the moral value of altruistic emotions transcends their conative value. An exclusive emphasis on motivation as being the source of moral value will be blind to this aspect of the value of emotions and emotional responses. Let us for the moment refer to this as the 'intrinsic' value of altruistic emotions.

The intrinsic value is not something inherently separate from the motivational value, though it can exist when the latter does not. Rather, it is also expressed in the motivation to beneficent action. We see this in the case of Joan, Dave, and Manny. For though Dave's concern and care are expressed in some ways which do not issue in action, they are also expressed in the actions he takes to attempt to help Joan. We saw this also in the four examples considered earlier — in all of them the concern or sympathy express themselves in the acts which they motivate.

The help, or beneficence, is an expression of the concern. It is only if we regard the beneficent response purely as a behavioral act that we think that the good of the beneficence and the good of the concern are always separable. This is why I have preferred to refer to what the agent does in these situations as his 'response,' a term which conveys a sense of emotional/actional unity. Just as the response is the totality of the action-as-expressing-emotion, so the good conveyed by the response is the totality of help-as-expressive-of-concern-for-one's-good.

Thus it is not the value of the conative or motivational aspect of altruistic emotion which the intrinsic good of altruistic emotion transcends; rather it is the confining of the former value solely to the beneficence itself, that is, to the concrete help which is motivated by the altruistic emotion. If 'motive' is conceived on the motive/act schema, then the acts which it prompts will be only behavioral acts, i.e., acts describable independently of any emotion which they express. If the motive is conceived in this way, as it generally is when one speaks of the moral worth of motives, then the full good of another's care or concern transcends the good of altruistic emotions as motives. But if the motivational aspect of altruistic emotions is properly regarded as an expression of the concern for the other's good; and if, therefore, the responses reflecting (and involving) those altruistic emotions are properly regarded as an emotional/actional totality; then we can see the motivational aspect of altruistic emotions as itself involving and expressing the intrinsic good of altruistic emotions.

IV

Can more be said about what I have called the intrinsic value of altruistic emotions? How exactly is it related to the good of beneficence? Why is it a good to someone that someone else be concerned about his weal and woe?

Several aspects of this good can be distinguished. First and most obviously, the concern is good because it leads to acts which help the person in question. Second, there is, distinct from this, a good in the fact that concern signifies that its subject is prepared to act beneficently towards the object of the concern, if he is in a position to do so. In this sense concern involves a beneficent disposition which is a good to its recipient beyond the present act of beneficence motivated by concern.

But what is the good in this beneficent disposition? Two different aspects can be distinguished. First is the good of the future (anticipated) acts of beneficence which the beneficent disposition promises. This good is limited to the occasions in which this help is actually provided. A second aspect is security or confidence; this is the good of knowing that one can count on the person with the beneficent disposition to help one out when one needs it. Security is distinct from the first good in being independent of the actual help we will receive. It is the good of knowing that we can depend on the other. Even if one never actually needs the other's help, his concern (and beneficent disposition) give one a security and confidence with regard to him which is a good to one.[2]

These two aspects of the good of the disposition of beneficence involved in concern depend only on the disposition itself, and not on the concern which is expressed by it. Any motive whatsoever could lie behind the disposition and, so long as the disposition were there, the good in question would be provided. For example, if the person's beneficent disposition were grounded in a sense of duty, or, to take an unlikely but theoretically possible case, if the beneficent disposition were grounded in fear of the other person (so that one knew one could count on him because he would be too afraid *not* to come to one's aid),

one would still have the security with respect to this person's beneficence because one would know one could count on it. In this way, the
two aspects of the good of beneficent disposition, and especially the
second which does not depend on actual beneficence, are entirely
dependent on the motivational/dispositional aspect of altruistic
emotions, that related to the production of behavioral acts of
beneficence.

The case of the astronaut helps us to see that the three aspects of the
good of altruistic emotions (actual beneficence, future beneficence,
security) do not exhaust the full value of altruistic emotion. For with
regard to all three aspects of good there is no distinction between
Manny and Dave (with regard to Joan). They are both equally disposed
to provide future beneficence, though this in fact may not be a good to
Joan at all, since she has no future (or none which Dave and Manny can
affect). Similarly, the security and confidence of Dave and Manny's
beneficent disposition towards Joan would be the same. (On the other
hand, this is at best a very minor good to Joan given her situation, since
it too is primarily a forward-looking good.)

Since Dave's response to the situation involves a greater good to
Joan than does Manny's, yet their responses are equivalent regarding
the three goods so far mentioned, there must be some further good
which is involved in Dave's concern and caring reaction, and which is
part of the intrinsic good of altruistic emotion. The good must not be
directly dependent on the beneficent disposition in the way the goods
so far discussed have been (though this is not to say that sympathy,
concern, and compassion could involve this sort of good without being
the kinds of things which do involve a beneficent disposition).

It is a good to us simply that someone else care about our welfare,
be sympathetic to us, have compassion for us when we are suffering.[3]
Concern from another is an affirmation that one's well-being matters to
that person, and that therefore one has some kind of importance to
him.[4] In turn, as James Wallace points out, this sense of mattering to
another serves to affirm one's own sense of self-worth.[5]

But there is no reason to think that the non-beneficence good
involved here is of only one kind. On the contrary, once it is acknowledged that emotional responses can convey goods beyond (though also
through) the beneficent dispositions which they involve, a fertile area
of exploration of values is opened.

Engaging in such an exploration is beyond the scope of my argument
here; but some brief remarks may help. First, there seems a difference

between the kind of good which a stranger's concern is to us, in comparison to a friend's concern. One values the human responsiveness to one's plight which leads a perfect stranger to go out of his way to help one out, e.g., when one is stuck by the side of the road with a flat tire (see above, p. 144). But the value of one's friend's care or concern for one, e.g., in the case of Joan and Dave, or Kate and Sue, seems different. In friendship there is a full-scale identification by the other with one's own good.[6] (Perhaps this difference is simply a matter of degree.) There are other forms of human responsiveness and human relationship in which the altruistic emotions convey a good to their recipient; e.g., the case of the teacher listening sympathetically to the student. It might be as Casey's teacher, or, more broadly, as someone whom Casey respects and admires, that Brown's sympathy is a good to Casey. Alternatively, it could simply be the good of any sympathetic human being, where it just so happens that Brown is the only one Casey has been able to find. The different types of human relationships – stranger, professional, friendship, etc. – and the different aspects of these relationships, seem to involve different ways in which the concern, sympathy, and compassion of one person for another conveys a good to the other. What the ultimate significance of these distinctions is I would not venture to say, but they seem worth noting as a preliminary step to understanding the variety and complexity of the intrinsic good of altruistic emotion.

V

In any case, one can note a pervasive individualism of a particular sort in much moral philosophy – certainly in Kantianism – which makes it difficult to see the intrinsic good of altruistic emotions. This form of individualism fails to accord ultimate and irreducible value to human relationships or to relationally defined attitudes, sentiments, and emotions (e.g., concern for another person). Value is defined only in terms of the needs, interests, desires, and wants of individuals as individuals, i.e., as not essentially related to others. It is difficult to pin down this notion of individualism, since anything that is of value to someone must, it seems, be connected to that individual's wants, needs, and the like. But, for example, placing value on being part of a community of a certain sort would fall outside the scope of this form of individualism, for it involves desiring to stand in certain relationships with other people.[7]

The notion of individualism has no generally agreed upon meaning in moral theory. It is therefore worth mentioning four other plausible meanings, all of which are distinct from my usage above, which I will call 'individualism₁':

1 A radical individualism, seen in Sartre's existentialism and in somewhat moderated form in R.M. Hare's work, in which moral values themselves are ultimately the choice of individuals. This view denies the objectivity of moral values, which individualism₁ does not necessarily do (Kant being an obvious example of an objectivist individualist₁).

2 The individualism of an ethical egoist system in which the ulimate vindication of moral conduct must be in terms of the individual agent's interests, however broadly construed. Individualism₁ involves no such requirement, and is compatible with the view that morality must at least to a substantial extent require consideration of the interests of others, whether or not the agent's own interest is thereby served.

3 Individualism not so much as a doctrine but rather as an orientation in moral philosophy, involving concern primarily with the behavior, attitudes, emotions of the moral agent towards other individuals, rather than, say, towards distinct social groupings, such as classes, economic groups, nations, races. My own view is largely individualistic in this sense (and this is one of its limitations).

4 Individualism as a focus solely on the individual as the paradigm moral agent, rather than on, say, groups, classes, nations as agents (or on persons primarily as members of such collectivities). The present work stays largely within the confines of this sort of individualism, as does most moral theory.

VI

Let us now consider some objections to the view developed in this chapter, that the value of altruistic emotions goes beyond the production of beneficence. Within the Kantian view one can find two sorts of objections — one, that only acts of beneficence have value to their recipient; two, that while emotions or sentiments may have value beyond the motivating of beneficence, the kind of value they have is not moral value.

The Intrinsic Value of Altruistic Emotions

The first line of thought can be seen in two passages from Kant's less theoretical moral writings:

> If . . . there is no way in which I can be of help to the sufferer and I can do nothing to alter his situation, I might as well turn coldly away and say with the Stoics: 'It is no concern of mine; my wishes cannot help him; for I can only sympathize with him and hope fervently that he would be rid of his misfortune.' . . . Men believe that sympathy in another's misfortune and kindness of heart consist in wishes and feelings, but when a man is indifferent to the wretchedness of others just insofar as he can do nothing to change it, and troubles only where he can do some good and be of some help, such a man is practical; his heart is a kind heart, though he makes no show; he does not wear it on his sleeve, as do those who think that friendship consists in empty wishes, but his sympathy is practical because it is active.[8]

> It is not possible that our heart should swell from fondness for every man's interest and should swim in sadness at every stranger's need; else the virtuous man, incessantly dissolving like Heraclitus in compassionate tears, nevertheless with all this goodheartedness would become nothing but a tenderhearted idler.[9]

One target of Kant's thoughts here is a certain kind of Romanticism, glorifying in dramatic and intense feeling for its own sake.[10] It should be clear that such a conception has little to do with my view, in which the point is for one to *have* sympathy, compassion, or concern when appropriate or desirable, not whether one is showy or dramatic about the emotion. 'Emotion for the sake of emotion' is alien to my view. Rather it is because altruistic emotions are forms of (appropriate) responsiveness to others' weal and woe that they are claimed to be morally desirable.

Another concern of Kant, expressed particularly in the second passage, is that a morality which places emphasis on feeling and emotion will end up substituting emotions for action, declarations of sympathy for concrete help. As is implied in the second passage, one gets so taken up with feelings that, so to speak, one never gets around to doing anything for those needing help. It is as if there is a choice where to put one's energies — into emotions, or into action.

The morality of altruistic emotions which I have put forth here is not susceptible to these criticisms. If we confine ourselves to situations in which the agent is in a position to help the other, sympathy or concern, far from being an alternative to action, actually require a willingness to engage in it on behalf of the other. The willingness to act is a test of the authenticity of the feeling, or of the profession of feeling. Certainly one can say (and even sincerely say), 'I am very sympathetic, concerned, etc.,' yet not be, and this can be shown in the failure to help when one has the opportunity to do so. Altruistic emotions can, as we have seen, be shallow, weak, ungenuine; then they are less likely to lead to action, to lead us to do that which requires some effort on our part. Against such instances of emotion the Kantian criticism is well-taken; but not against the genuine item.

So, developing one's capacities for sympathy, concern, and compassion is not a diversion from developing beneficent dispositions. Rather it is a way of developing them. It is not a morality of emotion rather than action that I advocate, but a morality of a certain kind of response to others, which encompasses both emotion and action.

There is perhaps also a false picture of the emotions working in Kant's views here, especially in the second passage; and that is of emotions as using up one's energies, taking over one's consciousness so that one does not focus outwardly on the situation and action appropriate to it. Such a conception is appropriate, perhaps, to what Hume called 'turbulent passions.' But the altruistic emotions are not essentially turbulent passions, though they can be; being compassionate, or feeling compassion, does not necessitate getting 'all worked up' and emotional over the situation prompting the compassion. It is true that if one cares about a certain bad situation being alleviated one opens oneself up to emotional reactions – concern, compassion, frustration, even despair if nothing can be done – which those who are not touched by the situation are protected from; but such reactions are not necessarily turbulent, debilitating to thought or action. And even a turbulent emotion can in any case lead to appropriate action (e.g., Dave's behavior in the face of Joan's plight).

But these arguments so far hold only for situations in which we are in a position to help, and I am arguing for the appropriateness and value of altruistic emotions even when no help is possible. Of such a view, Kant could be taken as making the criticism that one's energies are better spent in searching out those situations where one can help, rather than worrying about responding appropriately to those in which one cannot. Certainly if one already knows that one can help A but not B, though both are in bad straits, then one ought to give one's attention

154

to A rather than B. But this is no concession to the Kantian view. First, it does not deny the appropriateness of the sympathy for B. More important, it is a recommendation which the man of sympathy himself takes or can take, i.e., a piece of advice within a morality of altruistic emotions. For the help to A can still stem from sympathy or concern. Nowhere in this view is there a recommendation that one ought to prefer or give special attention to those whose situations one is not able to assist. Second, we are not normally presented with the sort of choice which this objection poses. Responding with compassion to those whom one is in no position to help does not normally preclude or divert one from helping those whom one is in a position to help.

It must be acknowledged that one can get too worked up over situations over which one has no influence at all, and can neglect others where one would have opportunities for help. So, making the distinction between these two types of situations is crucial to putting into practice a morality of altruistic emotions. Doing so requires good judgment. The compassionate person does more good to the extent that he is better able to distinguish cases in which he is able to help from those he is not. Good judgment is in no way guaranteed by sympathy, compassion, or concern. But neither is it in any way antagonistic to them.

This need of good judgment does not distinguish the compassionate person from the Kantian agent. For Kant's recommendation in the first passage is that it is better to turn away without further thought or feeling from situations in which one cannot help. But to do this one must already have assessed the situation as one in which one cannot help; and this requires the same judgment as the compassionate person makes. Hence the fact that a morality of altruistic emotion is not self-sufficient but requires, for its maximal application, good judgment does not distinguish it from the attitude Kant recommends in the passage.

Now these remarks on the role of good judgment are oversimplified, as we saw in the previous chapter. For one's judging is affected by one's emotions, by one's compassion or lack of it. The compassionate person will tend to see more situations as involving opportunities and possibilities of his help than someone lacking compassion would do. Having compassion means one is not so ready to consign a situation to the category of one in which nothing can be done (or in which one can do nothing oneself). The coldly realistic attitude of appraisal which Kant recommends overlooks the indeterminacy with which situations present themselves to us. It might not be so obvious whether someone is suffering, nor so clear whether there is something one could do to help. Thus, Kant's recommendation about the appropriate attitude to take up towards the well-being of others takes for granted a categorization of situations which that attitude itself will affect. Encouraging compassion and concern, rather than always a focus on duties of beneficence, can, among other things, reveal greater needs for and possibilities of beneficence.

It must be acknowledged, on the other side, that altruistic emotions can have a negative effect here, one which Kant seems concerned to warn against. And that is a reluctance to acknowledge that someone's negative situation might be hopeless, or in any case that one is oneself unable to help. Because one is concerned one wants to be able to help; and so perhaps one will not readily enough face up to the fact that nothing can be done. The coldly practical, though dutifully beneficent man will not have this problem.

Objecting to the morality of altruistic emotions on the grounds that it encourages us to put our energies into our emotional responses rather than into genuinely helpful activities falsifies that view in another way. For no matter how much of our own life we actively fashion, thus choosing where to put our energies, inevitably we are faced with many situations in which others are suffering or in difficulty, and in which we are not in a position to help. This will be so no matter how much we choose actively to pursue projects built around beneficent ends and actuated by altruistic motives. And so it is not a matter of coldly turning away from the former situations to seek out the latter. The point is, if my argument is correct, that it is good to respond with sympathy and concern, even when one cannot help, and doing so can convey a good to the person involved even if he is not thereby helped.

In the first passage, Kant seems to deny *any* value to sorts of response to another's plight which do not involve being able actively to help. At least, he can be taken to be emphasizing the much greater value of concrete help compared to emotional response which does not issue in such help. There is an important truth here. Often the good of altruistic emotions outside a context in which they lead to help is utterly valueless next to the help which someone really needs. A person out of work may get a lot of genuine sympathy and even concern from friends, employment agencies, places he goes to look for work. (But he will also no doubt get quite a few insincere or ungenuine professions of sympathy. These give the real thing a bad name, and I think contribute to some of the reluctance to see the value in altruistic emotions.) This might all be very well, and better than if he did not get any sympathy or concern. But what he really needs is a job, and the person who can convey the most good to him is the one who offers him or puts him onto a job.

I have said nothing about the relative value of the non-beneficence or intrinsic aspect of altruistic emotions in comparison to the beneficence aspect. Certainly, though nothing at a very general level could be said about this, there is room for exploration. My point, against Kant, has been only that the intrinsic aspect does have value, and that this value is or can be present as well in acts motivated by altruistic emotions, thereby adding a dimension to the overall value which is not present in the beneficence alone.

So while the Kantian thought, 'What really counts is what you do, not what you feel,' might be a true and important thing to say in some contexts, in others it glosses over a significant aspect of the value which other people's emotional responses to our weal and woe have for us.

Finally, one can also see in both the passages from Kant a more defensive line of thought than those considered so far, namely a concern to defend the helpful but emotionally unresponsive person. This too is a point worth making, a welcome corrective to an overemphasis on emotion and feeling. But several things must be said in response. First of all there is a problem or ambiguity with the terms emotional and emotionally (responsive). While it is true that concern, compassion, sympathy need not be turbulent, it is still true that they are not merely rational or intellectual attitudes; they necessarily have an affective dimension and thus involve emotion, in the ways spelled out in prior chapters. So, while the compassionate person may in one sense not be emotional, his emotions, in another sense, are involved in a way which distinguishes him from the dutifully helpful or beneficent person. One might, so to speak, only see the kind person's concern in the actions he engages in; he makes no declaration of it. ('His heart is a kind heart though he makes no show.') Yet if it is genuine concern or compassion, he must be having within himself some of the kinds of emotional responses discussed in chapter VI and elsewhere, and portrayed in the example of Dave and Joan.

This is not to denigrate the emotionally distant but dutifully helpful person. But it is to say that his way of being helpful fails to convey certain kinds of goods to the recipients of his beneficence which are conveyed by concern or sympathy-based helpfulness.

Let us next consider a more theoretical Kantian objection, namely that even if altruistic emotions and emotional responses are acknowledged to have value, it is not *moral* value. The objection can be spelled out in this way:

'You have argued that a human response conveys a certain good to its recipient, and you have argued that this good is to be conceived of as a whole, with parts which cannot be separated in reality. But you have admitted the possibility of acts ("behavioral acts") in which the emotional or motivational aspect of the good is non-existent. In these cases it is simply the "act" behaviorally described which conveys a good to the recipient.

'But it is only such behavioral acts which are of moral significance. For only they can be regarded as something which we ought to do, or are obliged to do. We can be obliged only to perform a certain act, and not to have a certain feeling or emotion. Hence it is only behavioral acts, and not responses as a whole, which can be made the object of obligation. And so it is only that aspect of the good to the recipient which can be brought about by an act independent of any emotion which is of moral importance. It is the conveying of this good which can be a "duty of beneficence." It cannot be a duty to feel anything, but only to perform certain acts.

'Therefore what has distinctively moral value can only be a motive to an act behaviorally described, that is, a motive which does not affect the nature of the act itself. The motive/act schema may be inadequate to express the nature of the relationship between emotion and action in general; but it is the appropriate model for discussing the specifically moral aspect of that relationship. So even if emotions do convey goods, and even if, when they do, those goods are not separable from the good of the response as a whole, nevertheless that aspect of the good conveyed by such responses which goes beyond what is conveyed by the behavioral act component of the response is without moral significance. Though it may be a genuine human value, the good involved is not a moral good.'

The answer to this line of thinking can be seen in retracing our steps. It emerged in the argument of chapter II that certain ways of responding or behaving in the situations described (teacher and student, friend in hospital) were the morally right or morally appropriate ones. But when, in the present chapter, we explored wherein this moral appropriateness lay, it seemed that it was appropriate not only that the agents perform some overt act but that they do so from a certain motive; or, rather, that their act express a certain emotion which it was appropriate for them to have; for otherwise it would fail to bring about the full good to the recipient which was involved in its being an act of beneficence.

Thus if the Kantian agrees that the act as originally conceived is morally appropriate or morally right, he must now agree that it is morally appropriate also that the agent's act express certain emotions.

The Kantian could, in line with this counter-argument, retreat from his earlier admission (in chapter II) and say that he was wrong to consider the acts in question (Brown listening sympathetically to Casey; Bob visiting Sue) morally appropriate, and say that all that could be morally appropriate would be a behavioral act — Brown and Bob exhibiting certain behaviors. But at this point such a move would seem entirely arbitrary. Why should the response of Brown and Bob get chopped up into artificial parts which were not originally perceived? Why (assuming this were possible) should we draw the line at the good which can be brought about by behavioral acts (i.e., as independent of emotion)? That is, why should we count the good which falls on one side of this line as morally relevant, and that which falls on the other as morally irrelevant?

In any case, it will not work to divide the good produced by the response in this way, since the response will not be the appropriate one unless it does involve the recipient regarding the act as done from a certain emotion.

VIII

There is, I think, one part of the Kantian view here which is correct — namely that the acts of beneficence which we are discussing cannot be objects of duty or obligation. For it is true that one cannot have a duty or obligation to have an emotion, or to act from an emotion. If the Kantian objector were to confine himself to this point, he would be on solid ground. But he goes much further when he says that that which cannot be made an object of obligation is therefore without moral relevance, though it may have some other kind of human relevance. The right view is that what has moral significance goes far beyond what can be made an object of duty or obligation. The good which is brought about by altruistic emotion is morally desirable, and sometimes even morally appropriate, but it is not therefore morally obligatory. It is morally good that we should respond to certain situations with care, concern, compassion, sympathy; but it is not and could not be morally obligatory to do so. It was morally good for Brown to listen sympathetically to Casey, and would have been for Jones to do so to Clifford; it would have been good for Bob to be concerned enough to visit Sue, and perhaps it was even bad that he was not. But he was not morally *obliged* to have such concern, nor were Brown and Jones morally obliged to listen sympathetically to Casey.

It is a characteristic feature of Kantian views to tend to focus moral inquiry on what is obligatory and dutiful. One important upshot of my argument has been that the area of the morally desirable and undesirable, appropriate and inappropriate, decent and indecent, admirable, estimable, and deficient is of much wider scope than the Kantian view allows for; and that moral philosophy ought to concern itself with this much wider territory, and must do so if the moral value of altruistic emotions is to be given adequate expression. This point began to emerge in chapter IV, when I argued that the moral merit of friendship could not be appreciated within a moral framework in which the notion of the *morally obligatory* retained a central place; and in chapter V when I argued that acts stemming from altruistic emotion are not generally, and are not regarded by the agent to be, morally binding on him.

That moral theory needs to make room for actions which lie outside the territory of the obligatory, Anglo-American moral philosophy has begun to recognize in the last two decades. Perhaps the most famous statement of this view is in J.O. Urmson's 'Saints and Heroes,' in which he argues that there is a large range of actions whose moral status is insufficiently expressible within the traditional classification of actions into morally impermissible/morally neutral/morally obligatory. We need also, Urmson argues, to allow 'for a range of actions which are of moral value and which an agent may feel called upon to perform, but which cannot be demanded and whose omission cannot be called wrongdoing.'[11]

While entirely agreeing with this point, my own argument is making an additional one: that moral philosophy needs to be concerned with more than overt actions. It must concern itself with our whole human response to situations and to other persons' weal and woe, which includes an emotional dimension. Thus it is not only, as Urmson says, that some morally good actions go beyond the realm of the morally obligatory. It is also that morally good responses which go beyond the realm of the morally obligatory also go beyond the realm of action itself.

IX

This brings us to the notion of 'supererogation.' This notion is often brought in within essentially Kantian-like moral theories to give room for actions which are not morally obligatory but which nevertheless have moral value. The most striking examples of these in the literature are the 'saintly' and 'heroic' acts discussed by Urmson. However, the notion is not meant to be limited to actions of an extraordinary degree of moral merit, but is meant also to cover other acts which, in being more than what duty or obligation requires, involve some degree of moral merit.[12]

The essential feature of the notion of supererogation in the accounts given of it seems to be that of action which *goes beyond duty*. If the notion is understood in this way, then, I will argue, it will not help us in understanding the moral significance of altruistic emotions and the realm of moral experience in which they operate.

There seem to be two ways in which an act can go beyond duty: (1) by involving a greater risk, cost, or sacrifice than is involved in duty; (2) by bringing about more good than is required by duty. But action from altruistic emotion does not characteristically or necessarily involve either of these features.

Action prompted by altruistic emotion need not involve greater sacrifice, cost, or risk than that involved in ordinary duties. Many acts prompted by sympathy, compassion, or concern involve only inconvenience to us, and no real risk, cost, or sacrifice at all. We have seen that altruistic emotions can prompt us to acts of some degree of sacrifice, and even extraordinary sacrifice. But one could not say in general that the degree of sacrifice is more than is involved in doing one's duty or obligation.

It must be pointed out that actions from duty do not themselves involve a uniform amount of risk, cost, or sacrifice, any more than do actions from altruistic emotion. As Joel Feinberg points out, some acts of duty require quite exceptional sacrifice, while others are routine and even pleasant.[13] But this fact does not help the category of super-erogatory to apply to action from altruistic emotion. For if one makes supererogatory refer to dutiful actions which require extraordinary sacrifice, then 'amount of sacrifice,' rather than going beyond duty in the sense of 'doing more than duty requires,' will become the defining feature of supererogation. In that case, actions from altruistic emotion which do not involve cost or sacrifice will not be supererogatory.

Nor does action from altruistic emotion characteristically involve going beyond duty in the second sense — bringing about more good than is brought about by acts of duty. Quite obviously, some acts of duty bring about a very substantial good to the recipient, while many acts from altruistic emotion involve fairly minor goods. More important, as I have argued in this chapter, the good brought about by acts motivated by altruistic emotion are often not directly comparable to those brought about by acts not so motivated. Certainly we cannot say in general that acts motivated by altruistic emotion involve bringing about more good than those motivated by duty. Hence action from altruistic emotion would not fall, as a whole, within the purview of supererogation on this understanding of it.

Though not generally spelled out in accounts of supererogation, there is a further implication of the notion of action going beyond duty, namely that the motive to a supererogatory act be something like the same motivation prompting normal dutiful acts, i.e., a sense of duty. Thus Urmson sees the saintly or heroic man as prompted by considerations which to him have the force of a duty, even though he cannot strictly regard his act as a duty, since he does not think that others would have a duty to perform it. G.R. Grice, elaborating this notion, sees supererogatory acts (which he refers to as 'ultra obligations') as ones which the agent regards as a duty for persons with the *character* which he has.

But, as argued in chapter V and elsewhere, the type of motivation involved in altruistic emotion is characteristically of a quite different sort than that involved in performing one's duty. A person acting from altruistic emotion need not and does not typically regard himself as compelled in any way (morally) to perform the act, even, to take Grice's suggestion, in a purely personal way which does not apply to others. In this sense too, the model of supererogation is inappropriate to action prompted by altruistic emotion.

Thus the notion of supererogation as 'going beyond duty' is not properly applicable to action from altruistic emotions. What action from altruistic emotion shares with supererogatory action is that it has moral value and that it is not morally obligatory. But there the similarity ends.

The important point here is that the notion of supererogation is meant to work within a framework in which obligation and duty remain the central notions. Supererogation, though itself defined as being other than duty and obligation, is meant as a supplement to a general framework dominated by those notions, rather than as an alternative to it. For example, it presupposes the motive/act schema.

Acting out of concern for a friend, or compassion for a stranger in need, are not properly conceived of as going beyond the requirements of duty. Nor are they acts which have more moral worth than acts of duty. They are best regarded as in an entirely different realm of moral experience, to which notions of duty and supererogation do not properly apply.[14] If one were to redefine supererogation so that it encompasses all morally desirable action and response not covered by the concepts of duty and obligation, then the moral value of altruistic emotions would count as supererogatory. But then one would have undermined any usefulness of the concept itself, by allowing it to refer to a heterogeneous group of actions and realms of moral experience.

X

The Kantian objections to regarding as morally significant the altruistic emotions and the full good conveyed by them as part of human responses will not hold. Now something must be said about the relationship between the good conveyed to the recipient and the moral good of altruistic emotion.

Basically, what makes the altruistic emotion morally good is that its object is the weal of another person. Why it is of moral value to have sympathy, compassion, or concern for someone is that one is thereby concerned for the good — the weal and woe — of another person. This is simply an extension of the view developed in chapter V, that action prompted by altruistic emotion has moral value in virtue of being motivated by regard for the weal and woe of particular other persons. That chapter was concerned with only the conative or motivational aspect of altruistic emotions. The present view, in contrast, attempts to articulate the moral value of altruistic emotions as a whole, i.e., why it is morally good to have altruistic emotions. In being grounded in concern for another's weal, the moral value of altruistic emotions goes beyond the moral value of their conative aspect. This allows us to see why an altruistic emotion can be morally good even though it does not lead to action. Dave's feeling concern for Joan is morally good because its object is Joan's weal and woe. Brown's response to Casey is good because it is Casey's difficulties and pain with his family which are the ground of Brown's concern.

That it is morally good to be concerned with the good of others is why, as we ordinarily think, it is good to be sympathetic, compassionate, concerned for others. These are morally good qualities of character whose moral value goes beyond their involving dispositions to perform beneficent acts.

We have been led to this broader view of the moral value of altruistic emotions through focusing on the good of a concerned or sympathetic response to a recipient.

Thus I have taken more seriously than does the Kantian view the good to the recipient as a touchstone of the moral significance of an emotional response, or human response, by an agent.[15] But not every good to a recipient confers moral value on the response of an agent which conveys that good. Not every preference or desire of a potential recipient of a response (or an attitude, action, emotion) gives moral significance to a response which satisfies this desire or preference. Suppose, for example, that what Sue wants from Bob is that Bob be infatuated with her. This is the attitude on her part which she would like his visiting her in the hospital to express. This desire of hers would not make it morally good for Bob to be infatuated with her. For one thing, not every desire is for a genuine good. Still, it often is a genuine good to person A that certain other persons like him; yet this does not make it morally good for these others to like (or, more generally, to have personal feelings towards) him.[16]

The reason that personal feelings, and human responses such as finding someone fascinating, are not moral emotions or attitudes is that they are not directed at or grounded in the weal and woe of others. What we humanly want from others in the way of emotional response towards us is a much wider territory than is covered by emotions which are morally significant.[17]

XI

What is the implication of the argument here for the question which might naturally be asked: 'Are the altruistic emotions superior to duty (as motives)?' As it stands, the question has no general answer, and it should not be thought to need one. Generally, the sense of duty and the altruistic emotions operate in different, if sometimes overlapping, areas of our lives, and comparison between them has no clear meaning. Similarly, there is no general answer to the question, 'Is courage better than honesty?'[18]

However, the question can be broken down into several others about which some things can be said. To do this it is useful to examine the views of two philosophers whom we have discussed before — W.D. Ross in *The Right and the Good*, and Philip Mercer in *Sympathy and Ethics* — who argue for the moral value of action from altruistic emotion, and who compare that value to the value of acting from duty.

Ross, while regarding sympathy as a morally good motive, sees it as inferior to the sense of duty.[19] He first argues that if we are drawn to do one act by our sense of duty and another by love, we should do what is our duty, since we thereby acknowledge it to be the right action: so that when duty conflicts with other motives it should take precedence. This shows, according to Ross, that in such a situation we accord sense of duty a superiority to other motives, including those of altruistic feeling and personal feeling. (Ross does not clearly distinguish these two types of motive.) This argument is acceptable, provided we assume that the act to which we are drawn by love is not also in fact a (prima facie) duty, and one of greater weight than the act to which we are drawn by duty. For it may be morally superior to perform from altruistic emotion an action which in fact is, and is believed to be, a more stringent duty than to perform a less stringent duty towards which one is drawn by sense of duty.

Ross next takes up the situation in which we are drawn to the same act by the two motives, and asks which is to be preferred. Ross says that if we give precedence to the sense of duty when they conflict then we must also do so when they do not.

But the situation of conflict does not transfer like this to the situation of the two motives prompting the same act. For we have seen that in general it is not the same act (or response) which is prompted by altruistic emotion and by sense of duty, in that the good conveyed to the recipient of the response is likely to differ in the two cases. In that sense, the act prompted by the sense of duty will convey less good than the act prompted by altruistic feeling, and may well not be appropriate to the situation. It would then seem perverse to argue that the dutiful act is still morally better, if it fails to convey the appropriate good to its recipient, which can only be conveyed by an action which expresses a certain emotion. Ross's working only within the motive/act schema does not allow him to see how the motive could be relevant to the moral appropriateness of the act.[20]

In any case, the general superiority of duty to sympathy — i.e., the moral superiority of a person disposed to act from one motive over one who acts from the other — could not be established by Ross's argument even if it were valid. For, as we saw in the previous chapter, it is characteristic of the sympathetic or compassionate person to perceive more situations as warranting beneficent action than does the merely dutiful person.

The argument of the present chapter in fact does carry the implication that often it is better — at least in one important respect — for sympathy to prompt a certain behavioral act than for the same behavioral act to be prompted by duty; for the total response in the first case will bring about more good than in the second case. And, therefore, it will be better to be a person who acts from sympathy in such cases than one who acts from duty. But again, this is not to say that the sympathetic person is in some general way superior to the dutiful person.

Thus, while Ross's account is an advance over the Kantian in according moral value to altruistic emotions, it suffers the defects of conceiving the relation between altruistic emotions and the acts in which they express themselves solely on the motive/act schema. It therefore fails to articulate the full moral significance of altruistic emotions when they do motivate action, including the perceptual/cognitive contribution of altruistic emotion to this significance.

Philip Mercer's view is much more complex than Ross's, and forms a major focus of his book, especially of chapters 6 and 7. I mention Mercer's account because it is addressed to countering the Kantian view and to explaining the moral significance of sympathy; and Mercer gives many of the same arguments that I do for the moral value of sympathy as a motive. Yet his account suffers from the weakness of confining itself to the motivational and cognitive aspects of sympathy when discussing its moral worth.[21]

Mercer argues that any act performed from the duty of beneficence ('conscientiousness') could also be performed from sympathy, so that sympathy could be substituted for conscientiousness as a motive.[22] He quotes with approval Nowell-Smith's statement:

Hence the conscientious man will do exactly the same thing a man with all the natural virtues will do. He does not do them for the same reason; and he is not brave or honest or kindly, since he acts for the sake of doing his duty, not for the sake of doing the brave, honest or kindly thing. But he will do what the brave, honest, and kind man does.[23]

But the kind man does not do the same things the conscientious man does. These two virtues work in different areas of our lives. Kindness does not lead us to work hard to fulfil our responsibilities, to adhere strictly to duty and principles, to do the right thing in the face of contrary inclination. Similarly, conscientiousness or duty does not lead us to notice the distress of a little boy wandering around lost, and to help him find his father or mother; or to volunteer to pick up the brother of a friend at the airport because the friend is not feeling up to it; and the like.

Also, even if we confine ourselves to situations in which the behavioral acts prompted by kindness and conscientiousness are the same, the total responses of the two agents will differ, as will the good conveyed by them. Actions (responses) expressive of sympathy convey goods which acts motivated by duty do not. Thus neither sympathy nor duty can properly be seen as a substitute for the other. Mercer thus fails to consider a crucial area in which he could draw support for his view that the sympathy is superior to duty.[24]

A third point against the Mercer/Nowell-Smith position is that the man of sympathy will tend to see the weal and woe of others as at stake more than will the conscientious man lacking sympathy, and so will be more likely to perform beneficent acts.

Mercer notes what he takes to be 'the interesting fact that most people would prefer to receive the help of someone who helped them because he sympathized with them rather than the help of someone who helped them because he thought it was his duty to do so.'[25] But Mercer fails to appreciate the significance of this point, because he sees sympathy only as a motive understood on the motive/act schema, and hence sees its moral value solely in its motivational dimension. The explanation of the 'interesting fact' is that acting out of duty and acting out of sympathy involve two different ways of regarding — different attitudes towards — the recipient of the beneficence. The argument spelling out this difference was given in chapter VI, pp. 118-21. Briefly, in acting from sympathy the recipient is seen as someone whose good matters to one, for whom one has some kind of concern: if one's attempted help is unsuccessful one is disappointed for the person; if it is successful one is pleased for him. When acting out of duty one regards the interests of the recipient as having some moral claim on one's action. But one does not thereby necessarily care about the person's good; it does not necessarily matter to one.

It is thus natural (though not inevitable) that in general one prefers to be helped from sympathy than from duty; for the former implies a fuller human response than the latter. The sympathetic response conveys a greater good than does acting from duty.

Mercer may appreciate some of this when he says, 'perhaps ... sympathy possesses a certain warmth that is lacking in conscientiousness.'[26] But this formulation still seems to make the difference between sympathy and duty a kind of adornment of the action, rather than a matter of real substance regarding the action — a difference in an attractive quality or tone rather than a real difference in the way one is regarded or related to by the other.

VIII

WILL, EMOTION, AND THE SELF

In chapter II I argued that to say that someone's altruistic emotions were capricious was to give a moral criticism of that person, to imply that his emotional response was insufficient or inadequate. I thereby argued that a person's characteristic or particular emotional reactions (or lacks thereof) reflect on him morally. In chapter VII I tried to bring out some of what constitutes the moral significance of our altruistic emotions, showing that they convey goods of human concern. I have therefore presumed that our altruistic emotions reflect on us morally. For this is necessary if one is to say that altruistic emotions have moral value.

The claim that our emotions and feelings can reflect on us morally is contrary to one of the deepest strains of thought within the Kantian view, according to which only our capacity for choice – our will – can reflect on us morally; feelings and emotions, in respect of which we are entirely passive, cannot reflect on a person morally. This view bears spelling out in detail, so that it can be met head on.

Moral assessment can be only of that in us which is directly producible by means of our will, or which is in the direct province of the will. Only that which we choose, or which we decide to bring about, can be a source of moral criticism, accountability, and assessment. That for which we can be morally blamed and praised must be something for which it is we who are fully responsible, who are its authors and initiators; it cannot be produced by something outside of ourselves. But that for which we are responsible is that which it is entirely within our power to produce, and this can only be actions; it cannot be feelings or emotions. For actions are what we do; emotions and feelings are something which we experience and which thus happens to us. We cannot help what we feel but only what we do.

Thus what is morally appropriate to do in a given situation must be that which is entirely within our power to produce or bring about in that situation. This is one meaning of the formulation, 'Ought implies can,' first brought out clearly in Kant, but accepted by many philosophers.

> Man must, therefore, judge that he is able to stand up to [his inclinations] and subdue them by reason — not at some time in the future but at once (the moment he thinks of duty): he must judge that he can do what the law commands unconditionally that he ought to do.[1]

Our feelings and emotions lie outside the scope of our will. It is not in our power directly to produce them within ourselves. Rather, we are entirely passive in respect to them. They are something we feel rather than something we do, and in that sense something which happens to us rather than something we bring about. We do not choose our feelings or decide to have them. We are not their initiators or authors. Thus our feelings and emotions cannot reflect on us morally.

The only relevance of our feelings to morality lies in whether we choose to act from them or not. If we choose to act from a feeling which is contrary to morality, we have acted wrongly and can be held accountable for this. But then it is not the feeling itself which is the source of this moral fault, but rather the fact that we chose to act from it. Thus the real locus of our moral responsibility is our will, our capacity for choice. The having of the feelings is a matter of moral indifference.[2]

This exclusion of feelings as reflecting on us morally is connected with the notions of *agency* and *activity*. It is because feelings are not products of our agency that they are excluded; for it is as agents that we are morally assessed. Morality has to do solely with that in virtue of which we are active (our will, our choices, our actions), rather than that in terms of which we are passive (our feelings, inclinations, emotions).

This viewpoint is intimately bound up with the Kantian view's grounding of morality in the notion of obligation. Morality takes the form of obligations, moral requirements that necessitate that we act in certain ways. Only that which we can bring about through the medium of our will is something which we can be obliged to do. And we cannot be obliged to have certain feelings; as Sidgwick says, 'it cannot be a strict duty to feel an emotion, so far as it is not directly within the power of the will to produce it at any given time.'[3] Thus feelings lie outside the scope of moral obligation. It cannot be morally required to have them, nor morally blameworthy to fail to.

This line of thought, regarding the role of emotions and feelings in the moral assessment of a person, emphasizes the notion of will as central, as the locus of moral assessment and of the self. But naturally accompanying this line of thought within the Kantian view are the notions of reason and deliberative judgment. (For Kant the will is (practical) reason.) Our reason is seen as fully an expression of ourselves. The idea that we are identified with our capacity for reason and judgment seems present in many philosophers in some form. R. Solomon articulates this tradition of thought when he says, 'Reason is that part of the soul that is most our own, the only part of the soul that is completely under our control.'[4] The exclusion of feeling from morality is connected with the dichotomy between reason and feeling, and the grounding of morality in reason. Thus, in acting according to reason we are most fully autonomous and in control of ourselves, according to this picture.

These arguments and the overall conception of the relations of will, reason, morality, and the self involved in them are powerful ones, and must be met if we are to be assured that it is possible for a person's emotions and feelings to reflect on him morally, if we are to be able to understand the ways we assess a person morally in light of his emotions, and if we are to see how it is possible for us to change in the direction of coming to have morally good and desirable emotions.

II

The Kantian view contains a certain conception of the moral self, i.e., of that in persons which is capable of being morally assessed, criticized, or, more generally, morally attributed. The conception is that the moral self includes only what is the outcome of the will, choice, decision, deliberative reason — only that of which we are fully the authors or initiators (such as our actions).

Against this Kantian view I will argue that the moral self cannot plausibly be conceived to exclude phenomena with regard to which we are passive, of which we are not the initiators or authors. Hence it is no argument against emotions and feelings being objects of moral assessment that we are passive with respect to them, that they are not within the province of the will. It is therefore also mistaken to identify the moral self with the will, or with deliberative reason, decision, and choice. The moral self must include emotions and feelings. They (in general) reflect on us morally as much as do our actual choices, actions, and rational judgments.

My argument will take the form of presenting some phenomena which we would ordinarily regard as reflecting morally on agents — namely attitudes and values regarding other persons. I will then argue that the Kantian view is unable to accommodate these phenomena within its own conception of the moral self, for they involve elements of passivity, and yet it has no independent argument against our ordinary notion that they are part of the moral self.

I will give several instances of the values and attitudes in question. (1) An attitude towards black persons which involves regarding them as inferior to white persons, and as less fully deserving of human consideration. (2) Values such as those attributable to Clyde Griffiths in Dreiser's *An American Tragedy* — placing supreme value on living in a manner expressive of having great wealth, on attaining social status or position; judging and reacting to people according to how well they exemplify a style regarded by one as appropriate to a person of wealth and position. (3) An orientation towards one's students which involves being generally unsympathetic to their professed problems and concerns, as they bear on their academic work. (4) Regarding others primarily as means to one's own pleasure, advancement, interest. Seeing others primarily in light of their usefulness to oneself. (5) Regarding blacks and whites as moral and social equals.

We would ordinarily regard these attitudes, orientations, values, ways of regarding, and the connected patterns of behavior, desires, typical judgments made, and setting of priorities in one's conduct as relevant to a moral assessment of a person.

I will call one's 'being-towards-others' those values, attitudes, orientations, and forms of regard towards other persons which bear on their weal and woe. This being-towards-others is not necessarily to be thought of as a kind of unity — for example, a person could have a sympathetic orientation towards Italians but a contemptuous attitude towards uneducated persons, and an unsympathetic attitude towards Slavs.

Nevertheless, it is also not merely a series of discrete attitudes and values. There will typically be certain interconnections.

Thus, we ordinarily think that our being-towards-others is part (though by no means the whole) of our moral self; for it comprises attitudes, values, and orientations towards others which are subject to criticism and assessment. Our being-towards-others reflects on us morally.

Moreover, our other-directed values and attitudes, and our being-towards-others generally, cannot be accommodated to a Kantian model of that which is, or which is solely a product of, will, decision, and reason. For, I will argue, (1) these phenomena — i.e., what it is to have a certain attitude or to hold a certain value — cannot be seen as the outcome of decision and choice, something which we will; (2) other-directed values and attitudes cannot be understood purely cognitively, as the outcome of a process of conscious rational thought, to which we give our assent; (3) they cannot be understood purely behaviourally, as a disposition to initiate certain actions.

III

Though analytically separable, the first two views can be considered together. According to them a person's values and attitudes can be portrayed in this way: the person chooses the values, or decides to adopt them. He weighs the various considerations for and against, and plumps for those values and attitudes most worthy of assent. The values and attitudes are then the result of conscious and deliberate thought and reason.

Let us first clear a possible irrelevancy out of the way. We certainly do not *in fact* come to hold most of our values and attitudes in this way. That is, we do not ordinarily reach them by a purely rational process, the outcome of which is a decision on our part to adopt these values. Rather, most of our values and attitudes are imparted by and absorbed from our upbringing, peers, surroundings, etc. We are often not aware of many of our values, and are not aware of their sources. Even the ratiocination we do engage in with regard to our values accounts only partially for the way we come to hold those values and for the actual ones we hold.

But this is not strictly relevant to the argument (though neither is it irrelevant). For the Kantian view requires not that we actually arrive at our values and attitudes in the way portrayed, but that we regard our values and attitudes as grounded in such processes of choice and rational deliberation and assent, and thus as potentially and ideally the outcome of such processes.[5]

But our values, attitudes, and being-towards-others cannot be so regarded. For even if it is possible, through rational processes alone, to regard a value or attitude as worthy of being held, and even if it is possible to choose or decide to assent to the value, it is not possible to come to hold or have the value or attitude in this way. It is thus not correct to see the values and attitudes as grounded in decision, choice, and reason. The Kantian view takes a picture applicable to the assessment of the validity or warrantability of values and attitudes, and uses it to portray what it is for someone to possess the value or attitude.

Let us examine the instance of racial attitudes.[6] Let us envisage someone who through rational deliberation comes to the view that blacks and whites are, and should be regarded and treated as, moral and social equals. He thinks it through, agrees that this moral viewpoint is worthy of assent, and gives his assent to it.

Is this sufficient to say that the man holds the value that blacks and whites are moral equals (have equal moral status)? It seems that it is not. Let us suppose, for example, that the man makes disparaging remarks about blacks. He supports policies which prevent blacks from achieving social equality. He is upset when blacks move into his neighborhood, and when his children associate with blacks in school. He feels uncomfortable with blacks.

It seems that these reactions, his behavior, emotional responses, and other attitudes would lead us to question whether the man genuinely regarded blacks and whites as equals, i.e., whether he truly held that value or attitude regarding blacks, even though he professed to do so and even though he arrived through a process of rational deliberation at the view that blacks and whites are moral equals.

An adherent of the Kantian view might respond to this by saying that if the man has the reactions attributed to him, then we have to question whether he really did actually go through a process of rational deliberation regarding these values and views and whether he did genuinely and sincerely assent to them. It may have all been a sham.

Well, it *may* have been a sham; we are not equating professing values with genuinely assenting to them. But the fact that the man subsequently behaves and reacts in the way described does not show that this process of apparent rational deliberation and assent was a sham.

All it shows is that it failed to bring it about that he actually held the values in question. But this is precisely my point. To say that someone holds or has a certain value or attitude, it is insufficient that he have assented to it on the basis of a conscious and rational deliberative process.

First of all, the man may not have even sincerely assented to the view or attitude, even though the view seemed to him to have reason on its side after the deliberative process. A person might deliberate as sincerely as possible, trying to weigh all the various considerations which he can think of, arrive at a result and yet still fail to be convinced by this result. If he fails to be convinced then he cannot sincerely give his assent, though he can say that the view seems to be right, or that it seems to have the weight of reason in favor of it. (He can also think that he is convinced, though he really is not.)

Thus rational deliberation is insufficient for conviction and therefore for rational assent. But, more important, rational assent itself is insufficient for it to be the case that the person has or holds, or comes to hold, the view (though it can be the beginning of his doing so). There must, in addition, be a context of certain reactions, feelings, other attitudes, desires, and behavior for the person actually to hold the view or have the value or attitude.

An objection could be made, on the other side, that the reactions I have described -- being upset when blacks move into the neighborhood, etc. − do not show that the man does not genuinely hold the view that blacks and whites are moral equals. These reactions are undoubtedly out of line with that view; but perhaps this just means that the man reacts in ways which are out of line with the views that he holds, not that he fails to hold the view at all. This would be like weakness of will (in which a person fails to do what he believes to be right), except that it is not only actions but emotional reactions and feelings which are out of line with the moral principle or value (alleged to be) held by the agent.

Evidently this does describe what is going on in some situations. It is possible to imagine a person with formerly racist attitudes, who now genuinely believes blacks and whites to be moral equals yet still has certain reactions which are contrary to those views. He could, for example, find himself assuming that a black colleague was unintelligent, when he really had no grounds for thinking this. Or he could have certain feelings of unease with blacks.

But if these are not to count conclusively against his holding the view that blacks and whites are equal, he cannot have such reactions too frequently. There is evidently a matter of degree here. A person can have *some* reactions which are out of line with a principle to which he has sincerely assented, without it necessarily being the case that he fails to hold the principle. But if the reactions are too extensive and frequent, than he will not be said to hold the principle even if he sincerely assented to it.

A further relevant consideration is the attitude the agent takes towards the out-of-line reactions. If he himself sees them as out of line, regrets them, and tries to change and avoid them in the future, this counts in favor of his holding the principle. (He may fail to notice that he is having these reactions; but if they are pointed out to him he must regard them as incompatible with his views and try to correct them. However, if he has too many such reactions without noticing that he does so, both the reactions and the failing to notice them will count against his holding the view.)

What this shows is that the fact that a sincerely assented-to principle can genuinely be held even though the agent has some reactions out of line with it does not confirm the Kantian view that sincerely assenting to it is sufficient for holding it. Emotional reactions play an essential role.

In our actual example (p. 174), in any case, it just does not seem plausible to say merely that the man's reactions are contrary to the professed views. If the man supports policies denying blacks equality, if he is upset that his children associate with blacks, if he makes disparaging remarks about blacks, if he is really upset when his children associate with blacks in school, etc., then this shows that he simply does not regard blacks and whites as equals (even if he believes that he does).

Suppose the man thinks, not that these reactions are contrary to his views and values regarding the equality of blacks, but that they are compatible with them. That is, he says that he regards blacks as equals, but he just does not want his children to play with them or for them to move into his neighborhood. And he says that though he regards them as having equal moral status, still it is true that they generally have certain undesirable qualities. And suppose he believes that the policies he supports are not incompatible with the belief in equality.

Perhaps without somewhat more detail in the example we cannot be absolutely certain what to say. Certainly there is disagreement as to what 'equality' means, and generally there can be disagreement as to what a certain moral view commits one to. But we can still be pretty sure that the man's view here serves only to confirm that he does not believe blacks and whites to be equal, rather than to support his truly holding that belief in the face of seeming counter-evidence to his holding it. (Suppose, for example, that the policy which the man opposes were one which encouraged and helped blacks to vote, or, more extremely, allowed them to vote at all.)

Thus for a certain attitude, value, or orientation to be truly held by a person, or to be a genuine part of himself, it is not sufficient that he give his rational assent to it, that he reach it by some outcome of rational deliberation, that he will himself to have it (or try to convince himself that it is justified, etc.). There must in addition be certain attendant emotional reactions, ways of responding, of treating others, other beliefs, etc. In short, more aspects of a person's being must come into play than merely his will, his capacity for choice, his deliberative reason, in order for us to say that the person holds certain values or attitudes towards others.

Bernard Williams puts this point well:

> The idea that people decide to adopt their moral principles seems to
> me to be a myth, a psychological shadow thrown by a logical
> distinction; and if someone did claim to have done this, I think one
> would be justified in doubting either the truth of what he said or the
> reality of those moral principles. We see a man's genuine convictions
> as coming from somewhere deeper in him than that.[7]

This argument implies that the notion of the moral self cannot be seen on a model of pure *activity*, of that which is a product of choice. The moral self cannot be identified solely with that of which we are the initiators or authors. It is not generally within our power to bring it about, merely through an effort of will and focused attention, that we possess a certain attitude or adhere to a certain value; nor is it generally within our power to rid ourselves of unwanted attitudes and values (and emotions) in this way. Nevertheless, the values and attitudes we have do reflect on us morally. Aspects of ourselves — our values and attitudes — which are fit objects of moral assessment involve some element of passivity, of feeling and emotion.

So the moral self inevitably comprises a dimension of feeling and passivity. But the original Kantian objection to the notion that our emotions reflect on us morally is that we are passive with respect to our feelings — we do not choose them or decide to have them. If it is granted that the moral self inevitably involves passivity, and cannot be restricted to what is an outcome of choice, then this objection to considering our emotions as part of our moral self no longer holds. A person's sympathy (or lack of it), contempt (or lack of it), etc., reflect on him morally as surely as do the actions he performs (and the views to which he gives assent).

IV

The third way in which values and attitudes cannot be accommodated to the Kantian view is that they cannot be analyzed in terms of dispositions to perform certain acts. (This preserves a Kantian element, in that we are the initiators of our acts — they are something we do.) We have seen that possessing these attitudes involves having certain emotional reactions and feelings, certain thoughts, etc. which are not themselves merely dispositions to act. The racist man's attitudes are not merely dispositions to perform certain acts; they also involve his having certain thoughts, feelings, and inner reactions to and concerning black people.

Also, the fact that certain actions can be manifestations of certain attitudes and values does not mean that the attitude or value involves an actual disposition to perform the act. For example, an attitude of superiority towards a class of persons (e.g., uneducated) can express itself in saying something disparaging about an uneducated person. But it is surely not the case that this attitude involves a disposition to say disparaging things. For it might just as (or even more) naturally express itself as failing even to notice such persons, failing to take account of them. Both of these represent natural expressions of an attitude of superiority, but the latter is not a disposition to behave in certain ways, and its existence precludes the former from constituting what it is to have the attitude.

Further, even when a form of behavior is a natural manifestation of an attitude, it is so only in certain contexts, defined in not purely behavioral terms. For example, it is not the case that ignoring or failing to take account of uneducated persons is in itself a manifestation of a sense of superiority towards them. In addition there must be a certain view of them, which involves, at the least, regarding them as not worthy of one's consideration. This is to be distinguished from, for example, failing to take account of them simply because they are different from one (whether one is conscious of this reason or not). Further, 'ignoring' or 'failing to take account of' does not name an act-type; it is not a purely behavioral description. There are many different behavioral acts which constitute ignoring someone. What makes them all cases of ignoring has to do with the settings of the acts, as well as the way that the persons are regarded by the agent, his motives, etc.[8]

I would not want to say that no value or attitude could be given a purely behaviorist account; but I would want to claim that very few could. In particular, the values and attitudes mentioned in the beginning of this chapter seem clearly to involve emotional reactions, ways of regarding, judgments about, and the like, which are more than mere acts, behaviorally described. That values are manifested in behavior does not mean that they can be analyzed behavioristically.

V

The Kantian could take another position compatible with what I have argued so far. He can admit that values and attitudes cannot be analyzed without loss of meaning as dispositions to act; and that what it is to have a certain value or attitude cannot be analyzed in terms of something which one has arrived at through a process of rational deliberation. But he could claim that the only aspects of attitudes and values which are morally relevant are those which can be so analyzed. Even though values and attitudes involve more than assenting to certain principles and performing certain acts, nevertheless, he could argue, it is only the principles to which we assent and the acts which we perform which are appropriate objects of moral assessment and which reflect on us morally.

Such a view could not be decisively refuted, but it seems arbitrary and question-begging. For it normally seems to us that our attitudes and values do reflect morally on us — that if anything reflects morally on us, it is our values and attitudes. It seems to us that we regard it as morally undesirable to have a contemptuous attitude towards someone, to regard someone as inferior because of his race, to regard people primarily in terms of their usefulness to oneself, etc. And we ordinarily think that it is the full attitudes themselves, and not merely their behavioral manifestations, or the principles to which we have assented, which are appropriate targets for moral criticism and assessment.

It seems, then, that the Kantian view is asking us to revise our normal moral judgments, but without giving us an adequate reason for doing so. I have said in chapter I, and throughout, that the Kantian view involves an entire alternative conception of morality, one which cannot be decisively refuted. I aim only to articulate a coherent alternative view, and to ply what arguments I can muster. But there comes a point — and this is one of them — when the best that one can hope for is to attempt to place the Kantian view in a certain light, to try to reveal a certain arbitrariness in it, to try to address what seem some of the sources of its appeal and to show that they do not stand on the foundation which they seemed to.

VI

One consequence of my argument is that the passivity of emotions cannot be identified with what is external to our moral selves. Passivity signifies that emotions are something we experience, rather than something we choose or initiate. But that concern, compassion, hatred, or contempt are things we feel or experience does not mean that they are not fully a part of us, that they are external to our true selves, morally speaking.

A person who has a contemptuous attitude towards persons who are uneducated will necessarily sometimes have feelings of contempt (or related feelings) towards such persons.[9] These feelings cannot be seen as external to his moral self, for his contemptuous attitude is very much a part of him, rooted in an entire way of looking at persons of a certain type, and connected with other ways in which he regards himself and views society.

A teacher who does not have high regard for students will not take fully seriously problems and concerns of theirs, especially if they detract from a student's work, or might potentially do so. Such a person will have weak feelings of sympathy towards students in such situations. But such feelings of sympathy are not external to his moral self, though they are passive, i.e., something which he experiences. Rather they are an integral part of the way he regards students.

My argument here is *not* that anything which is genuinely part of our experience is as much a part of the self as anything else, although there is one sense in which this is true — the momentary irritation I feel towards a friend who has not conformed to my admittedly irrational and misplaced expectation is an experience of mine as much as are my feelings or care for my friend.

180

But from a moral point of view there is, I think, an important distinction, if only one of degree, to be drawn between feelings and emotions, between those which can be seen as external to the self and those which are part of it. I think it is possible to speak of ourselves as having dissociated ourselves from an emotional reaction, so that when we have it it feels as if it comes upon us, is external to us. If it is a dishonorable, regrettable, or otherwise morally undesirable reaction we are nevertheless not to be thought ill of for it, for it does not in a sense really reflect on us morally. (To be more accurate, since we are dealing with matters of degree, we can say that an emotional reaction from which a person is, by and large, dissociated reflects on him morally much less than does a reaction which is fully a part of his moral self.)[10]

Let us then examine the phenomenon of dissociation. The formerly racist man who now believes in equality (p. 175) can serve as an example. Occasionally he finds himself having a reaction of dislike or distrust towards a black person. He regards such reactions as entirely baseless and inappropriate. He sees them as the remnants of his racist upbringing rather than as grounded in any features of the persons in question. He wishes he did not have these reactions. He tries to rid himself of them, by focusing on his understanding of their source and on their groundlessness. He does find himself less and less subject to such emotional reactions.

Such reactions are very much out of line with the man's real view of blacks, and with his values regarding social equality. He is not 'color-blind' (on the contrary, he attempts to be aware of the different social and historical situations of blacks and of whites as groups); but his likes and dislikes, trustings and distrustings, do not correlate with people's race.

In this case I think we can say that the man has dissociated himself from his occasional feelings of dislike and distrust towards blacks. He can no longer be identified with them. He is not to be criticized for having them. They are thus external to his moral self. Metaphors of externality can be applied to such feelings – they 'assail' him, they 'come upon' him, he is 'saddled with' them. Such metaphors are inapplicable to feelings in general, i.e., feelings merely in regard to our passivity with respect to them. Feelings of concern for a friend in trouble do not assail me or come upon me. They, as it were, arise from within my (moral) self, not from outside it, though they are nevertheless happenings rather than actions.

These notions of passivity, dissociation, and externality are applicable to thoughts as well as to feelings. Many thoughts simply occur to us, or come into our heads, in this sense we are passive with respect to them. Nevertheless they do reflect on us. But I can try to dissociate myself from a thought which keeps occurring to me. I may succeed in dissociating myself from it. It is then no longer part of myself, morally speaking, even if it is a morally undesirable thought. Even though it is genuinely a thought of mine, it does not reflect on me morally. (This indicates that the distinction between active and passive does not correspond to that between thought and emotion; nor does the distinction between internal and external.)

Dissociation and externality do not bring the Kantian view in at a new level. Dissociating ourselves from a feeling involves more than deciding not to identify with it, or regarding it as inappropriate. For we can choose (or try) not to identify ourselves with a feeling which is nevertheless very much a part of us, internal to our (moral) self, so that we do not actually succeed in dissociating ourselves from it. Andy might recognize in himself contemptuous feelings towards women. He does not approve of such feelings, and in fact thinks them reprehensible. Nevertheless they are very much a part of him. He constantly regards women in contemptuous ways, reacts to their opinions with belittling comments, or, more generally, fails to take what they say seriously. He finds it difficult to have a genuine heartfelt respect for very many women. He is not dissociated from his feelings of contempt.

Deciding not to identify himself with these reactions and feelings, or regarding them as inappropriate, is insufficient for his actually dissociating himself from them. They have too deep and pervasive roots in his being, as was not the case with the racist feelings of the formerly racist man discussed above. They are reprehensible feelings and attitudes, for which Andy is properly thought ill. (However, sincere, even if unsuccessful, attempts to change do affect the *overall* moral assessment of a person.)

Dissociating oneself from a reaction involves an entire structure of one's moral being – including feelings, attitudes, behavior, thoughts, desires, etc. – and not merely an act of one's will or deliberative judgment.

We should not misconstrue this notion or metaphor of externality. That a feeling or emotional reaction can be seen as external to the self, morally conceived, does not mean that the reaction has no significance for our moral self. The formerly racist man's reactions do say something about him. They say that he retains vestiges of reprehensible attitudes in himself. A man happy to be brought in as a strikebreaker could find himself with passing feelings of sympathy for the strikers, feelings which he regards as inappropriate and shameful and from which he entirely dissociates himself. But the existence of such feelings says something about this person, though his successful disavowal of them means that he is not to be thought well of for having them, desirable as they are in themselves.

The relation between the moral self and reactions external to it is not a simple one. Certainly such reactions are improperly thought of as like bodily conditions, which have no human meaning for us but which simply have causes into which we can inquire. Emotional reactions almost always have some personal meaning to their subjects, so that a purely causal account of them cannot be fully adequate, even if the reactions are genuinely external to the moral self. (Of course, bodily conditions can be psychosomatic, so that they will have human meaning also.) One may be able to dissociate oneself from the reaction without inquiring into its meaning for one. But this will not deny that meaning.

VII

I have argued that we are passive with respect to our emotions and feelings but that, nevertheless (except when and to the extent that we are dissociated from them) they are properly seen as genuinely a part of us, no less a full part of us than are the actions we perform and the judgments that we make. This view involves some revision of the traditional notion of passivity in philosophy. For passivity has been portrayed as being identified not only with what we experience rather than what we do, but also with what is external to us rather than what is internal to us. Revision of the notion of passivity to exclude the latter association involves a revision of the contrast between activity and passivity. On my view this distinction is to be conceived no longer as a contrast between that which, from a moral point of view, is part of us and that which is not; rather it is a contrast between two ways in which something is part of us.

But could I not be taken as arguing that, in a sense, our emotions and feelings are something which we can be regarded as *doing*, as being active with respect to? Harry Frankfurt argued in 'Identification and Externality' that we should distinguish, among our passions, between those with respect to which we are active, and those with respect to which we are passive.[11] For him, the distinction corresponds to Aristotle's between something regarding which the moving principle is within us and that regarding which the moving principle is outside us; it is exemplified in the difference between directed attention, thought, and deliberation, and thoughts which beset us, obsessions, and thoughts which strike us willy-nilly.[12]

In his book *The Passions*, Robert Solomon puts this view in a particularly striking way:

> The Myth of the Passions has so thoroughly indoctrinated us with its notion of passivity that we are no longer capable of seeing what we ourselves are doing. Once the Myth is exploded, however, it is obvious that we make ourselves angry, make ourselves depressed, make ourselves fall in love.[13]

> An emotion is a judgment (or a set of judgments), something we do.[14]

Perhaps Solomon is exaggerating for effect. But in rightly rejecting the myth of pure passivity he goes all the way to the other side, and sees emotions as something we do, very much like what the Kantian view has in mind as the model of what we do, i.e., something which we entirely bring about. But this is to accept the very dichotomy which I am trying to undercut. For we do not, it seems to me, characteristically make ourselves angry, fall in love, etc. We become angry, feel angry, get angry − it is genuinely our true self which is involved, but these are not things which we do, conceived as something like performing an action.

Nor is an emotion a judgment, though it involves beliefs, cognition, ways of regarding others (all of which Solomon himself brings out very well in his book). There is an element of passivity in emotions which Solomon is not recognizing here, and which should not be regarded as disturbing, once we realize that the notion of the moral self must include a notion of passivity.[15]

Similarly, Frankfurt's distinction seems to preserve the very dichotomy which is in need of revision, though he does rightly argue, as we saw above, that some of our passions, thoughts, etc., can be regarded as external to the self (see note 13). The problem is that he identifies what is external to the self with passions regarding which we are passive; and this leaves him with failing to distinguish − among passions, thoughts, etc., which are part of the self − between those which are really like directed attention and deliberation, and those which are more like something which we experience. The latter, which include, in general, altruistic emotions fall into neither his category of directed attention and judgment, nor his category of obsessions or thoughts which strike us willy-nilly.

It is true that altruistic emotions involve judgment in some way — e.g., the judgment that someone is in pain, in need, suffering. In that sense, perhaps, one might want to say that they involve activity. But they are not mere reflections of such judgment, nor are they grounded in judgment, nor are they brought about (primarily) through a deliberate process of judgment. In this sense they are not active. Moreover, even if one wants to say that in involving judgment our emotions involve activity, this is not a form of activity which excludes passivity. For it remains true that our emotions are something we experience or feel.

It is not so important whether one wants to say that emotions (which are internal to our moral selves) involve activity, as long as one does not see this activity purely on the Kantian model of it; as long as one does not see such activity as incompatible with passivity (understood as that which is experienced); and as long as one does not identify that regarding which we are *not* active with that which is external to the self.

VIII

In summary then, the moral self cannot be identified solely with will, choice, decision, and deliberative reason. It cannot be identified with that regarding which we are active. Our feelings and emotions are as much a part of our moral self as are the actions we perform and the moral views to which we give assent. Though we are passive with respect to our emotions, in that they are something experienced rather than something done or brought about, they are no less a part of ourselves than that which we do bring about through our will. They are not rightly portrayed as external. However, it is possible for one to dissociate oneself (or disidentify oneself) from a particular feeling or thought, which will then be external to one's moral self and will no longer be a proper object for moral criticism or assessment.

Emotions, attitudes, beliefs, values, feelings, reactions, cannot be sharply distinguished from one another. They are interdependent, and are all part of the moral self. None of these elements (including the more cognitive or intellectual ones: attitudes, beliefs, and values) can be analyzed in a purely Kantian fashion. What it is to have a certain attitude, belief, emotion, or reaction cannot be seen purely as a matter of rational deliberation about, and rational assent and commitment to, certain propositions. This is true of holding moral beliefs (such as the belief that blacks and whites are equal) no less than it is of having certain emotional reactions.

The other side of this first point is that attitudes, emotions, values, etc. all involve an aspect of passivity to them. What it is to have them always involves something which is experienced – it involves reactions, feelings, emotions.

What this means is that having attitudes and values involves having feelings and reactions. Similarly, many emotions and feelings (and in particular altruistic emotions) involve values, attitudes, ways of regarding others. In fact, sympathy, compassion, and concern can be regarded as something like 'emotional attitudes,' in that they involve ways of regarding others, of perceiving others, etc. The differences between attitudes, (moral) beliefs, values, emotions, feelings must be largely a matter of degree on the dimensions of activity/passivity and cognition/affect.

It may be that altruistic emotions are, perhaps, more like what are generally thought of as attitudes than like what are generally thought of as feelings. It does not matter if this depends on inaccurate conceptions of 'attitude' and 'feeling.' The point is that, in arguing that attitudes and values are part of our moral self, I can be taken as arguing directly that altruistic emotions are part of our moral self, as well as doing so indirectly, through arguing that failure to conform to the Kantian picture (of activity) does not exclude something from being part of the moral self.

The argument so far has been addressed to showing that an emotion, feeling, or emotional response on a particular occasion reflects morally on the person who has it. But the actual argument given implies more than this. It implies that our patterns of emotional response, our traits of character involving emotions, our emotional attitudes, our ways of regarding and treating other persons in general – all are fit objects of moral assessment and criticism. All are part of our moral self.

This leads to the notion of being-towards-others, which I have introduced. Being-towards-others includes those aspects of our attitudes, emotions, sentiments, ways of treating and regarding, patterns of behavior, feelings, emotional responses, values, and moral beliefs which have to do with the weal and woe of other persons. This constitutes a subset of those attitudes, beliefs, emotions, etc. which are part of the moral self, for some attitudes and beliefs are morally significant yet not because of a connection to the weal and woe of others – e.g., the values of integrity or courage, or a persevering attitude.

But our being-towards-others constitutes an important part of our moral self. What allows the concept of being-towards-others to have some usefulness is that beliefs, attitudes, and emotions regarding the weal and woe of others are interconnected and interpenetrating with one another, so that our being-towards-others is not just a congeries of disparate and separable elements, but can be seen as a genuine kind of totality (which can nevertheless allow for diversity and even contradiction with it).

IX

I have argued that our emotions are, in general, proper objects for moral assessment, criticism, and admiration, just as are our actions and considered judgments (regarding moral matters). I have not yet said anything about *how* our emotions are to be assessed, or how a person is to be assessed in light of his emotions and feelings.

To give such an account of moral assessment of emotions is not central to my main purpose, which is to show that the altruistic emotions have moral value and reflect on us morally. Nevertheless, a few words are in order here.

First, I think we can distinguish two levels of the moral assessment of an emotional reaction. The first involves considering the reaction in itself, abstracting from its context in the character of the person who has it and in the wider circumstances of its occurrence. In this sense it is, one can say, morally bad to dislike someone because he is black. It is morally undesirable to show insufficient sympathy to someone whose situation warrants it. It is good for Dave to feel concern for his dying astronaut friend Joan; it is not good that Manny fails to feel that concern (chapter VII, pp. 146-51).

A second level of moral assessment of an emotion or emotional reaction or response involves seeing that emotional response in the context of the person's character or his being-towards-others. We discussed this point in chapter II (pp. 37-40). In order to have a full moral comprehension of Jones's 'capricious' sympathy for Clifford, we have to look at his reaction to Clifford in light of his general attitudes towards students, and his being-towards-others in general. The inadequate sympathy will have a certain moral significance if Jones is generally sympathetic to students but fails to be in this case, because of being tired and therefore less patient and attentive than usual. It will have a different significance if Jones's failure of sympathy is part of and typical of his general way of regarding students, i.e., unsympathetically. The difference in being-towards-others and in the circumstances surrounding the response in the two cases is reflected in a difference in our moral assessment of the persons, in light of the particular situation. In both cases we say, perhaps, that Jones ought to have been, or that it would have been good or appropriate for him to have been, more sympathetic. But in the first case we might think less poorly of Jones, for there are mitigating circumstances (he is tired), and because Jones generally does not react in these ways.

The distinction being drawn here applies in some measure to actions as well as to emotional responses. We distinguish between a judgment on a particular action – that it was wrong, ill-considered, or blameworthy – and a judgment taking into account the wider circumstances of the action, including mitigating circumstances relating, for example, to certain pressures on the agent.[16] (This is not a distinction between the rightness of the act and the moral worth of the act-cum-motive; rather it is a distinction within moral worth itself. Nor is it a distinction between a prima facie good action and a good action all things considered. The action in question is either good or bad, all things considered, in both cases; the contextual view can only mitigate, but not change, the fundamental moral value of the act.) For example, it is bad of someone to cheat and lie in order to obtain a job; but our judgment of the person in light of the action is affected by the pressures which exist on him. Was getting the job a matter of great urgency or even necessity for him? Would he have found it very difficult to support himself without it? If so, we would perhaps think less poorly of him. Nevertheless we do think poorly of him for lying and cheating. The act is still a morally bad one. The distinction here is essentially the same one as is being made in connection with emotional responses.[17]

In discussing how our feelings reflect on us morally, I have avoided the concepts of praise and blame. I have not argued that a person is to blame for his emotional reactions; nor that he can be praised for having them. I do not want to say that Jones is morally to blame for failing to be sympathetic to Clifford; but only that his failure reflects on him morally.

I suggest that notions of blame and praise, and blameworthiness and praiseworthiness, are closely connected with notions of will, of that of which we are the initiators. They are concepts appropriate to those aspects of what we are which conform to the Kantian view; if my argument is right they comprise only a subset of the concepts in terms of which we can be morally assessed and criticized. To say that someone is to blame for something, seems to me to imply that he could have brought it about through his will that he did otherwise. But a person cannot always, or even typically, bring it about through his will — i.e., just by deciding and trying (exerting effort) — that he fail to have an undesirable or inappropriate emotion, or that he have a desirable or appropriate one. The notion of blame seems to me connected closely with the notion of moral agency, rather than with the wider notion of moral being.

There seems to me a notion of responsibility which is connected with this notion of blame and praise, although there seems also a notion of responsibility which is more closely connected with the wider notion of moral reflection which I have developed. To illustrate the first, we might say of someone whose upbringing and social milieu very strongly reinforced racist attitudes and values, that he is not responsible for his attitudes, that he is not to blame for having them, that he could hardly have been expected to think differently than he does, etc.

But that a person is not to blame for some of his values and attitudes, nor, in one sense, is he responsible for them, does not mean that they cannot reflect on him morally. It is still bad for the racist man to hate black persons, to discriminate against them, to treat them badly, to regard them as moral inferiors. These are morally bad actions, responses, ways of regarding persons. A person is thought ill of for having them. In another sense of 'responsibility' I think we can say that a person must 'take responsibility' for attitudes and values which are genuinely a part of him, no matter what their source. This means that a person cannot use the fact of his racist upbringing to excuse himself from moral criticism for discriminating against blacks, responding to them in contemptuous ways, etc. If these reactions are truly part of his actual attitudes and values regarding blacks, then he cannot absolve himself from moral assessment in light of them; and in this sense he must take responsibility for them. (This is a different situation from one described earlier (p. 185), in which a person no longer has genuinely racist attitudes, but occasionally has reactions not consonant with his present values of equality between blacks and whites, reactions from which he dissociates himself in the ways discussed previously, and for which he is therefore not properly morally assessed.)

The issue of blame (and its associated sense of responsibility) differs from the issue of whether a person is a genuine moral being or not, i.e., whether he is a fit subject for moral assessment at all. The psychopath is not responsible for his psychopathy; nor (I am envisaging) is the racist for his racism. Nevertheless the latter is a genuine moral agent, and therefore can be morally criticized for his racist reactions and attitudes (and is, in the second sense, responsible for them); whereas the former cannot be morally criticized at all.

I do not mean this discussion of the notions of blame and responsibility to have done more than scratch the surface of a difficult problem. I have said nothing about the relationship between moral assessment in terms of blame and the wider notion of moral assessment appropriate to a person's emotional reactions, values, and attitudes. Another question is whether a person can ever be said to be blameworthy for his attitudes and values; that is, whether some persons can more properly be regarded as the authors of their own values and attitudes than can others, and thus more blameworthy or praiseworthy for them. Can some people's racist values and attitudes be accounted for primarily by external forces and others not? Or are everyone's values and attitudes equally to be accounted for (ultimately) in terms of forces external to themselves?

I leave these questions unanswered. I intend this discussion primarily to explain that, when I speak of moral assessment and moral reflection, these are not to be thought of in terms of blame, praise, and (in one sense) responsibility.

X

The notion of the moral self is particularly crucial for the phenomenon of moral change — i.e., of how it is that we become morally better persons. Moral change cannot be explained without some notion of moral self. And differences in theories of the moral self show themselves particularly clearly in their application to the phenomenon of moral change. There are several distinct views of moral change which can justly be seen as Kantian or Kantian-like.

I want to begin with a view which is grounded in two elements within the Kantian view of the moral self, and results from following out their implication for a view of moral change. This view may seem extremely unsympathetic, one which no one would actually hold; but it is useful as a point of reference.

The two elements are these: (1) The identification of the moral self with the will, the capacity for choice and decision, deliberative reason, that of which we are fully the initiators or authors and which is fully within our control. (2) Regarding emotions and feeling as lying outside the moral self, external to us.

These two premises have the consequence that as moral agents we have no control over the nature of the feelings and emotions which we experience. We have no control over whether we experience a particular feeling or emotion; for our feelings and emotions come upon us from outside. What they are is due to something which is not part of our moral selves.

This view does allow for some relationship between our moral selves and our feelings. For what *is* within our control is the effect of the feelings on our actions, on what we do, on what is the outcome of our rational deliberation. Since it is within the capability of the will to choose our actions, it is also within the capability of the will to determine whether our feelings will influence those actions or not. We can choose whether or not to act in accordance with our feelings or emotions, whether to accede to the feelings or not.

What are the consequences of this view for moral change? It seems that what is within our power is to try to keep our feelings and emotions from diverting us from acting in accord with what our moral principles tell us is right to do. Becoming more moral, on this view, consists in a progressively increasing ability to keep our feelings and emotions from affecting our actions and the principles to which we assent. This is not because all our feelings and emotions will necessarily incline us to act contrary to morality. Rather it is because, since we have no control over what our feelings and emotions will be, there is always the possibility that our feelings and emotions will go against the dictates of morality. And since our feelings and emotions play no role in what it is which constitutes moral actions, it will be entirely a matter of chance whether they do in fact lead in a morally good direction.

Thus, becoming morally better will mean increased self-control in our actions and rationality in our moral thinking. The progress towards increased self-control will have to be continually renewed.[18] There can be no guarantee that we have reached a plateau in which we can be assured of acting morally, across a certain range of sorts of action; for we are truly only our will, and are powerless to affect the nature of the material which affects our ability to act in accordance with morality. This material is always liable to affect us so as to draw us away from morality.[19]

But increased self-control is a very limited aspect of all that is involved in moral change, especially when the self-control rests on somewhat precarious ground. Self-control does not bring about any fundamental change in moral attitudes, values, and principles. And it seems that this version of the Kantian view leaves no room for such fundamental changes. For as we have seen, what it is to hold a moral value or principle involves having certain emotional reactions, feelings, etc. Thus changing one's values will involve new ways of responding, different emotional reactions, etc. But if we cannot affect the nature of our emotions, but only their effect on us, we cannot bring it about that we have different emotional reactions from the ones we do have. Hence we cannot bring about a fundamental (or even not-so-fundamental) change in moral principles and values.

Moreover, with regard to altruistic emotions, the prime moral task is not to control them but to bring them about in ourselves, to become a person who is prone to altruistic response when it is good and appropriate to do so.

By locating the moral self in the will, this version of the Kantian view forbids us access to most of what is actually necessary to bring about substantial moral change in ourselves: our attitudes, ways of regarding others, emotions, and feelings.

XI

What does the view of the moral self which I have put forth in this chapter imply for moral change?

By broadening the view of the moral self to include emotions, and, more generally, to include one's being-towards-others, my view allows for a much richer and more realistic view of what it is to become a better person in regard to the altruistic virtues. How, then, do we become more compassionate, sympathetic, concerned, and caring persons? The first thing to say is that, in contrast to the Kantian model, the will must be seen as playing a much diminished role. It now becomes only one element in both the source and the material of change.

It is beyond the scope of this work to give a detailed theory of moral change. What can be said is that moral change will involve at its most fundamental level an engagement with and reorientation of our being-towards-others. I say 'will involve,' but the point is really that it *can* involve this. That is, because our being-towards-others is part of the moral self, it becomes something which is capable of change, something with which we can engage (because it is part of what we are). If I am a person who lacks compassion, this will mean that I have a certain kind of regard to others, a certain orientation of my being-towards-others. If this orientation can be engaged with and changed, then I could perhaps become a more compassionate person.

How is one's being-towards-others engaged with? Without trying to say anything general about this, one way to look at it is to ask the question, what are the *obstacles* to a person's being sympathetic, compassionate, caring, etc.? Some may be: self-absorption; competitiveness; regarding others solely in terms of their usefulness to oneself; an inflated sense of one's own importance; various kinds of prejudices against particular groups of people; lack of imagination; and lack of experience or knowledge of what others are like, of what is going on with them. All these sorts of things affect our being-towards-others, and stand as obstacles to being a person prone to the altruistic emotions. It is in some cases possible to do something about these obstacles, to work at changing. One tries to understand why one is competitive, self-centered, etc. One tries to change, one subjects oneself to better influences, one focuses one's attentions on certain things rather than others.

We can see these points in the case of the unsympathetic teacher, Jones (chapter II, p. 36). Let us envisage Jones as having a generally unsympathetic attitude towards students. What would it be for Jones to come to regard his students sympathetically rather than unsympathetically?

Let us imagine that central to Jones's ways of regarding students is the kind of importance he gives to different aspects of his life – his teaching, his intellectual pursuits, etc. It would be possible for him to undergo a kind of value shift in his life, so that he came to feel that educating students was what was most important, and that other pursuits were secondary. He would then give much more of himself to his teaching and to his students. Such a shift in value would almost certainly involve a more sympathetic attitude towards students, since it would involve giving them a kind of importance in his life which they did not heretofore have. He would care more what was going on with them, with how well they were doing. He would be more inclined to understand the different elements of their own lives, which play a part in their learning and education.

We can imagine several ways that such a shift in values would come about in Jones — influence of respected colleagues, certain experiences with students, frustrations in his own intellectual life. Whatever motivates the change, the point here is that involved in the process of change will be an engagement with Jones's being-towards-students. His attitudes, sentiments, values, emotions, beliefs regarding students will all have to undergo some kind of change. This change cannot come about simply through willing or wanting to do so, or becoming convinced that it would be a good thing to do so — though all these can be the beginning of change and can play a continuing role within it.

The obstacles within Jones to a different attitude towards students might well be deep ones, not readily amenable to change. Thus, he might harbor a kind of resentment against his students, because he feels that his talents deserve what he regards as a more desirable academic environment. He may feel that he ought to be teaching at a more prestigious institution, in which his students are better prepared and more academically oriented, and in which his colleagues are more prominent in their fields. He may feel that it is unfair to him that he is teaching where he is, and he may be quite frustrated by this. He may take this frustration out on his students in the form of the unsympathetic attitude described above. Perhaps a quite profound change in Jones would be required to bring about a sympathetic attitude towards his students, if this sort of thing is the source of his unsympathetic attitude.

XII

In the next sections I want to consider three views regarding the kind of access we as moral agents have to our emotions, and the kind of moral change of which we are capable. All of these views offer some kind of alternative or modification of the extreme Kantian view elaborated in pp. 190-2. Each of the views, while accepting the notion that we are essentially passive with respect to our feelings and emotions, nevertheless sees them as subject to moral criticism and change, in a way which the extreme Kantian view does not strictly allow for. They argue that we are not confined simply to accepting the feelings and emotions which happen to come upon us, while trying not to allow them to affect our actions. Rather, we are able, at least to some extent, to affect the actual nature of the feelings and emotions which we experience.

While each of these views makes an advance on the extreme Kantian view, I will argue that each one retains too much of the identification of the self with the will or with conscious reason. While they are limited as adequate accounts of the relations of will, self, emotion, and moral change, each one contains valuable insights regarding ways that it is possible for us to change in regard to sympathy, compassion, and concern.

XIII

The first view can be found in Henry Sidgwick, and in some sections of Kant's *The Doctrine of Virtue*. According to this view, it is possible for us to bring it about that we have a greater amount of altruistic feeling than we might otherwise have, by placing ourselves in circumstances which we know to be causally related to producing altruistic feelings in ourselves; and that in fact it is some sort of moral requirement to do so. Thus, though Sidgwick agrees with the view (which he attributes to Kant) that it cannot be a strict duty to feel an emotion, insofar as it is not directly within the power of the will to produce it, nevertheless he says:

> It would seem to be a duty generally, and until we find the effort fruitless, to cultivate kind affections towards those whom we ought to benefit . . . by placing ourselves under any natural influences which experience has shown to have a tendency to produce affection.[20]

In *The Doctrine of Virtue*, section 34 ('Sympathetic Feeling is a Duty in General'), Kant, departing from doctrines central to other aspects of his moral writings, argues that nature has implanted within us the capacity for sympathetic joy and sorrow, and that we have a duty to use these feelings to foster our performance of beneficence ('active and rational benevolence') towards others:

> Thus it is our duty: not to avoid places where we shall find the poor who lack the most basic essentials, but rather to seek them out; not to shun sick-rooms or debtors prisons in order to avoid the painful

sympathetic feelings that we can not guard against. For this is still one of the impulses which nature has implanted within us so that we may do what the thought of duty would not accomplish.[21]

This view progresses further than the previously discussed Kantian view, in allowing us to have some responsibility and choice in the kind of emotions we have, not directly through the will itself, but indirectly through our power to place ourselves in circumstances which we know will cause us to have certain emotions. It does not reject a radical separation between will and emotion, but it does allow ways in which we can bring it about that we have the emotion.[22]

But if we are really to imagine someone becoming a more sympathetic or compassionate person, a person more prone to feeling sympathy or compassion,[23] the conception that this can be brought about through placing ourselves in certain circumstances which cause us to have these feelings is an incomplete one. If someone does come to be more compassionate or prone to sympathy as a result of being in certain circumstances, this will mean that in some way his general being-towards-others has been engaged with; so that there will not be a direct causal link between the situational influences that Kant is talking about and the person's becoming a more sympathetic and compassionate person. Rather, as I will argue below, the link will be by way of the person's other values, ways of regarding others, etc., which must be seen as fundamental. On the other hand, if we try to abstract from a person's being-towards-others, imagining the natural effect of being placed in the circumstances Kant envisions, it is not clear that this effect would be the sympathy and compassion desired by Kant (and Sidgwick).

Kant assumes that contact with suffering and misery, for example, in sick-rooms or debtor's prisons, will naturally and automatically bring about sympathy for those suffering. But it might very well have a contrary effect, producing feelings of disgust, revulsion, or even contempt, rather than sympathy. The main effect might be to cause the person to flee, to stay away from such places, to want not to have anything to do with them, to want the suffering out of his sight, rather than to cause him to have sympathy for the people involved. Kant assumes a morally positive effect stemming from such experience, but this is by no means assured or even necessarily the most likely.

The same circumstances will have different effects on different people, depending on other features of themselves. A person with a certain kind of 'aristocratic' morality, for example, will consider persons in the circumstances Kant describes to be in some ways beneath him, in terms of their full humanity, or as having lesser claim on his human consideration than persons of his own station. Face-to-face with 'the poor who lack the most basic essentials,' such a person's compassion is less likely to be aroused than his revulsion, or at best his pity.[24]

There are many ways of failing to allow oneself to confront the full humanity of another human being in his suffering: prejudices, rationalizations, defenses, etc. Whether a given person will react in the way that Kant says, rather than in these less morally desirable ways, will depend on other aspects of his attitudes, values, and orientations towards others.

This is not to deny that exposure to circumstances involving human suffering can play an important role in moral change and moral development, in the direction of sympathy, compassion, and human concern. It is only to say that it cannot do so in abstraction from other elements of the person's moral orientation. One would have to be open to feeling the full human force of the circumstances in question, or to not have various obstacles within oneself which would block such an effect.[25]

This argument connects with a hidden orientation of Kant's remarks. He presumes to address anyone, since he sees the envisioned effect as an entirely natural one, and since bringing about this effect is seen as a duty applicable to anyone. But what lends his view plausibility is that he tacitly presumes a person who already acknowledges it as a duty to produce sympathetic feelings in himself, who already acknowledges the duty of beneficence to others, and who has the intention of promoting his adherence to duty by causing himself to have feelings of sympathy.[26] Such a person is already oriented toward trying to bring about these feelings in himself, and is thus already open to experiencing them in situations where others are suffering. It is thus much more likely that such a person will be affected in the way Kant describes than in some of the other ways I have mentioned. But this is because he already has a certain moral orientation towards others, signified by his clear acknowledgment of the duty of beneficence and by his desire to become more sympathetic than he is. He already regards other persons in a way different from that of the aristocratic person described above. Thus other elements of his being-towards-others are presupposed when we envision that the circumstances described will produce sympathy and compassion in him. The circumstances do not produce the effect merely naturally, independent of the moral being of the person in question.[27]

This same conclusion can be reached by a different route. We can imagine that a person is caused to have momentary feelings of compassion or sympathy by going to a poorhouse, hospital, debtor's prison, or into circumstances of suffering or misery. But what will preserve such feelings after the person leaves the poorhouse? What will turn the momentary feelings into a genuine and full sympathy and compassion for the inmates? Only if the fleeting feelings take root in a person's wider sentiments, emotions, and moral attitudes will this take place. One can easily imagine, for example, a selfish and self-centered person being moved to flickers of compassion for destitute people who have somehow been brought to his attention. But because of his fundamental self-centeredness, and the structure of his values built around this, he simply will not come to be genuinely compassionate and sympathetic towards these people. He will not have a true appreciation of their plight. He will not have the disposition to help when it is possible for him to do so. He will not come actually to have compassion, concern, or sympathy.

Thus, although momentary feelings of sympathy or compassion can be caused in someone by the circumstances which Kant mentions, they will not constitute genuine sympathy, compassion, or concern unless other aspects of a person's being-towards-others are engaged.[28]

Sidgwick also suggests one other way in which we can cultivate our affections towards others which lead to beneficent acts — namely to engage in repeated beneficent resolves and actions, 'since, as has often been observed, a benefit tends to excite love in the agent toward the recipient of the benefit, no less than in the recipient toward the agent.'[29] But again, affection for the person benefited is not an inevitable, nor necessarily even a natural effect of kindly acts when some positive regard does not already exist, at least to some extent. If, for example, the acts are done strictly from duty, the agent might very well as naturally have resentment towards the person he benefits as have affection for him, especially if the duty were unanticipated and regarded as a burden. Whether an agent will come to have sympathy rather than resentment, indifference, anger, or irritation for recipients of his beneficence will very much depend on the way the agent already regards this other person, and the way he understands his beneficent acts towards him. But this is to say that wider aspects of a person's moral being must be taken into account if the connection which

Sidgwick asserts as natural is to take place.

Though Kant and Sidgwick have noted a significant way in which we can come to increase our sympathy towards others, they both overstate its significance and misrepresent its nature. Their views still regard our feelings primarily on a model of pure passivity, as too separate from other aspects of our moral being, and as external to our true selves. The self is still primarily identified with the will, seen as our ability to engage in actions which place us in certain circumstances.

XIV

A second view of how emotions can be brought into morality begins from the consideration that it is sometimes possible for us to bring it about that we have sympathy or compassion directly, through summoning up that feeling within ourselves. In this way feelings and emotions are in fact available to our will, and directly so. Therefore, as Philip Mercer says, we can 'exercise some kind of choice in the matter of whether or not we experience a particular emotion.'[30] Feelings become something we can choose to have.

In order to understand the significance of the consideration on which this viewpoint rests, we must understand that it is only on some occasions that emotions are able to be summoned.[31] Earlier in the chapter (p. 188) I described a way of understanding the reaction of Jones to Clifford, in the situation described in chapter II, in terms of Jones's being basically a sympathetic and responsive person who fails to be sympathetic and to do the sympathetic thing in this situation, because of his mood or temporary state of tiredness. It is in such situations that we can imagine a person summoning up his sympathy. Suppose Jones is aware of his mood and aware that this mood would tend to make him feel less sympathetic than he would otherwise be. He recognizes the difficulty of Clifford's situation, and, though not spontaneously feeling sympathy for Clifford, is able to summon up some sympathy, managing by force of will to overcome the contrary tendency of his present mood. In such a situation the picture of someone bringing it about through his will that he feels sympathy seems a plausible and appropriate one.

This picture is not appropriate, however, with regard to the Jones-Clifford situation described on p. 188 of this chapter, in which Jones is basically unsympathetic to students. His response to Clifford as described is typical of the ways he does respond to students. In such a situation it does not really make sense to imagine Jones summoning up sympathy for Clifford and thereby bringing it about that he feels sympathy.

First of all, it is extremely unlikely that he would be motivated to do so, or even that we can make sense of the notion of his attempting to do so. For, in contrast to Jones in the previous example, the values and attitudes which Jones here brings to this situation mean that he does not experience Clifford's situation as containing the elements which would warrant a stronger and more substantial sympathy for him than he already feels. He brings a general unwillingness to give much of himself to students, especially if this requires sacrificing something which he really wants, such as the talk which he wishes to attend. He brings a general failure to fully acknowledge the difficulties of students, a suspicion that they are trying to weasel out of something, etc.

In such a context, how can Jones be envisioned to summon up sympathy for Clifford? Whatever sympathy he would manage to bring about through his will alone would necessarily be extremely weak and flimsy, mere shadows of real sympathy.

Though Mercer is correct to speak of one's attending to certain features of the situation in order to bring it about that one has certain feelings,[32] it would be misleading to think of this option as genuinely available to every moral agent. For such features of the situation will not really be available immediately to a person whose moral outlook or being-towards-others does not incline him to see those features. It holds only for those who, like the first Jones, generally see and respond to those features but whose 'taking them in' is temporarily clouded in a particular situation by a mood or other feeling, whose influence they can, by force of will, counteract.

What this argument suggests is that the will can operate to bring about altruistic feelings only in people (or people in certain situations) who are already normally prone to that altruistic feeling. For people not prone to that feeling, this effort will not be possible, or at least not generally successful. Consequently, what the fact that feelings are sometimes summonable up by the will shows is not so much that the will really is primarily in morality, and that feelings have a role in morality insofar as they are mediated through the will; but rather that what is primary in morality is our moral being, our being-towards-others, our character structure, taken in the widest sense. The will functions in a subsidiary role to this.

This second Kantian view notes an important source of access to our emotions, but still gives the will primacy and centrality in the moral life and in moral assessment, and gives feelings and emotions a subsidiary role, grounded only in their direct availability to the will. It tries to give a role to the feelings only insofar as they approach the inappropriate ideal of being self-produced or chosen.

Moreover, this view leaves no room for fundamental moral change. For we can choose or cause ourselves to have certain feelings only if our being-towards-others is in a certain state. The model gives us no way of engaging with and changing our being-towards-others itself.

XV

The final view to be considered is related to an important strand in contemporary thinking regarding the emotions, namely that emotions are intentional, i.e., that they have objects to which they are necessarily related, and in that way they involve beliefs, and can thus be seen as having a cognitive component (see chapter II, pp. 12f).[33]

It is through rational assessment of the objects of emotions, or the beliefs on which they are based, that we as rational persons can have an effect on our emotions, that we are able to direct, control, and change them. 'The most obvious influence of rational thought or advice on the emotions [is]: that of convincing one that a given object is no proper or appropriate object of that emotion.'[34] I might have compassion for someone who seems to be being grievously abused, but subsequently discover that the man is getting exactly what he deserves; my compassion, found thereby to be inappropriate, ceases to exist.

This view enables us to be accountable for our emotions, in that we are able to assess the appropriateness of their objects. It is within our power at least to attempt to have only emotions which are appropriate, in the sense that their objects are appropriate ones for the given emotion. The moral self, on this view, is identified with thought, conscious reason, and cognition. Emotions are seen as secondary to judgment, and as morally significant primarily in relation to their cognitive element.

This view suffers from an initial limitation, if it is meant to capture an important part of how we have access to our emotions, or, more generally, if it is to serve as a model for moral change in the area of altruistic emotions. The limitation is that it applies only to our assessing *already existing* emotions as to their appropriateness. It allows us to try to rid ourselves of inappropriate emotions, but not to acquire appropriate or desirable ones.

Nevertheless, it could be argued that the notion of assessing objects can be extended to cover acquiring desired emotions, and this is in fact suggested by Hampshire, who speaks of 'desires and attitudes [one could just as well say, "emotions"] *being formed by* considering the appropriateness of their objects'[35] (my emphasis).

One might imagine an altruistic emotion coming to be formed in something like this way. Suppose I hear that an acquaintance, Peter, has been laid off from his job. On the grounds of this belief about Peter I come to have sympathy or even concern for him, for I believe he will suffer financially and emotionally from losing his job. I believe that Peter is an appropriate object for sympathy and concern, and I do in fact come to feel concern and sympathy for him.

The grounds on which my concern rests can be a matter for rational assessment. Suppose, for example, that someone tells me that, unbeknownst to me, Peter has another job lined up − one which he prefers to the one which he has just lost − and that he was prepared to quit if he had not been laid off. I am skeptical about this, given the present job situation, but if I come to believe that what the person says is true this will affect the appropriateness of my sympathy and concern for Peter. In this way, we can regard my sympathy and concern as outcomes of a process by which I come to assess the appropriateness of a certain object, or potential object, of those emotions.

Nevertheless, this process just described cannot be regarded as portraying the whole of how we have access to our altruistic feelings and emotions. For we can come to be convinced of the facts on which it is appropriate to feel certain emotions, and yet nevertheless not come to feel them. I might acknowledge that an acquaintance has been laid off from his job and yet not feel sympathy or concern for him.

There are different ways in which this could happen. Other feelings regarding Peter might get in the way of sympathy or concern − e.g., personal envy, anger, or resentment towards him. More generally, one might simply not allow the acquaintance's plight to touch one's feelings. One might simply not focus on what this might mean concretely for the acquaintance, though one readily admits, when pressed, that it is going to be bad for him. One might be more taken with feelings of relief that one has not lost one's own job. Or, one might think of the much worse things that do happen to people, and think that, compared to these things, the acquaintance is fortunate. In another direction, the news about Peter, coming on top of one's knowing so many people losing their jobs or not being able to find jobs, is something one is simply unable to take in, to allow to engage with one's emotions. One is, so to speak, emotionally numb regarding this sort of situation, though readily acknowledging that Peter is an appropriate object of sympathy or concern. One might be convinced that Peter is an appropriate object for sympathy, and even hope that someone does have sympathy for Peter, without oneself having sympathy for him. One might not let one's feelings, one's sympathy or compassion, be engaged with, knowing that one could very well do so if one let oneself.

Thus there seems to be a gap between acknowledging something as an appropriate object of an altruistic emotion, and coming to have that emotion. Other elements in our attitudes, feelings (towards particular people or towards people in general), or general being-towards-others can prevent the connection from being made. Thus, though assessing objects and beliefs can play some role in moral change regarding our altruistic emotions, there are distinct limits to that role. Therefore the conception of assessment of objects is a limited one as a view of how it is that we have access to our emotions, and how we are able to change them. But, in addition, even when we do succeed in bringing it about that we have a certain desirable emotion, through assessment of objects, this conception does not allow us an adequate understanding of the process involved.

Within emotions cognition cannot be regarded as having any particular primacy. Our being-towards-others must always be seen as a necessary context for understanding our altruistic emotions, and no notion of pure cognition can allow for this. We saw in chapter VI that emotions often determine how one perceives a situation, and in that way the cognitive judgments made about that situation. So emotions are not determined by or grounded in cognition. The cognitive component which we have seen that emotions characteristically involve cannot be seen as having any particular primacy in the nature of emotions or in their moral significance.

XVI

In the preceding three sections I have considered three different views of the way that our emotions can play a role in the assessment of ourselves as moral beings. Each marks a departure from the Kantian view I spelled out in the beginning of the chapter, in which our emotions do not reflect on us morally. In articulating a more substantial role for the emotions in the moral life, each of these views involves a conception of the way that we as moral beings have access to our emotions, a conception of what is involved in moral change regarding emotions, and a conception of the self insofar as it is relevant to morality. Yet none of the views departs sufficiently from the Kantian identification of the self with will, deliberative reason, judgment, choice, decision, cognition.

I have agreed that each of these three views shows us some of the ways that we as moral beings have access to our emotions, and thus tells us something of the ways that we are capable of moral change. We are able to place ourselves in circumstances which can cause us to have certain desirable emotions, such as sympathy. We are sometimes able directly to summon up desirable emotions within ourselves. We are able to assess the object of our emotions and can thereby come to rid ourselves of inappropriate emotions, and even come to possess appropriate or desirable ones.

Against these three views, I have argued that each is incomplete as a fully adequate conception of how we have access to our emotions, and thus of how we are able to change morally. Not only does each view give us only some of the ways that we are able to change morally; but in addition, they all fail to portray adequately what is involved in the processes of moral change which they do articulate. What all fail to bring out is that our being-towards-others is fundamental to moral change.

XVII

Finally, I want to make some brief remarks regarding the relationship between the moral self, being-towards-others, and the notions of 'virtue' and 'character.' There are some important similarities between a moral philosophy focused on the notions of character and virtue (such as Aristotle's), and one which involves the notion of the moral self which I have tried to articulate. There are similar divergences from the Kantian view. Morality is not seen primarily as a matter of the exercise of the will. For a morality of virtues, we cannot bring it about through our will that we have virtues, or desirable traits of character. What it is to possess a morally good trait of character is more than to have a disposition to perform certain acts. It involves, in addition, patterns of emotional response. On Aristotle's view we cannot simply bring it about that we have a certain virtue, such as courage or liberality. Rather we must learn, and learn to take pleasure in, certain habits of action and response which take time to acquire. Moreover, we must have had a certain kind of upbringing which provides the foundation for the development of such habits.

Therefore character, like being-towards-others, is a kind of totality which encompasses ways of behaving, attitudes, and emotions. The perspective of character requires and involves a richer and fuller notion of the moral self than is involved in the Kantian view.

It is possible to cast much of the argument of this book in the language of character and of virtues. To some extent I have done this explicitly. For I have regarded compassion, sympathy, and concern (or concernedness) as virtuous traits of character, associated with the emotions denoted by the same terms. I have wanted to argue that it is morally good to be a compassionate person – to be a person who possesses the character trait of compassion (or compassionateness) – as well as that it is good to have (the emotion of) compassion for others.

An aspect of the concepts of virtue and of character which leads me to prefer my own formulations, in terms of attitudes, values, emotions, and our being-towards-others, is connected with the phenomenon of moral change just discussed. The notions of virtue, and especially of character and trait of character, seem to me to imply a kind of fixity or permanence which I wish to avoid in my account of a person's moral being. It seems to me that to refer to something as a quality of someone's character is to imply a deep-rootedness in the person's being which would make the person very resistant to change with regard to the quality. Let us consider, for example, a person (called Bemis) who we want to say has the quality or trait of competitiveness in his character. Let us contrast with this the formulations, 'Bemis has a competitive attitude towards others'; 'Bemis regards others in a competitive way', and 'Bemis acts in a competitive manner.' It seems to me that the formulation in terms of character implies the other formulations – it implies ways of regarding others, ways of behaving, and attitudes.[36] But it implies, I think, more than this.

The formulation in terms of attitudes, behavior, and ways of regarding imply possibilities of change which the formulation in terms of character does not. We can inquire into the sources of Bemis's competitive attitudes. Let us say that Bemis is competitive with his colleagues. Perhaps this competitiveness is connected with a sense of insecurity regarding how he is viewed by them. He feels he has to establish his position by belittling others, because he does not feel that he is really valued by them. Let us imagine that, were he to be convinced that he has the respect of his colleagues, then he would cease to be so competitive with them. In this case I think we would be loath to say that competitiveness was a part of Bemis's character, or that he possessed the trait of competitiveness; though we would say that he had a competitive attitude and behaved in a competitive manner.

To say that competitiveness is part of Bemis's character seems to me to imply that it could not be changed in the manner suggested, whereas to speak of attitudes and ways of regarding and behaving leaves such a possibility open. If this is true, it is an important point in regard to moral change. For competitiveness is something which is a natural obstacle to developing sympathy or concern for others.

It seems to me that a person who has struggled to overcome his competitiveness, through coming to terms with its sources in his insecurities, is less usefully spoken of as 'changing his character,' or as losing a trait of character, than as having changed his attitudes, his ways of regarding others, his patterns of behavior.

If this verbal intuition is correct it means that regarding persons in terms of traits of character, rather than in terms of being-towards-others, can discourage us from looking for the ways that persons can change. For example, if we think of a person as 'a selfish person' — as having the character trait of selfishness — then we tend to regard this as a relatively permanent and unchanging feature of him. We are not encouraged to look at the meaning and sources of his selfish attitudes, ways of regarding others, ways of behaving, etc. It might turn out, to be somewhat oversimplistic, that the person is selfish because he feels no one cares for him or could care for him. His selfishness is grounded in a kind of bitterness regarding others. Perhaps this is an attitude which could be changed, e.g., if he saw that his own behavior involved the 'self-fulfilling prophecy' of turning others away from him. In this case perhaps the person could come to be less selfish.[37]

I do not want to quarrel about the word 'character' or 'trait.' The main point is that we not look at a person's (undesirable) attitudes, patterns of behavior, and ways of regarding others in a manner which implies less of a possibility of change than really exists. If someone uses the concepts of character and trait in ways which leave room for this sort of moral change, then I have no quarrel with this.

Finally, I am obviously not denying that it often is appropriate to apply concepts of character and trait to persons (given my understanding of those concepts). In many cases, patterns of behavior, attitudes, and ways of regarding are so substantially rooted in a person's being that it is true that they constitute part of his character. He simply *is* selfish, competitive, shallow, kind, compassionate. These are qualities of his character. My point is only to discourage a conceptualization of a person's moral nature in these terms when it is not appropriate to do so.

NOTES

I ALTRUISTIC EMOTIONS AND THE KANTIAN VIEW

1 I have in mind some contemporary works on Kant such as Mary Gregor's *Laws of Freedom*, Keith Ward's *The Development of Kant's View of Ethics*, and John Rawls's reading of Kant in *A Theory of Justice*, as well as increased attention to Kant's *Metaphysics of Morals* — all of which argue for a less formalist account of rationality, a less severe dichotomy between reason and inclination, the presence of empirical elements in morality, and the like, as part of a sound interpretation of Kant.

2 For support for this view of morality see Alasdair MacIntyre, *A Short History of Ethics*, Joel Feinberg, 'Supererogation and Rules'; and W.D. Falk, 'Morality, Self, and Others.'

3 Iris Murdoch, *The Sovereignty of Good*, pp. 49-50.

4 *Ibid.*, p. 77.

II ALTRUISTIC EMOTIONS AS MORAL MOTIVATION

1 'Weal' (a translation of the German 'Wohl') will be useful for my purposes in distinguishing among several concepts of 'good' for which the German language provides different words (*Wohl, Gut, Güte*) while the English does not. It is approximately equivalent to the philosophical use of the word 'welfare,' but is somewhat broader in scope. I will also use its opposite, 'woe' (in German, 'Übel').

2 A fuller account of the cognitive dimension — as well as of the other features mentioned below — of the altruistic emotions is given in my 'Compassion.'

3 Nor, I would claim, can emotions be analyzed as dispositions to have such feeling-states.

4 Philip Mercer, *Sympathy and Ethics*, p. 10.

5 It is worth noting also that, though impulsive, an action might turn out well, because though the agent did not really have enough information to understand his situation adequately, his spontaneous 'take' on it turned out to be right (so that it was not merely an accident that it did turn out well). Moreover the sympathetic or compassionate impulse can be admirable even if the act, taken as a whole, is morally defective. That is, it can be a good thing about the agent that he is a concerned person who so wants to help, though it is a deficiency in him that this concern takes such impulsive forms, i.e., that he acts without sufficient understanding or grasp of his situation. These considerations mitigate the defectiveness of impulsive though altruistic action.

6 That there are degrees of the strength of the desire for the other's good, and thus of the motivation to help the other involved in different altruistic emotions and sentiments, is recognized by Aristotle, in his discussion of *eunoia* ('well-wishing' or 'goodwill' in Thomson's translation) which Aristotle contrasts to 'friendship,' *philia* (*Nichomachean Ethics*, book 9, chapter 5). Of persons who have *eunoia* towards others Aristotle says, 'All they wish is the good of those for whom they have a kindness; they would not actively help them to attain it, nor would they put themselves about for their sake' (p. 269). The contrast Aristotle is drawing is with friendship rather than with altruistic emotions (which play a minimal role within Aristotle's ethical theory), but it is the same contrast which I am drawing between well-wishing and altruistic emotions: between a sentiment which does not, and one which does (or does to a much greater degree) involve a disposition to help the other.

7 Important steps in this direction (focused primarily on the concept of generosity) — to which my brief remarks above are indebted — are Lester Hunt, 'Generosity,' and James Wallace, chapter 5 ('Benevolence') of *Virtues and Vices*. See also my 'Compassion.'

8 Immanuel Kant, *Foundations of the Metaphysics of Morals*, p. 14:398.

9 For a development of this point see Jean Baker Miller, *Toward a New Psychology of Women*.

10 One might perhaps imagine extreme forms of depression in which a person is unable to find virtually anything in the world in which to find meaning or interest, or to which he can form a commitment or attachment. His inability to be touched by the plight of others so as to be moved by sympathy or compassion would then be part of a general inability to value anything, including his own pursuits. But this case, though not without its own philosophical significance, is of a fairly serious form of emotional disturbance. It is much more than a mere state of mind or mood of depression, and so is not strictly relevant to the issue of the effect of negative moods on altruistic feelings.

11 In considering the significance of this admission for the adequacy of altruistic emotions as moral motives, it is important to point out that we are capable of counteracting, or attempting to counteract, this effect. If I know myself to be someone who, when in bad moods, is less sympathetic than usual, and if I desire that this not be the case, then I might be able to compensate for this tendency in myself. When I feel myself to be in a bad mood I can make a special effort to be attentive and receptive to others.

On another level I may attempt to understand what it means about myself that I tend to get into moods which have the effect of closing me to altruistic feelings. There may be deeper sources of this in my personality. Though it may be difficult in particular cases for me to counteract its effects, a more powerful method such as psychotherapy might get at the root of this condition.

12 W.D. Ross, *The Right and the Good*, p. 144.

13 C.D. Broad, *Five Types of Ethical Theory*, pp. 117-18.

14 Whether one could like or feel affection for another person and yet have no more inclination to feel sympathy or compassion for him or her than if one did not is another issue. All I am arguing here is that sympathy and affection do not always occur together.

15 Immanuel Kant, *The Doctrine of Virtue*, p. 63:401(Academy edition page number). Henry Sidgwick, *The Methods of Ethics*, p. 239.

16 Kant, *ibid.*, pp. 53:392. 62:400, and Kant, *Foundations of the Metaphysics of Morals*, p. 16:399.

17 Kant, *The Doctrine of Virtue, loc. cit.*

18 See, e.g., Kant, *Foundations of the Metaphysics of Morals*, pp. 15-16:399, and *The Doctrine of Virtue*, p. 62:400. In the latter passage one sees Kant's ambivalence about whether to call beneficence from duty 'love' at all, or to restrict love to what is a matter of feeling. The former view, seen in the *Foundations* passage and elsewhere, preserves Kant's roots in the Christian tradition in which love is a commandment, a duty; the latter view more accurately follows through on the Kantian view that it is strictly only conduct which can be commanded of us, and not feelings at all.

19 Kant, *The Doctrine of Virtue*, p. 63:401.

20 'For when incentives other than the law itself (such as ambition, self-love in general, yes, even a kindly instinct such as sympathy) are necessary to determine the will to conduct conformable with the law, it is merely accidental that these causes coincide with the law, for they could equally well incite its violation.' (Kant, *Religion within the Limits of Reason Alone*, p. 26.)

See also *Foundations of the Metaphysics of Morals*, p. 6:390, and *Observations on the Feeling of the Beautiful and the Sublime*, p. 57.

21 Bernard Williams articulates this notion of being moral as equally within everyone's capability as a central Kantian line of thought in 'The Idea of Equality,' from *Problems of the Self*, p. 228.

22 See, e.g., Kant, *The Doctrine of Virtue*, p. 37:379.

23 In this stage of the argument I follow Kant in using the following interchangeably: 'sense of duty', 'sense that (firm conviction that) something is morally right or wrong', 'sense of obligation', 'sense that one ought morally to do . . .', though there are in fact not insignificant differences between them.

24 Kant, *Foundations of the Metaphysics of Morals*, pp. 23-4:407-8, and elsewhere.

25 The notion is spelled out explicitly in Thomas Nagel's *The Possibility of Altruism*. It is expressed in Kant in the idea that moral considerations make an appeal to the rational nature which all human beings share.

26 Arthur Schopenhauer, *On the Basis of Morality*. All subsequent references to Schopenhauer's views are based on this work, which is a cantankerous, mostly unsympathetic, and often grossly distorted account and critique of Kant's ethics, and an attempt to replace Kant's ethics with one built on compassion. The tone, the sloppiness, and the distortions in this book have, in my opinion, led moral philosophers to neglect its several powerful insights and perspectives on moral philosophy.

27 Imagining the sympathy as actually disappearing seems to mean envisioning a scenario such as the following: Jones alters his view of Clifford or of his situation, perhaps coming to feel that the latter is blowing a minor family problem out of proportion, or that Clifford is exaggerating or dissembling in order to win Jones's sympathy, so that Jones will excuse him for turning his work in late.

III FRIENDSHIP, BENEFICENCE, AND IMPARTIALITY

1 Charles Fried's *Anatomy of Values* spells out such a conception of morality explicitly, as seen in the conjunction of the following passages:
   'The principle which specifies the content of morality is an expression of the concepts of equality, impartiality, and of regard for all persons as ends in themselves.' (p. 42)
   'The domain in which the concept of morality . . . applies is the domain of all ends and actions which impinge in any significant way on other persons.' (p. 41)
   'The interests, preferences, or desires of the agent have no special status or higher priority just because they belong to the agent; that is, an agent may not prefer his own interests as such.' (p. 42)

2 Fried, *ibid.*, sees that his conception of morality appears to pose a problem for personal relations. For example he worries whether it is morally permissible for a father to take his son fishing, in preference to taking some other child from the neighborhood (p. 54).
   Elizabeth Telfer, in 'Friendship,' shows a similar concern that friendship involves a breach of impartiality, and hence an injustice:

Those who oppose the idea of duties to friends might well go on to argue that friendship seems prima facie to involve a kind of injustice, in that it means giving preferential treatment to those who differ neither in need nor in desert – in other words so far from being duties our services to friends might be construed as positively immoral. (p. 235)

It might be argued at this point that I have not met the objection that it is unjust to view friends as having very special claims, for since friendship is, and is bound to be, very unevenly distributed, the rights which it confers will also be unevenly distributed. I think the only possible answer is that this is a case where the utility of a practice is high enough to compensate for the fact that some measure of injustice is involved in it. (p. 236)

Both Fried and Telfer believe that these worries can be met within an impartialist moral framework.

3 Sidgwick, *op. cit.*, p. 253. The view that we have natural duties and that beneficence is one of them is developed by John Rawls, *A Theory of Justice*, sections 19 and 51. I am not so much endorsing this view as citing it, as one plausible source of an alleged conflict between morality and friendship.

4 See Fried, *op. cit.*, p. 226 and elsewhere.

5 Sidgwick, *op. cit.*, p. 268.

6 Telfer, *op. cit.*, p. 235.

7 A few remarks are in order here on Bernard Williams's 'Persons, Character, and Morality', an article to which my argument of this chapter is greatly indebted. Williams recognizes impartiality and impersonality to be central to Kantian moral theory and shows that utilitarianism is not far from Kantianism in this regard. He points out that the sense we normally have of our own attachments to other people, or to the projects and endeavors which give meaning to our lives, can clash with this impartialist perspective, and that the Kantian claim to be the pervasive and final arbiter to our projects and actions is not acceptable.

The weakness in Williams's argument lies in its tendency to accept the Kantian identification of impartiality with morality itself, thus portraying the possible clash between personal relations (or personal projects in general) and impartiality as a clash between those relations and morality as a whole. This alarming view is not necessary, since it is not morality itself which clashes with personal relations but the false Kantian/impartialist conception of it. Morality, in its complexity, itself places limitations on impartiality and gives a proper place for personal relations (and other personal commitments) generally outside the bounds of impartiality's demands.

This is in no way to deny the potential clashes between our personal commitments and impartialist morality; but it is to minimize their significance in the overall scheme of things.

Nevertheless, Williams's view finds it difficult to take fully seriously those situations in which impartiality is properly demanded of us, compelling us to overlook personal ties even though it might be painful to do so.

Williams's implied view that morality demands the impartial perspective of us in a global way leads him to an unnecessary attack on morality itself. In general he fails to distinguish in any clear way between morality and the Kantian conception of it; so his attack on the Kantian conception becomes an attack on morality itself. This is a lapse in Williams's article, for in most of Williams's other writings on ethics he tends towards a view much closer to my own, in which a fundamental demarcation of the realm of the moral lies in the distinction between concern for others and concern for self. See, e.g., his *Morality* (esp. chapter 1), 'Egoism and Altruism' in *Problems of the Self*, and 'Utilitarianism and Moral Self-Indulgence.' Williams is also concerned to emphasize a related point that there is no single unified concept of morality.

8 Telfer, *op. cit.*, p. 235.
9 This does not mean that one always enjoys drinking with a friend more than drinking with someone one does not know. It is not a matter of the degree of pleasure but of its kind, of the meaning of the experience to the person.
10 This argument is made in my 'Friendship and Moral Commitment.'
11 This sort of justification is one to which, as mentioned in note 2, both Telfer and Fried appeal in their defense of beneficence to friends, in the face of Kantian worries.
12 A detailed defense of this point is made in my 'Friendship and Moral Commitment.'
13 John Rawls's 'Two Concepts of Rules,' pp. 3-32 is the seminal work on this reconciliation.
14 In *Rights and Persons*, A.I. Melden has argued powerfully that the 'institution' model is inappropriate, and distorting of the moral nature of family relationships and of promises.
15 Nicholas Rescher, *Unselfishness*, pp. 77-8.
16 The line of thought presented here, and some of the response to it, was suggested to me by Bernard Williams, in private conversation. In general the next sections owe much to this brief conversation and to Williams's three lectures on 'Ethical Theory and the Individual,' delivered at Johns Hopkins University in March 1977. These sections are also strongly influenced by Stanley Cavell's 'The Claim to Rationality' (PhD, Harvard University, 1961). This has now been published as *The Claim of Reason*.
17 This line of thought owes much to Cavell's 'Rules and Reasons,' chapter 8 of 'The Claim to Rationality' (chapter 11 of *The Claim of Reason*), mentioned above. There Cavell argues that knowing that I ought to keep my promises, or more generally my commitments, is fundamental to being a competent moral agent at all. It is not a judgment which I make, say in some particular case, on the

basis of some scheme or principles of justification which tells me that I ought to keep my promises. On the contrary I could not even understand what a moral principle was unless I already understood such things as that I ought to keep my promises and honor my commitments.

I am suggesting a similar argument with regard to impartiality and its related moral conceptions (fairness, justice): that it is a basic moral notion, an understanding of the general range of applicability of which is part of being a competent moral agent. I recognize that this argument, to be adequately made out, would require a good deal more expansion.

IV FRIENDSHIP AS A MORAL PHENOMENON

1 On this issue see Anna Freud, 'A Form of Altruism,' in *The Ego and the Mechanisms of Defense*; Max Scheler, *The Nature of Sympathy*, pp. 42-3 and *passim*; and Blum, Homiak, Housman, and Scheman, 'Altruism and Women's Oppression.'

2 Bernard Mayo, *Ethics and the Moral Life*, p. 198.

3 This line of thought should make one suspicious of an interesting argument put forward by Bernard Williams in *Morality*, chapter 1, that a person who is generally selfish but who cares for just one person could be led to extend his caring to others, the transition from one to many being a fairly natural one (a matter of quantity rather than quality), and the gap between one and many being much smaller than that between none and one. If my own argument is right, then the kind of caring which a selfish person has for only one person is likely to be minimal and deficient, and not such as could be readily extended to a genuine caring for others.

I am not denying here that a person could care genuinely and deeply about only one person, but only that such a person could be a fundamentally selfish person, essentially unresponsive to the weal and woe of others.

4 A selfish person will have many relationships which are not friendships at all, but which are sustained solely by his deriving some pleasure or advantage from them. If he does not wish the other well at all, nor really like him or enjoy being with him, then there is no friendship. But if these elements do exist, then even if the man's primary concern with the other is the advantage he derives from him there is still some sort of friendship. And so the basically selfish person can have friendships of a minimal sort. (I follow Aristotle's account of friendship here: *Nichomachean Ethics*, books 8 and 9, and in particular John Cooper's reconstruction of that account in 'Aristotle on the Forms of Friendship.')

5 Part of the problem here is that the language and antitheses of 'activity/passivity,' 'doing something/something happening to one,' are ill-suited to express how our friendship is a reflection of

ourselves morally. This issue is taken up explicitly in chapter VIII.
6 The previous and following sections owe their existence to some
   well-taken criticisms by Jennifer Radden of a previous draft. I
   fear, however, that I have inadequately addressed the issues raised
   in those criticisms.
7 This conception of caring is powerfully spelled out by M. Mayeroff
   in *On Caring*.
8 This unhealthy form of pseudo-friendship is described by Scheler,
   op. cit., p. 42.
9 See chapter III, pp. 55-7, concerning good to others within and
   outside of friendship.
10 The general inapplicability of the notion of self-sacrifice and the
   limitations of the concepts of egoism and altruism in the context
   of friendship have wider implications for moral and social philosophy. For it can be argued that such concepts are misleading in
   the context of any genuinely cooperative endeavor, i.e., one in
   which there is a shared goal among the participants, a goal regarded
   by them as a good, and thus a good which is in essence shared
   rather than being merely an aggregate of individual and private
   goods. Such a cooperative enterprise, even if it can be seen also as
   fostering the individual and private interests of its participants,
   becomes a context of meaning which is essential to understanding
   the significance of actions which individuals take within that
   common endeavor. Acting for the sake of the good-of-cooperation
   is here analogous to acting out of friendship. (In fact friendship
   can be seen as a type of cooperative relationship, on this definition.) It cannot typically be seen as involving self-sacrifice; nor,
   on the usual understanding, can concepts of egoism and altruism
   be usefully applied. For a discussion of this perspective, on the
   concepts of egoism and altruism see Alasdair MacIntyre, 'Egoism
   and Altruism.' In 'Community,' chapter 5 of *The Poverty of
   Liberalism*, R.P. Wolff makes an important beginning to defining
   concepts necessary for conceptualizing cooperative relationships
   and endeavors.
11 Soren Kierkegaard, *Works of Love*, part 1, chapter 2B.
12 Kant, *The Doctrine of Virtue*, pp. 140-6:468-73, and *Lectures on
   Ethics*, pp. 200-9.
13 John Cooper, 'Aristotle on the Forms of Friendship,' p. 620, has
   argued that Aristotle uses the concept of friendship (*philia*) to refer
   to many different forms of social connection between people
   ('civic friendship'), all of which are different ways in which, or
   contexts in which, we come to care about another for his own sake.
14 Some reference to C.D. Broad's 'Egoism as a Theory of Human
   Motives' is in order here. Broad is one of the few writers I have run
   across who distinguishes out conditional altruism as a particular
   type of motive. He calls it 'self-referential,' distinguishing it from
   'self-regarding' motives. The former are genuinely altruistic, he
   acknowledges, though their operation is dependent on an 'egoistic

motive-stimulant,' such as a pre-existing relationship to the other person.

Yet Broad confuses the issue by implying that it is useful to group self-referential motives together with self-regarding ones to yield a possible and plausible definition of psychological egoism (i.e., the view that all motives are either self-regarding or self-referential — see pp. 109, 111, 112). He thus implies, seemingly contrary to his original definition, that self-referential motives are best seen as in some way egoistic.

It may be that Broad believes that all self-referential motives are as a matter of fact accompanied by egoistic motives of the self-regarding kind. (See, e.g., p. 108.) As a matter of empirical fact this does not seem true, and Broad's support for it seems weak. For example Broad is certainly wrong (as well as sexist) in saying that a mother's desire for her child's happiness is always accompanied by 'the desire that other women shall envy her as the mother of a happy, healthy, and popular child' (p. 108). In any case, even if the general claim were true, it would not make the self-referential motive itself any less genuinely altruistic.

Broad's discussion seems to involve, though not consistently, a kind of universalist bias — a tendency to class other-regarding motives which are not grounded in universal considerations (e.g., love or duty to human beings simply *qua* human beings) as somehow egoistic or otherwise morally deficient.

15 Charles Fried's discussion of love (which he sees as very akin to friendship, differing primarily in intensity) in *Anatomy of Values* illustrates this false view. Fried explains love almost entirely in terms of the willingness to give of oneself to the other beyond what is deserved (pp. 77-80). He gives insufficient emphasis to the role of liking, enjoying being with the other, etc. Sidgwick in his discussion of love warns against precisely this error: *The Methods of Ethics*, pp. 244-5.

16 Nor, I would add, is a friendship in which the friend's moral virtue is the grounds of the friendship necessarily a morally superior form of friendship. Such a grounding does not seem to me what we mean by 'caring for another for his own sake.' If this is right it seems to me a point against Aristotle's view of friendship; but I cannot be certain of this, for the interpretation of what he means by love (*philia*) for another for his own sake is not entirely clear to me. On this see John Cooper, *op. cit.*, and 'Friendship and the Good in Aristotle,' pp. 290-315.

17 The arguments of Joseph Butler in *Fifteen Sermons Preached at the Rolls Chapel* (especially the Preface and sermon) and of C.D. Broad in 'Egoism as a Theory of Human Motives' (note 14) seem to me particularly worthy of note here. These arguments are not, however (in my opinion), conclusive against more subtle forms of egoism, such as in 'self-realization' theories.

V DIRECT ALTRUISM, UNIVERSALIZABILITY, AND CONSISTENCY

1   The universalizability implication which regarding an act as morally right carries with it is complicated. Peter Winch has argued, I believe successfully, that in situations with competing moral considerations, to regard a certain act as the right one to perform does not require one to believe that the act would be right for any agent similarly situated. It requires only the belief that any such agent should take seriously the moral considerations which one regards as present in the situation. If another agent, having conscientiously allowed those considerations to weigh with him, sees a different act as right, one is not required to regard him as having acted wrongly. ('The Universalizability of Moral Judgments' in Peter Winch, *Ethics and Action*.)

   If this argument is right the universalizability involved in regarding an act as right is, strictly speaking, a universality regarding the considerations which must weigh with any similarly situated agent, rather than a universality regarding the actual act itself. Of course in many cases there will not be, so to speak, any room for someone both to conscientiously take into account the considerations which one regards as grounding the rightness of one's action, and yet come up with some alternative action as right. In such cases universalizability will indeed require one to view any action other than the one which one regards as right, as wrong for any similarly situated agent.

2   Mayo, *op. cit.*, pp. 193-4. I do not endorse the characterization of this view as 'existentialist.'

   It should be noted that Mayo's interest in this view is in the alleged uniqueness of the situation facing the moral agent, rather than in the uniqueness of the good of individuals. In focusing on the latter I am making use of this quote in a way which Mayo would not necessarily approve.

3   E.g., see *ibid.*, chapter 9.

4   Ross, *op. cit.*, p. 163.

5   It is beyond the scope of this work to enquire which of the two interpretations is the better one of Kant on the whole. Two recent works on Kant argue that Kant's categorical imperative or universalization test cannot coherently be understood to do any more than provide a test or criterion for morally right acts; that is, it cannot do what the strong universality interpretation envisions – namely by itself generate morally correct principles. R.P. Wolff, *The Autonomy of Reason*. Onora Nell, *Acting on Principle*.

6   Murdoch, *op. cit.*, pp. 1, 2.

7   Sidgwick, *op. cit.*, p. 225.

8   Bernard Williams, in 'Utilitarianism and Moral Self-Indulgence,' makes something like these points also.

   Sidgwick too recognizes that acting virtuously does not require regarding one's act *as* virtuous, or right. See *ibid.*

9 To be precise, those actions which are required, hence generated, by strong universality are also generated by weak universality. But what I am concerned with here are those actions regarded merely as permissible but not required, which hence conform to weak but not to strong universality.

10 On the weak universality interpretation of the Kantian view, it is not really possible to determine the rightness of an act independent of the agent who intends or proposes to perform it, in that it is the particular agent's maxim of action which is tested for its universalizability.

11 Broad, *Five Types of Ethical Theory*, p. 118.

12 Ross, *op. cit.*, pp. 162-3.

13 Kant shows a more accurate understanding of the nature of poverty and its relationship to charity when he says, 'The ability to practice beneficence, which depends on property, follows largely from the injustice of government, which favors certain men and so introduces an inequality of wealth that makes others need help' (*The Doctrine of Virtue*, p. 122:453).

14 I owe this distinction to Mercer who calls it 'helping' and 'assisting,' *op. cit.*, p. 100.

15 I owe much in this section's discussion to Richard Norman.

16 Mercer, *op. cit.*, pp. 105-6.

VI ALTRUISTIC EMOTION, REASON, AND PERCEPTION

1 See Kant, *The Doctrine of Virtue*, pp. 34-5:376-7, where it is asserted that there is a kind of moral happiness or pleasure which comes from consciousness of having done one's duty.

2 Thomas Nagel, *The Possibility of Altruism*, pp. 79-80.

3 *Ibid.*, pp. 15-16.

4 *Ibid.*, p. 1.

5 This view can be given an egoist rendering, as Nagel does in the following passage:

> Egoism holds that each individual's reasons for acting and possible reasons for acting, must arise from his own interests and desires, however those interests may be defined. The interests of one person can on this view motivate another or provide him with a reason only if they are connected with his interests or are objects of some sentiment of his, like sympathy, pity, or benevolence. (*The Possibility of Altruism*, p. 84)

However, though Nagel is not entirely clear about this, in general he allows a distinction between a desire or interest which is egoist, in the strict and most useful sense of being a desire for something for oneself, and a desire or interest which is genuinely for the good of others for their own sake. Thus the above passage represents a lesser strain in Nagel's thought.

6   Nagel, *op. cit.*, p. 1 and elsewhere.

7   This description is drawn from, though it is not meant actually to reflect, the character of Rosamond in George Eliot's *Middlemarch*, especially in her encounter with Dorothea in chapter 81.

8   Needless to say, a person can apprehend a situation very clearly as involving someone's weal and woe and yet not act altruistically. For instance, in example 1, I might very clearly perceive the woman's discomfort and yet fail to give up my seat to her, not because I feel that I would be equally uncomfortable standing up, but simply because I do not want to. Apprehending weal and woe at stake is not a sufficient condition for acting with beneficent intention, since the agent may lack the altruistic motivation. It is only a necessary condition.

9   I am assuming here that the sympathy-warranting description is accurate. Of course in many situations in which sympathy is not warranted (e.g., the student is lying in order to get the teacher to excuse him for failing to do his work on time) a non-sympathy-warranting description will be accurate.

10 Kant, *Foundations of the Metaphysics of Morals*, pp. 14-15: 398-9.

11 Kant's discussion of this part of the passage has been examined in chapter II, pp. 21-2.

12 One could, in response to this argument, say that Kant's man of duty might have an especially strong and wide-ranging notion of duty, so that he regards it as his duty to perform acts of beneficence which, strictly speaking, are not matters of duty at all, and which include the acts which I claim the altruistic agent will perform. This man's notion of duty will cover actions which are supererogatory rather than dutiful in the strict sense. But such a stringent sense of duty can not be grounded in rational considerations alone, ones applicable to all rational beings. In any case, one can not derive a general argument regarding duty from cases of supererogatory conceptions of duty; for not all persons who have a sense of duty have such a strict sense of duty, nor does strict attention to their duty compel them to do so. Thus an especially strong sense of duty will not address the criticism of Kant's views being made here.

13 Murdoch, *op. cit.* Murdoch includes existentialism, Kantianism, and, in a general sort of way, most contemporary British moral theory in this critique. See also her 'Vision and Choice in Morality,' p. 39.

VII THE INTRINSIC VALUE OF ALTRUISTIC EMOTIONS

1   It should be noted that my argument, that the actions must express certain emotions in order to convey the full appropriate good to

the recipient, depends not so much on the actual emotional motivation as on the emotional motivation as perceived by the recipient. I think that for the kinds of cases we are discussing, we can regard the actual motivation and the perceived motivation as the same, though in some cases it might be morally appropriate to attempt to disguise one's true motivation. In any case this complication does not, I think, seriously affect the argument.

2 John Rawls in *A Theory of Justice*, pp. 338-9, draws the distinction between actual beneficence (present and future) and the sense of security, confidence, and trust attendant upon knowing that one can count on others to come to one's aid when one is in need. Rawls thus notes a value which goes beyond the direct receipt of beneficence, though I will argue below that such a value, in not going beyond that involved in the disposition to beneficence, fails to articulate the full value of sympathy and concern. The context for Rawls's discussion is a rationale for the duty of mutual aid. Rawls argues that it would be a good to individual members of society if the duty of mutual aid were observed. In contrast to my own argument, Rawls's takes place on a social level — what is good to the individual is that fellow citizens generally have a disposition of beneficence (connected with an acknowledgment of the duty of mutual aid) towards him. I have claimed only that it is a good to an individual that another individual have such a disposition.

3 Functioning on the same social level as Rawls, R.M. Titmuss in *The Gift Relationship* — a discussion of the social and moral dimensions of the giving of blood — seems to me to go beyond Rawls in noting the intrinsic value of altruistic emotions and sentiments in non-personal contexts. Titmuss's discussion is a complex one: I will mention only two of his major conclusions.

Titmuss contrasts two systems for the organization of giving of blood. In the 'voluntary' system it is forbidden to sell blood, so that all giving of blood is uncompensated and in that sense voluntary. In the 'market' system, blood is treated as a market commodity; it can be purchased in a number of ways, and persons who give blood can be compensated. Titmuss argues for the superiority of the voluntary system on two grounds: first, more blood of a higher quality is generated; second, the voluntary system encourages, while the market system discourages, a sense of social solidarity, altruism, responsibility towards others, and responsiveness towards the needs of others, in and between members of society personally unknown to one another.

Titmuss, like Rawls, notes the beneficence value of mutual aid (voluntary blood-giving), i.e., the value of the blood to its recipients. And both Rawls and Titmuss see the value of the principle of mutual aid as transcending this concrete beneficence. Both see it as involving a value to the society in general.

But Titmuss goes beyond Rawls in seeing intrinsic value in the social sentiments, attitudes, and emotions which he is discussing.

They are good in themselves, beyond the good attached to them as derived from being productive of beneficent acts. It is a good to us merely that someone, unknown to us, cares about our weal and woe.

Titmuss's view is worth mentioning also because he shows the importance of the question of the forms of social organization which encourage and discourage the altruistic emotions. I have mentioned something of this issue in chapter 4 in the discussion of conditional altruism. But my own endeavor in this book shares with most mainstream moral philosophy the failure to investigate the social conditions of morally good conduct, an inquiry which has a philosophical as well as an empirical dimension.

4 This insight and others regarding the good of concern derive, for me, from Nicolai Hartmann's discussion of 'Brotherly Love' especially p. 273.
5 James Wallace, *Virtues and Vices*, pp. 154-5. Wallace's discussion of the good of benevolence is valuable on these points.
6 Accounts of the good of friendship often fail to bring out the inherent good of being the object of another's care, concern, and love. For example, Telfer, in her account of the value of friendship, mentions four factors. (1) Promotion of the general welfare. (2) Usefulness to the friend (beneficence). (3) Pleasures of friendship (e.g., of shared activity). (4) Life-enhancement: friendship enhances life by increasing the things to which we are attached and in which our emotions are bound up, by enhancing our involvement and absorption in activities shared with friends, and by increasing the range of our knowledge of other people and their needs and natures, and of other points of view (and Telfer compares this last with something which can be gained by reading a great work of literature). (Telfer, *op. cit.*)

But this list omits — or at least fails clearly to articulate — the good to the friend in the fact that his friend cares about him or loves him.
7 There is a trace of individualism$_1$ in the view of Wallace's mentioned above (p. 150) that altruistic sentiments are a good to their recipients because they support their sense of self-worth, and in a similar argument regarding friendship made by John Cooper in 'Friendship and the Good of Aristotle' pp. 302-10 — that a central good to us of friendship is that it affirms our self-worth. Both Wallace's and Cooper's accounts are grounded in Rawls's emphasis in *A Theory of Justice* on self-respect as 'perhaps the most important primary good' (p. 440).

The basic insight of these views seems to me entirely correct and important; but there is a tendency for it to obscure the fact that the good to us in being the object of an altruistic sentiment is not only having our self-worth affirmed but knowing ourselves to be of value to a particular other person. Rawls's insight goes beyond the individualism of much traditional liberal political theory, with its strong emphasis on individual autonomy, by recognizing that others' valuing of oneself is normally required in order for one to be able to sustain a sense of one's own self-worth. Yet this insight does not quite accord a fully autonomous and intrinsic value to a relationship between persons, or to a relationally-defined attitude.

8   Kant, *Lectures on Ethics*, p. 200.

9   Kant, *Observations on the Feeling of the Beautiful and the Sublime*, pp. 58-9.

10   Because of this focus on Romanticism Kant does not sufficiently distinguish what I call altruistic emotions from emotions as conceived by the Romanticist view.

11   J.O. Urmson, 'Saints and Heroes,' p. 208.

12   The account given here of supererogation draws mainly on Rawls, *op. cit.*, especially pp. 117, 191, 435, 478; Feinberg, 'Supererogation and Rules'; Urmson, 'Saints and Heroes'; and G.R. Grice, *The Grounds of Moral Judgment*, chapter 4.

13   Feinberg, *op. cit.*, p. 399.

14   Something like this point is made by Feinberg (*op. cit.*) when he argues that doing favors for someone 'is not similarly commensurable with duty' (p. 397), and, more generally, that notions of duty and obligation apply within institutional-like contexts which cover only a part of the moral life.

15   A few remarks on Hume's moral theory (as expounded in *Enquiry Concerning the Principles of Morals*) are in order here, for Hume gives a central role to emotions in general and to the altruistic virtues (see e.g., pp. 9, 10). In addition, Hume distinguishes from the 'utility' of these virtues (i.e., their leading to acts of beneficence), a second source of their value, namely their 'agreeableness':

> It will also be allowed that the very softness and tenderness of the sentiment [of benevolence], its engaging endearments, its fond expressions, its delicate attentions and all that flow of mutual confidence and regard which enters into a warm attachment of love and friendship — it will be allowed, I say, that these feelings being delightful in themselves, are necessarily communicated to the spectators and melt them into the same fondness and delicacy. (p. 80)

Here Hume recognizes an intrinsic value in benevolence, not merely a utilitarian one. Yet this value is expressed less in terms of the good to the recipient of the benevolence than in the pleasingness to someone contemplating the sentiment in another person. This accords with Hume's characteristic approach to moral philosophy, which is from the point of view of, as he says, 'the spectator' (a person approving or disapproving of traits or actions in others) rather than that of the agent or the recipient of actions. Thus, even though Hume acknowledges and gives an important role to the fact that human beings are capable of sympathy with others, or concern with their happiness, this element in human nature is given moral importance not so much as the foundation of particular virtues or morally desirable emotions, but rather as the source of our disinterested moral approbation of certain qualities of character. (On this aspect of Hume's moral philosophy, see Mercer, *op. cit.*, chapters 2-4.)

16 Note that I have not argued here that infatuation, liking, etc., fail to be morally relevant because we are entirely passive with respect to them, and have no control over whether we have them. For one thing, I do not think this characterization is entirely true. For another, as I will argue in the next chapter, these are misleading as criteria for what can have moral significance and value.

17 In 'Morality and the Emotions' (in *Problems of the Self*) Bernard Williams says,

> Is it certain that one who receives good treatment from another more appreciates it, thinks the better of the giver, if he knows it to be the result of application of principle, rather than the product of emotional response? He may have needed, not the benefits of universal law, but some human gesture. It may be said that this is obviously true enough in many cases but has nothing to do with morality; it just shows that people place other sorts of value on human conduct besides moral value. Well this may be said, and Kant indeed said it, but it leads to an uncomfortable dilemma. Either the recipient ought to prefer the ministrations of the moral man to the human gesture, which seems a mildly insane requirement; or, alternatively, if it be admitted that it is perfectly proper and rational of the recipient to have the preference he has, the value of moral men becomes an open question, and we can reasonably entertain the proposal that we should not seek to produce moral men, or very many of them, but rather those, whatever their inconsistencies, who make the human gesture. While there is something in that conclusion there cannot be anything in it for Kant (p. 227).

While I agree with Williams that looking at Kantian morality from the standpoint of the recipient finds that morality wanting, I believe he goes astray in implying that when we give importance to an aspect of human life which cannot be encompassed within a Kantian framework, that importance will be non-moral. (This tendency in Williams's work was noted and criticized in chapter III, note 7.)

Williams speaks of a 'human gesture.' Altruistic emotions are one kind of human gesture, and I have tried to show why they bring about a good to someone which is not brought about by acting from duty or principle, and thus why someone might prefer that sort of human gesture to action from universal principle. But, contrary to Williams, I have tried to make it clear that the altruistic emotion has *moral* value, which not every kind of human gesture which we might value (e.g., a personal feeling) possesses. Hence to question the value of the Kantian way of being moral, at least in certain circumstances, is not to question the value of moral persons altogether, as Williams seems to do.

18 This is not to say we never can rank virtues in terms of importance. For example, we can say that honesty and compassion are in general superior to punctuality and amiability.

19 Ross's argument is found mostly on pp. 164-5.

20 In some cases it is the same act which can be prompted by either motive, e.g., a case in which the non-motivational aspect of the altruistic emotion is not a good to the recipient. But this will be a restricted class of cases, and, more important, a general theory of the superiority of duty to feeling cannot be built on it.

21 In earlier chapters, Mercer discusses other aspects of sympathy in Hume's and Adam Smith's moral philosophies, in particular sympathy as a source of moral judgment. (See note 15 above, on Hume.) Mercer finds this view of the moral role of sympathy basically unsatisfactory, and it is for this reason that he turns in the later chapter to a consideration of sympathy as a moral motive.

22 Mercer, *op. cit.*, p. 114.

23 *Ibid.*, citing G. Nowell-Smith, *Ethics*, p. 258.

24 On p. 123 Mercer seems almost to recognize the sort of point I am arguing for here, when he says, 'sympathy affects the *nature* of our help.' But this turns out to mean that sympathy allows us to understand better what someone needs, and thus to help him in a more appropriate way. The 'help' here is still seen as entirely distinct from the emotion which prompts it, so it is still the value of the beneficence itself which Mercer is talking about, rather than an intrinsic value of the sympathy.

25 *Ibid.*, pp. 101-2.

26 *Ibid.*, p. 102.

VIII WILL, EMOTION, AND THE SELF

1 Kant, *The Doctrine of Virtue*, p. 37:379.

2 This view is connected with what Kant and other philosophers regard as the autonomy and freedom required by morality, i.e., that in being moral it is only and wholly ourselves on whom we are dependent for our action; to be dependent on anything outside ourselves is to be unfree, 'heteronomous,' and not moral. But it is only our will, our capacity for rational choice, which is fully and wholly ourselves.

3 Sidgwick, *op. cit.*, p. 239.

4 Robert Solomon, *The Passions*, p. 11.

5 The views being discussed here may seem to have strayed too far from anything like what can be found in Kant to be usefully called Kantian. But the point is that I am examining resources possessed by a Kantian outlook (as described in the beginning of the chapter)

to attempt to accommodate the presumption that our values and attitudes reflect on us morally. The use of the term 'Kantian' in the first half of the chapter should be understood in this way.

6 The argument in the remainder of this section draws on P.L. Gardiner, 'On Assenting to a Moral Principle.'

7 Williams, 'Morality and the Emotions,' in *Problems of the Self*, p. 227.

8 For arguments regarding the impossibility of a purely act-dispositional account of character traits, see G.H. von Wright, *The Varieties of Goodness*, chapter 7, and Marcia Homiak, *Character, Virtue, and Self-Respect*, chapter 1.

9 A contemptuous attitude cannot be identified with the attitude of superiority discussed above. The former is *focused on* the persons who are its object, whereas the latter is *about* the persons (regarding them as inferior, etc.) without being so substantially focused on them. So, for example, failing to pay attention to the persons in question is more a manifestation of a sense of superiority than it is of contempt. (I owe this point to Martin Andic.)

10 The argument of this section draws on Harry Frankfurt, 'Identification and Externality.' Frankfurt argues that some passions can be regarded as external to the self.

11 *Ibid.*, p. 241.

12 *Ibid.*, pp. 241-2.

13 Solomon, *op. cit.*, p. 193.

14 *Ibid.*, p. 186.

15 *Ibid.*, p. 58. It should be said that despite such tendencies to exaggeration, Solomon's book is a sustained and powerful attack on the Kantian conception of emotions, and is an important contribution to an adequate conception of emotions.

16 The distinction I am drawing here with regard to actions comes from Elizabeth Beardsley, 'Moral Worth and Moral Credit.'

17 A condition for moral assessment in either sense is that the person in question be, one might say, a moral agent, someone capable of acknowledging the force of moral considerations. This would exclude a person with certain sorts of moral/psychological aberration and incapacity, such as a psychopath. Such a person is not simply unresponsive to the weal and woe of others (and to other moral considerations) in the way that a selfish person is. In addition he has a type of deficiency which makes him incapable of grasping moral considerations at all, which is not true of the selfish person.

This point applies to the actions of the psychopath as well as to his emotions. If he acts in a way which harms the interests of others he is not blameworthy for this, and it does not reflect on him morally, even though he acted from a morally bad motive, i.e., harming another in order to promote his own interest. For he is not really a moral agent at all.

The example of the psychopath is not uncomplicated and more

needs to be said about how to characterize the nature of his moral incapacity. On this see Hervey Cleckley, *The Mask of Sanity*.

18 The notion that self-control is fundamental to morality is a not unfamiliar one. 'The various virtues, it may be said, are so many forms of self-control' (von Wright, *op. cit.*, p. 149).

19 A contemporary statement of this view can be found in the writings of Stuart Hampshire, who has elaborated a subtle and powerful moral philosophy and moral psychology connecting morality with will, and emphasizing control over unfit emotions as central to this conception. In addition, especially in *Freedom of the Individual*, the notion of reason, and the grounding of emotions as much as possible in reason, plays a central role. (See also *Thought and Action*, and 'Commitment and Imagination.')

Though such views represent the dominant tendency in Hampshire's writings, some passages lend support to the anti-Kantian views which I am developing here.

> the concept of action itself is [not] by itself sufficient to mark the domain of the essential human virtues. One has before one, for reflection and comment, whether in one's own person or in the person of another, always a whole person, including the way he thinks and expresses his thoughts and feelings, the things he notices and neglects, the attitudes he adopts, the feelings he restrains and the feelings to which he allows free play, the words that he chooses to use. (*Thought and Action*, p. 91)

20 Sidgwick, *op. cit.*, p. 239.

21 Kant, *The Doctrine of Virtue*, p. 126:456.

22 In the sections (34 and 35) from which this quote is taken, Kant seems in some way to locate the feelings in the will itself. I am not certain how he can do this, in any case the more dominant picture in these sections is the one seen in the passage, in which the feelings are not themselves part of the will, nor directly available to it.

23 I am overlooking the fact that for Kant the *point* of arousing this sympathy is to become more dutiful in our actions. I am considering the goal to be the arousal of the feelings themselves.

24 A good description and discussion of this sort of 'aristocratic' insensitivity to the sufferings of social inferiors is given in Alexis de Tocqueville's *Democracy in America*, vol. 2, book 3, chapter 1. ('Madame de Sevigny had no clear notion of suffering in anyone who was not a person of quality.')

25 Even if a person does not have the appropriate orientation of his being-towards-others, or if he does have such obstacles to sympathy within him, it is still possible, though much less likely, that confrontation with misery and suffering would have the effect which Kant wants. For example, it could shake a certain kind of person out of his complacency and narrow concerns. He might come to realize that his life had been built around a fairly limited outlook on the world (primarily because he had not been exposed

to much else), one which had left no serious place for the fact of extreme misery, deprivation, and oppression which some people face.

Yet, for such a person this reaction would not be typical. More likely the person's moral outlook would allow him to assimilate the experience without being moved or shaken by it. He might be momentarily affected, but could think, 'The people are in poor-houses, debtor's prisons, etc., because they cannot do any better for themselves.'

In any case, no matter what the reaction, an understanding of it will have to take into account the person's being-towards-others.

26 See Kant, *The Doctrine of Virtue*, p. 125:455.

27 We can imagine two sorts of person here. One is already generally sympathetic, but his sympathy has been flagging lately, and he is looking for a revitalization of it. The second person is not so sympathetic, but regrets this and would like to become more sympathetic. The experience Kant refers to will not trigger an existing reservoir of sympathy in the latter case. But if the man genuinely acknowledges the duties of beneficence, and is as I have described him, then he is at least open to feeling sympathy in a way that someone else might not be.

28 It should be noted that even if momentary sympathy does not automatically turn into a fuller and more substantial sympathy, nevertheless it could have the effect which Kant himself is talking about in the passage, namely strengthening one's resolve to act from duty of beneficence.

29 Sidgwick, *op. cit.*, p. 239.

30 Mercer, *op. cit.*, p. 105.

31 Mercer points out that some emotions, e.g. fear or anger, can hardly ever be directly summoned up, but rightly claims that sympathy is not one of these. *Ibid.*, p. 108.

32 *Ibid.*, pp. 108-9.

33 This view is meant as a corrective to a dominant view of emotions, found in Descartes as well as most empiricist philosophers, which regards emotions as feeling-states and thus as only contingently connected with their objects. A. Kenny, *Action, Emotion, and Will*, discusses this conception of emotions.

34 Williams, 'Morality and the Emotions', in *Problems of the Self*, p. 224. This conception is emphasized by Hampshire in *Freedom of the Individual*.

35 Hampshire, *Freedom of the Individual*, p. 93.

36 That traits of character involve patterns of behavior seems evident. That they involve attitudes and ways of regarding persons and situations is argued by M. Mandelbaum, *The Phenomenology of Moral Experience*, chapter 4, especially p. 144, and is a major focus of Homiak's interpretation of Aristotle in *op. cit.*

37 Two things should be said here. First of all I do not regard the attribution of a trait of character as implying the absolute

impossibility of change, of ridding oneself of that trait. Persons can undergo extremely dramatic personal changes which involve change of character. But such cases seem to me unusual. They comprise a minor portion of instances in which substantial moral change takes place within one's behavior, attitudes, or ways of regarding others.

Second, it may be worth pointing out that for Aristotle, who is generally regarded as the foremost exponent of a philosophy of virtue and character, traits of character are extremely resistant to change. In fact, Aristotle often implies that possessing virtues is almost entirely dependent on having had a certain kind of upbringing, without which one would find it nearly impossible to acquire those virtues.

BIBLIOGRAPHY

Aristotle, *Nichomachean Ethics*, trans. J.A.K. Thomson, Baltimore, Maryland, Penguin Books, 1955.

Beardsley, Elizabeth, 'Moral Worth and Moral Credit,' *Philosophical Review*, July 1957.

Blum, L.A., 'Compassion,' in Amelie Rorty (ed.), *Explaining Emotions*, Berkeley, University of California Press, 1980.

Blum, L.A., 'Friendship and Moral Commitment,' unpublished manuscript.

Blum, L.A., Homiak, M., Housman, J., and Scheman, N., 'Altruism and Women's Oppression,' in C. Gould and M. Wartofsky (eds.), *Women and Philosophy*, New York, G.P. Putnam's Sons, 1976.

Broad, C.D., 'Egoism as a Theory of Human Motives,' *Hibbert Journal*, vol. 48, October 1949-July 1950.

Broad, C.D., *Five Types of Ethical Theory*, New Jersey, Littlefield, Adams, 1965.

Butler, Joseph, *Fifteen Sermons Preached at the Rolls Chapel*, New York, Bobbs-Merrill, 1950.

Cavell, Stanley, *The Claim of Reason: Wittgenstein, Skepticism, Morality and Tragedy*, New York, Oxford University Press, 1979.

Cleckley, Hervey, *The Mask of Sanity: An Attempt to Clarify some Issues about the So-Called Psychopathic Personality*, 4th edition, St Louis, C.V. Mosby, 1964.

Cooper, John, 'Aristotle on the Forms of Friendship,' *Review of Metaphysics*, June 1977.

Cooper, John, 'Friendship and the Good in Aristotle,' *Philosophical Review*, July 1977.

Dreiser, Theodore, *An American Tragedy*, New York, Dell, 1959.

Eliot, George, *Middlemarch*, Harmondsworth, Penguin, 1965.

Falk, W.D., 'Morality, Self, and Others,' in G. Dworkin and J. Thompson (eds.), New York, Harper & Row, 1968.

Feinberg, Joel, 'Supererogation and Rules,' in G. Dworkin and J.

Thompson (eds.), *Ethics*, New York, Harper & Row, 1968.

Frankfurt, Harry, 'Identification and Externality,' in Amelie Rorty (ed.), *The Identities of Persons*, Berkeley, University of California Press, 1976.

Freud, Anna, *The Ego and the Mechanisms of Defense*, revised edition, New York, International Universities Press, 1966.

Fried, Charles, *Anatomy of Values*, Cambridge, Mass., Harvard University Press, 1970.

Gardiner, P.L., 'On Assenting to a Moral Principle,' in G. Dworkin and J. Thompson (eds.), *Ethics*, New York, Harper & Row, 1968.

Gregor, Mary, *Laws of Freedom*, Oxford, Basil Blackwell, 1963.

Grice, G.R., *The Grounds of Moral Judgment*, Cambridge University Press, 1967.

Hampshire, Stuart, 'Commitment and Imagination,' in M. Black (ed.), *The Morality of Scholarship*, Ithaca, New York, Cornell University Press, 1967.

Hampshire, Stuart, *Freedom of the Individual*, New York, Harper & Row, 1965.

Hampshire, Stuart, *Thought and Action*, London, Chatto & Windus, 1959.

Hartmann, Nicolai, 'Brotherly Love,' *Ethics*, vol. 2, London, George Allen & Unwin, 1932.

Homiak, Marcia, *Character, Virtue, and Self-Respect: A Reading of the Nichomachean Ethics*, PhD dissertation, Harvard University, 1976.

Hume, David, *Enquiry Concerning the Principles of Morals*, New York, Liberal Arts Press, 1957.

Hunt, Lester, 'Generosity,' *American Philosophical Quarterly*, July 1975.

Kant, Immanuel, *The Doctrine of Virtue*, trans. Mary Gregor, New York, Harper & Row, 1964.

Kant, Immanuel, *Foundations of the Metaphysics of Morals*, trans. Lewis White Beck, New York, Bobbs-Merrill, 1959.

Kant, Immanuel, *Lectures on Ethics*, trans. L. Infield, New York, Harper & Row, 1963.

Kant, Immanuel, *Observations on the Feeling of the Beautiful and the Sublime*, trans. Goldthwait, Berkeley, University of California Press, 1965.

Kant, Immanuel, *Religion within the Limits of Reason Alone*, trans. Greene and Hudson, New York, Harper & Row, 1960.

Kenny, A., *Action, Emotion and Will*, London, Routledge & Kegan Paul, 1963.

Kierkegaard, Soren, *Works of Love*, trans. Howard and Edna Hong, New York, Harper & Row, 1962.

MacIntyre, Alasdair, *A Short History of Ethics*, New York, Macmillan, 1966.

MacIntyre, Alasdair, 'Egoism and Altruism,' in Paul Edwards (ed.), *Encyclopedia of Philosophy*, vol. 2, New York, Macmillan, 1967.

Mandelbaum, M., *The Phenomenology of Moral Experience*, Baltimore,

Johns Hopkins University Press, 1955.

Mayeroff, M., *On Caring*, New York, Perennial Library, 1971.

Mayo, Bernard, *Ethics and the Moral Life*, London, Macmillan, 1958.

Melden, A.I., (ed.), *Essays in Moral Philosophy*, Seattle, University of Washington Press, 1958.

Melden, A.I., *Rights and Persons*, Berkeley, University of California Press, 1977.

Mercer, Philip, *Sympathy and Ethics*, Oxford, Clarendon Press, 1972.

Miller, Jean Baker, *Toward a New Psychology of Women*, Boston, Beacon Press, 1976.

Murdoch, Iris, *The Sovereignty of Good*, New York, Shocken, 1971.

Murdoch, Iris, 'Vision and Choice in Morality,' *Proceedings of the Aristotelian Society*, 1956.

Nagel, Thomas, *The Possibility of Altruism*, Oxford, Clarendon Press, 1970.

Nell, Onora, *Acting on Principle: An Essay on Kantian Ethics*, New York, Columbia University Press, 1975.

Rawls, John, *A Theory of Justice*, Cambridge, Mass., Harvard University Press, 1971.

Rawls, John, 'Two Concepts of Rules,' *Philosophical Review*, January 1955.

Rescher, Nicholas, *Unselfishness: The Role of the Vicarious Affects in Moral Philosophy and Social Theory*, University of Pittsburgh Press, 1975.

Ross, W.D., *The Right and the Good*, Oxford, Clarendon Press, 1930.

Scheler, Max, *The Nature of Sympathy*, trans. Werner Stark, London, Routledge & Kegan Paul, 1965.

Schopenhauer, Arthur, *On the Basis of Morality*, trans. E.F.J. Payne, New York, Bobbs-Merrill, 1965.

Sidgwick, Henry, *The Methods of Ethics*, 7th edition, University of Chicago Press, 1962.

Solomon, Robert, *The Passions: The Myth and Nature of Human Emotions*, New York, Anchor Press/Doubleday, 1976.

Telfer, Elizabeth, 'Friendship,' *Proceedings of the Aristotelian Society*, supplement, 1970-1.

Titmuss, R.M., *The Gift Relationship*, London, George Allen & Unwin, 1970.

Tocqueville, Alexis de, *Democracy in America*, vol. 2, New York, Alfred A. Knopf, 1945.

Urmson, J.O., 'Saints and Heroes,' in A.I. Melden (ed.), *Essays in Moral Philosophy*, Seattle, University of Washington Press, 1958.

Wallace, James, *Virtues and Vices*, Ithaca, Cornell University Press, 1978.

Ward, Keith, *The Development of Kant's View of Ethics*, Oxford, Blackwell's, 1972.

Williams, Bernard, *Morality: An Introduction to Ethics*, New York, Harper & Row, 1972.

Williams, Bernard, 'Persons, Character and Morality,' in Amelie Rorty (ed.), *The Identities of Persons*, Berkeley, University of California Press, 1976.

Williams, Bernard, *Problems of the Self*, Cambridge University Press, 1973.

Williams, Bernard, 'Utilitarianism and Moral Self-Indulgence,' in H.D. Lewis (ed.), *Contemporary British Philosophy*, vol. 4, New Jersey, Humanities Press, 1976.

Winch, Peter, *Ethics and Action*, London, Routledge & Kegan Paul, 1972.

Wolff, R.P., *The Autonomy of Reason: A Commentary on Kant's Groundwork of the Metaphysics of Morals*, New York, Harper & Row, 1973.

Wolff, R.P., *The Poverty of Liberalism*, Boston, Beacon Press, 1968.

Wright, G.H. von, *The Varieties of Goodness*, London, Routledge & Kegan Paul, 1963.

INDEX

activity (of emotions), 172, 177-8, 183-5

altruism: conditional, 77-81; and co-operation, 215; defined, 9-10; direct, 83-7; and friendship, 43-4, 67-8; and obligation, 91-2; and universalizability, 87-91

altruistic emotions: account of, 12-15; as (allegedly) egoistic, 18-22, 83; and apprehension of situation, 132; capriciousness of, 36-41; and cognition, 201-3; and conflict with duty, 105-7; and consistency, 110-15; as essential to the good of beneficent action, 144-6; good of, 148-51; and knowledge, 108-10; and moods, 16, 18, 20; moral value of, 163-4; non-motivational value of, 140, 148-9, 152-7; and personal feelings, 23-7; and rational altruism, 117-24; and strength of desire for other's good, 18-20; as summonable by will, 199-201

Aristotle, 81, 82, 184, 204-5, 228

Broad, C. D., 23, 108, 215
Butler, J., 10

character, 204-7
charity, 107-9
choosing values, 173-8
consistency, 110-12, 115

duty (of beneficence), 45, 105, 136-7

duty, sense of (as moral motivation, contrasted with sympathy), 22-3, 30-6, 118-21, 164-8

examples: changing flat tire, 144, 151; clerical worker friends, 68-9; dying astronaut, 146-9, 150, 187; formerly racist man, 175-6; friend in hospital, 37-8, 142-3, 159, 164; helping dig car out of snow, 87-8; inconstant but sympathetic person, 112-15; racist man, 174, 176; sympathetic college instructor, 40-1, 151, 159; unsympathetic college instructor, 36-7, 37-41, 187-8, 193-4, 199-200

Feinberg, J., 161, 222
Frankfurt, H., 183-5
Fried, C., 211-12, 216
friendship: and altruism, 43-4, 67-8; caring for friend, 69-70; its conflict with impersonal obligations, 45-6; effort and struggle in, 73-4; and egoism, 75-7, 83; good of, 221; and impartiality, 58-61, 211-12; levels of caring in, 71-3; personal significance of, 43, 64, 82; and universalistic altruism, 77-8

generosity, 20
Grice, G. R., 162

Hampshire, S., 226

233